Tastefully Oregon

Healthy Culinary Treasures From The Pacific Northwest

Oregon Dietetic Association

First Printing March 1996
Second Printing December 1997

Published by
Oregon Dietetic Association
PO Box 6497
Portland, Oregon 97228

The Oregon Dietetic Association (ODA) is an organization of approximately 700 dietetic professionals. Registered Dietitians (R.D.), Dietetic Technicians Registered (D.T.R.), and other dietetic professionals work in:
- hospitals and other health care facilities
- schools and universities
- government and community agencies
- business and industry
- private practice settings

Dietetic professionals have met a rigorous set of criteria established by the American Dietetic Association:
- completed a program of study at accredited colleges/universities
- received post graduate training or supervised job experience
- taken a national examination to become registered
- met continuing education requirements

Oregon dietitans are licensed by the State (L.D.) and have additional professional certification in specific areas of expertise.

Printed by
Jumbo Jack's Cookbook Co.
PO Box 247
Audubon, Iowa 50025

Copyright © 1996 Oregon Dietetic Association
Cover Art and Illustrations: Copyright © 1996 by
Apridesign and Thomas K. Weeks, *Art and Design*
ISBN 0-9650697-0-2

Many Thanks To Many People!

Cookbook Committee

Emma Steen, R.D., Chair
Tanya Boynay, R.D.
Sonja Connor, R.D.
Karlyn DeBow, R.D.
James Fox, R.D.
Cindy Freer Francois, R.D.
Joyce Gustafson, R.D.
Kimra Warren Hawk, R.D.

Cover Art and Illustrations © 1995

M. Teresa Cochran, R.D.,
Apridesign

Computer Graphics and Colorization

Thomas K. Weeks,
Art and Design

Nutrition Analysis

Marcia Whitman, R.D.

Editors/Writers

Sabine Artaud-Wild, R.D.
Sonja Connor, R.D.
Connie Evers, R.D.
James Fox, R.D.
Cindy Francois, R.D.
Anne Goetze, R.D.
Joyce Gustafson, R.D.
Kimra Warren Hawk, R.D.
Shirley Papé, R.D.
Peggy Paul, R.D.
Doris Pavlukovich, R.D.
Emma Steen, R.D.

Recipe Contributors

ODA members (see recipes)

Testers & Cooks

ODA members
Cheryl Laughlin
Roxanne Ruyle Griswold, R.N.

Marketing Committee

Sharon Brown, R.D.
Christie Digman, R.D.
Pat Fischer, R.D.
Joanne Lyford, R.D.
Kevin Monti, R.D.
Janet Muckridge, R.D.
Kathy Schwab, R.D.

A Word From Oregon Dietitians

A spirit of adventure and a love of nature characterize Oregonians. These traits came from courageous pioneers who traveled
to Oregon from the midwest in the mid 1800's during "The Great
Migration." Drawn by the promise of free land, they stuffed their
belongings into covered wagons and headed West.

**The Oregon History Center's display, *OREGON--Land of
Promise, Land of Plenty* depicts foods recommended for one
adult for 110 days:**

150 lb. flour	**30 - 40 lb. dried fruit and vegetables**
25 lb. bacon/pork	**25 lb. fresh beef (acquired on the trail)**
20 lb. beans	**1 cow for milk**
8 lb. rice	**1 jug molasses**
25-40 lb. sugar	**5 lb. baking soda**
15 lb. coffee or tea	**yeast powder for bread**
salt/pepper	**buffalo/antelope/fish/rabbit/sage hen**

During the 2000 mile trek they faced dust, mud, bugs, boredom,
danger, disease and death. Along the way, Indians taught them
to hang strips of fish, buffalo and antelope on poles to dry. Nothing
was wasted. The hides were dried, tanned and made into clothing
that fared well in thorny, rough country and during harsh winters.

Diaries provide insight into the struggle against the elements and
the emotional toll. In 1846, eleven-year-old Lucy Ann Henderson
Deady wrote of the decision to throw away surplus weight to
speed the journey, "A man named Smith had a wooden rolling pin
that it was decided was useless and must be abandoned. I shall
never forget how that big man stood there with tears streaming
down his face as he said, 'Do I have to throw this away? It was my
mother's. I remember she always used it to roll out her biscuits,
and they were awful good biscuits.' The pioneers were very
resourceful with what they had as they replaced scarce wood with
"buffalo chips" over which they cooked their buffalo steaks,
saying "they have the same flavor they would have had on hickory
coals" (from Tamsen Donner's diary, 1846).

In staggering numbers these people came to Oregon--10,000 arrived in 1852 alone. From those simple beginnings Oregon has become number one in the country in eleven commodities. Food growing and processing are major industries. Oregonians are strong advocates for the environment. We support policies and practices that affect food packaging, recycling, reduction of waste and promote environmentally safe agricultural practices.

The fertile soils of the Williamette Valley and mid-state provide apples, pears, cherries, watermelon, grains, hazelnuts, walnuts, strawberries, blueberries, and raspberries, in addition to grapes from which first class wines are produced. Salmon and other succulent seafood come from the coastal waters and fish abound in our rivers and lakes. From the open spaces of Eastern Oregon come meats and grains, and the state is renowned for excellent cheeses and dairy products.

The abundance of these foods plus the adventurous spirits of the members of the Oregon Dietetic Association motivated us to compile our favorite recipes that combine good food with good health. Dietetic professionals throughout Oregon submitted recipes that were carefully taste-tested and analyzed. Some of these recipes represent family favorites that have been passed down over several generations and revised to meet specific healthy guidelines that are delineated later. All are creative combinations of tastes, textures and colors. There was a little bit of fun, too, in the decision to spice up the pages of this book with personal photographs related to food and Oregon. Some go back a long way. We hope you enjoy them all.

Good Food & Good Health--A Winning Combination. The past 150 years have brought tremendous advances in the sciences of medicine and nutrition. It is widely recognized that a definite correlation exists between eating and health. The 1988 Surgeon General's Report on Nutrition and Health states that eating and drinking habits contribute to eight of the ten leading causes of death in the U.S., including coronary heart disease, cancer, stroke and diabetes. According to the June 1993 issue of the *Journal of the American Dietetic Association,* "more than $200 billion per year, or one-fourth of all health care expenditures, is spent for the treatment of these diet-related diseases." The good news is that those statistics can be improved with changes in lifestyles. The dietetic profession plays a major role in the promotion of optimal nutrition, health and well-being, and supports the notion that food can be both nutritious and delicious!

All parents want to give their children a healthy start. Children who begin their lives consuming large amounts of fat, sugar and sodium acquire a taste preference for them which will be more difficult to change as the years go by. How much healthier it is to develop a taste for the crispness of fresh vegetables and fresh fruits and the wholesomeness of grains early in life! Over a lifetime these habits make a tremendous difference. To arrive at later years with strong bones and teeth, clean arteries, strength and vitality, a healthy foundation needs to be laid in the early years of life.

EATING STYLE, rather than diet, more accurately descibes a way of eating that implies choosing healthy foods, eating in moderation and balancing high-fat foods with low-fat ones. A low-fat eating style, along with regular exercise and a positive outlook, are the keys to achieving optimal health throughout life. We proudly offer you our collection of healthy culinary treasures.

BON APPETIT and STAY HEALTHY

The Food Guide Pyramid

The most important dietary changes we can make to lower the risk of chronic diseases are to increase the intake of foods rich in complex carbohydrates and fiber and to reduce the intake of fat. Scientific information was translated into recommendations for the public in 1980 with the USDA "Dietary Guidelines for Americans" and updated in 1990. Recently, the USDA created a "Food Guide Pyramid" to convert the Dietary Guidelines into practical eating advice.

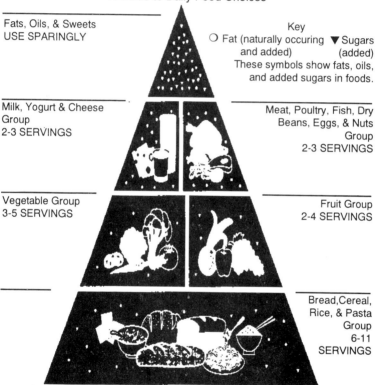

SOURCE: U.S. Department of Agriculture/U.S. Department of Health and Human Services

The Food Guide Pyramid shows that eating a variety of foods from the lower five food groups is the key to a healthy eating style. The fats, oils and sweets group at the top should be used sparingly. Foods should be consumed in amounts specified to provide a balance of nutrients.

Designing the Recipes

Our goal was to offer you a variety of tasty recipes that meet the USDA Dietary Goals and Guidelines:

30% or less calories from fat
10% or less calories from saturated fat
300 milligrams cholesteol or less/day
2000 milligrams sodium or less/day

Nutrient Guidelines For Recipes

Upper Limits for One Serving
(Many Recipes Contain Less than the Upper Limit)

ENTREES:
10 grams fat
100 milligrams for cholesterol
500 Calories for pasta entrees
300 Calories for other entrees
600 milligrams sodium

SIDE DISHES (pasta, grains, salads, vegetables):
5 grams fat
500 milligrams sodium

BREADS/MUFFINS:
5 grams fat

DESSERTS:
10 grams fat

Recipes were analyzed using The Food Processor Plus, Version 6.0, ESHA Research, Salem, OR. Selected nutrients for one serving are listed with each recipe. When there was more than one choice for an ingredient, the first ingredient listed was used in the analysis. Ingredients listed as optional were not included in the analysis.

Table of Contents

Appetizers & Beverages.................................... 1-30

Breads & Muffins...31-56

Breakfasts, Brunches
   & Lunches...57-74

Soups, Stews & Chili.....................................75-106

Salads & Salad Dressings 107-142

Side Dishes, Sauces
   & Condiments.. 143-158

Vegetarian Main Dishes............................. 159-176

Seafood Main Dishes.................................. 177-188

Chicken & Turkey
   Main Dishes.. 189-218

Beef, Veal & Pork
   Main Dishes.. 219-238

Desserts... 239-276

Especially for Children................................ 277-288

Index... 289-292

FAVORITE RECIPES

FROM MY COOKBOOK

Recipe Name	Page Number

Appetizers & Beverages

Tastefully Oregon

Snacking--The Way To Go

- Low fat, nutrient-rich snacks can be part of a healthy diet. The problem is that many commercially prepared snack foods contain excess fat and many calories.

- Snacking and impulse eating are often synonymous, so it is very important to have healthy snacks on hand. As a first step, check your impulse buying of high fat snacks. Remember, if they are not in the house...you will not eat them.

- Great snack ideas are included in *Tastefully Oregon*, especially in "Breads and Muffins," "Breakfasts, Brunches and Lunches" and the large section on "Desserts." The section "Especially for Children" has wonderful snacking recipes.

- Leftovers make good snack foods.

- Don't forget the "ready made" snack foods in the food stores: fruits have their own "wrappings" ready to be peeled off at any time; any cut up vegetable can be spiced up with the dips from the "Appetizers and Beverages"; beverages can fend off hunger pangs. Low fat yogurts, low fat cheeses, low fat milk, sorbets and low fat frozen desserts contribute much-needed calcium to the diet. Breads, low fat crackers, low fat cookies and cereals are good choices for an afternoon or evening energy boost.

APPETIZERS & BEVERAGES

Baked Garlic

Stephanie Langton

An appetizer that is definitely "IN". I am sending this recipe in honor of my husband, Scot, a true garlic lover! Try it, you'll be pleasantly surprised.

5 heads garlic, about 40 cloves
1 (14 1/2 oz.) can chicken broth
1/4 tsp. cayenne pepper

Heat oven to 350°. Remove papery outer skins from garlic, but do not separate heads. Place garlic in small baking dish. Pour chicken broth and cayenne pepper over them. Bake, uncovered, for 1 1/2 hours. Spoon broth over garlic several times during baking.

Serve with small slices of French bread. Remove a clove of garlic and squeeze garlic purée onto bread. Enjoy!

Servings:
  10 for most people, or 5 for "garlic lovers"

Serving Size:
  4 to 8 cloves

Nutritional analysis per serving:
  Calories: 28
  Fat: trace gm
  Cholesterol: trace mg
  Protein: 2 gm
  Carbohydrate: 4 gm
  Sodium: 193 mg

TASTEFULLY OREGON

Marinated Mushrooms
Jodie Donnelly Perry, R.D.

May also be mixed with cherry tomatoes for more color.

1 qt. (1 1/4 lb.) sm. to med. fresh mushrooms
1 (16 oz.) btl. *Kraft Reduced-Calorie Zesty Italian* dressing, or your favorite low-fat or fat-free Italian salad dressing

Lightly clean mushrooms. If more than 3/4-inch diameter, cut in half. Place in saucepan; cover with cold water and bring to a boil. Remove from heat and drain immediately. Put into 1-quart jar (or deep glass bowl) and pour dressing over mushrooms. Cover and marinate in refrigerator at least 24 hours before serving. These marinated mushrooms will keep in refrigerator for 2 weeks.

Drain off marinade before serving with wooden picks as an appetizer.

Servings:
16 servings

Serving Size:
1/4 cup

Nutritional analysis per serving:
Calories: 39
Fat: 3 gm
Cholesterol: 2 mg
Protein: <1 gm
Carbohydrate: 3 gm
Sodium: 224 mg

APPETIZERS & BEVERAGES

No-Guilt Nachos

Luanna Squires Diller, R.D.

Healthy nachos you can feel good about serving. Preparation time is only 15 minutes.

8 oz. ground turkey, or extra-lean ground beef (opt.)
1 (15 oz.) can vegetarian refried beans, or 2 c. cooked pinto beans, mashed
1 T. taco seasoning
1 (7 oz.) bag *Guiltless Gourmet No-Oil Tortilla Chips*
8 oz. low-fat cheese, grated (I like Jarlsberg Lite)
2 lg. tomatoes, chopped, or 1 (16 oz.) jar salsa or picante sauce
8 oz. fat-free sour cream (*Land O'Lakes* tastes the best)

Brown turkey or hamburger until no longer pink, if using. Mix refried beans with taco seasoning and warm slightly. On 8 plates, or 1 large platter, layer the ingredients in equal portions in this order: chips, refried beans, meat and cheese. Cover with plastic wrap and microwave on HIGH 15 to 20 seconds. Then add layers of salsa and sour cream.

Servings: 8

Serving Size: 1 cup

Nutritional analysis per serving (not including ground meat):
Calories: 265
Fat: 5 gm
Cholesterol: 19 mg
Protein: 16 gm
Carbohydrate: 36 gm
Sodium: 536 mg

TASTEFULLY OREGON

Special Shrimp
Ruth Hayden, R.D.

This wonderful treat was served at a special party as an appetizer and was very well received.

1 T. olive oil
2 lb. lg. prawns, shelled (except tail)*
1/4 tsp. fresh-ground black pepper
1/4 tsp. Lite Salt
1/4 c. dry vermouth (Martini-type) or water
1/4 c. fresh-squeezed lemon juice (about 2 lemons)
1 clove garlic minced

Heat olive oil in a large skillet. Add shrimp and cook until golden brown. Reduce heat and add garlic, Lite Salt and pepper. When well blended, increase heat to very hot. Add lemon juice and dry vermouth, cooking for about 1 minute, constantly stirring or shaking.

*To save time, use frozen, precooked shrimp.

Servings:
  12

Serving Size:
  2 ounces of prawns

Nutritional analysis per serving:
  Calories: 72
  Fat: 2 gm
  Cholesterol: 108 mg
  Protein: 12 gm
  Carbohydrate: <1 gm
  Sodium: 147 mg

APPETIZERS & BEVERAGES

Hummus Dip

Robin Stanton, R.D.

Quick, easy and healthy.

2 (15 oz.) cans garbanzo beans, drained & rinsed
1/4 c. fresh-squeezed lemon juice
2 T. sesame oil
2 cloves garlic, minced
Pita bread, cut in wedges

Purée beans, juice, oil and garlic in blender or food processor. Transfer to a bowl and serve with pita bread.

Servings:
  10

Serving Size:
  1/4 cup

Nutritional analysis per serving:
  Calories: 128
  Fat: 4 gm
  Cholesterol: 0 mg
  Protein: 4 gm
  Carbohydrate: 20 gm
  Sodium: 255 mg

Moroccan Eggplant
Kathy Schwab, R.D.

Serve as a dip with toasted pita bread or crackers. This dish, along with hummus, veggies and pita bread, makes a great, light lunch. It also works well as a nice side salad or relish.

2 lg. eggplants, about 2 lb.
2 lg. tomatoes, diced
2 tsp. minced garlic
1 tsp. paprika
1/2 tsp. ground cumin
Pinch of cayenne pepper
3 T. fresh-squeezed lemon juice
1/4 tsp. Lite Salt

Preheat oven to 400°. Line a baking sheet with foil and spray foil with non-stick cooking spray. Slice eggplants in half lengthwise, and lay cut-side down on the foil. Bake for 30 minutes, until soft. Let cool until can be handled. Scoop flesh out of the eggplant skin onto a cutting board and cut into 1/2-inch pieces.

Put eggplant cubes, tomatoes, garlic, paprika, cumin and cayenne pepper into a large skillet and cook over medium heat until most of the liquid has evaporated (about 5 minutes). Cool to room temperature and add lemon juice and Lite Salt.

Servings:
8

Serving Size:
1/2 cup

Nutritional analysis per serving:
Calories: 43
Fat: trace gm
Cholesterol: 0 mg
Protein: 2 gm
Carbohydrate: 10 gm
Sodium: 42 mg

APPETIZERS & BEVERAGES

Party Vegetable Dip

Barbara Lanning, R.D.

This is that great dip which is very nice to serve at a family gathering or party for friends. I like to surround it with raw vegetables such as carrot and celery sticks, cherry tomatoes, cucumber slices, cauliflower or broccoli pieces. This recipe makes a fairly large amount, but can be easily cut in half.

1 c. fat-free mayonnaise
1 c. fat-free sour cream
1/2 c. finely-chopped onions, or 1/2 tsp. onion powder
1/2 c. finely-chopped green bell pepper
1/4 c. chopped pimentos
1/4 tsp. Lite Salt
1/4 tsp. pepper
1/8 tsp. garlic powder
1/8 to 1/4 tsp. Tabasco sauce

Mix all ingredients. Cover tightly and chill overnight.

Servings:
12

Serving Size:
1/4 cup

Nutritional analysis per serving:
Calories: 31
Fat: trace
Cholesterol: 0 mg
Protein: 2 gm
Carbohydrate: 7 gm
Sodium: 263 mg

Russian Bean Dip

Kathy Schwab, R.D.

Serve this crunchy dip with toasted whole wheat pita triangles, low-fat crackers, or use as a sandwich spread.

1 (15 oz.) can kidney beans, drained & rinsed
1 T. red wine vinegar
1 T. water
2 tsp. olive oil
1/3 c. finely-chopped red onion
1/4 c. ground walnuts
2 cloves garlic, minced
1/4 c. finely-chopped fresh cilantro
Dash of cayenne pepper
1/2 tsp. Lite Salt

Put beans, vinegar, water and olive oil in blender or food processor fitted with a steel blade and process lightly, just until mixture is coarsely chopped. Transfer beans to a bowl; add remaining ingredients and mix well. Cover and refrigerate at least 8 hours before serving.

Servings:
   6 to 8

Serving Size:
   1/4 cup

Nutritional analysis per serving:
   Calories: 105
   Fat: 3 gm
   Cholesterol: trace mg
   Protein: 5 gm
   Carbohydrate: 15 gm
   Sodium: 290 mg

APPETIZERS & BEVERAGES

Spicy Garbanzo Bean Dip
Kathy Schwab, R.D.

Use as a dip for crackers, vegetables or toasted pita bread wedges. For a sandwich filling, spread in a pita pocket and top with sprouts, lettuce, tomatoes, broccoli, etc.

1 (15 oz.) can garbanzo beans, drained & rinsed
2 T. sesame tahini
3 T. lemon juice, about 1 med. lemon
3 cloves garlic, minced
1 tsp. ground cumin
1 tsp. ground coriander
1/8 to 1/4 tsp. cayenne pepper
1/2 tsp. Berbere* or paprika
2 to 3 T. water

*Berbere is an Ethiopian spice blend available at Nature's Fresh Northwest.

Mix all ingredients together in food processor and blend until smooth, adding water until desired consistency is reached.

Servings:
  6

Serving Size:
  1/4 cup

Nutritional analysis per serving:
  Calories: 122
  Fat: 4 gm
  Cholesterol: 0 mg
  Protein: 5 gm
  Carbohydrate: 19 gm
  Sodium: 213 mg

Tangy Dip
Juanita Dodd, R.D.

This dip is delicious served with raw vegetable sticks. It is also wonderful with fresh steamed artichokes.

1 c. fat-free mayonnaise
1/3 c. Dijonnaise
1 tsp. garlic powder
1 T. fresh-squeezed lemon juice

Mix all ingredients together. Chill.

Servings:
5

Serving Size:
1/4 cup

Nutritional analysis per serving:
Calories: 67
Fat: 3 gm
Cholesterol: 9 mg
Protein: trace gm
Carbohydrate: 12 gm
Sodium: 516 mg

APPETIZERS & BEVERAGES

Tofu Paté

Nancy Ludwig-Williams, R.D.

This filling tastes similar to egg salad and is very easy to make. I like it best as a sandwich spread on whole grain bread with lettuce or sliced cucumber.

16 oz.) firm tofu,
   rinsed & drained
2 T. nonfat mayonnaise
2 T. yellow prepared or
   Dijon mustard
1 tsp. sage
1 tsp. curry powder
1/2 tsp. Lite Salt
1/2 tsp. thyme leaves
2 T. fresh-squeezed
   lemon juice

Place all ingredients in blender or food processor and blend until smooth. If more texture is desired, mash with fork or potato masher. Serve cold.

Servings:
   8

Serving Size:
   1/4 cup

Nutritional analysis per serving:
   Calories: 91
   Fat: 5 gm
   Cholesterol: 0 mg
   Protein: 9 gm
   Carbohydrate: 4 gm
   Sodium: 214 mg

TASTEFULLY OREGON

Tzatziki

Carol DeFrancesco, R.D.

This is a very popular Greek appetizer. To achieve a thick, creamy yogurt like the one you would find in Greece, drain the yogurt overnight or for several hours. Add garlic according to your taste, but the original Greek dish has lots of it! When prepared, the tzatziki will keep a day or two in the refrigerator. Serve with small pieces of thickly-sliced whole grain bread.

2 c. plain, nonfat yogurt, or use part nonfat sour cream
1 med. cucumber
1 to 3 lg. cloves garlic, minced
Freshly-ground black pepper
1/2 tsp. Lite Salt

Line a strainer with cheesecloth, paper coffee filter or linen napkin. Place over a bowl and pour in the yogurt. Refrigerate overnight, or for several hours, while it drains. The yogurt should be quite thick.

Peel the cucumber, scoop out the seeds and grate enough to make 3/4 cup. Let dry for a few minutes on a paper towel. Beat the thickened yogurt (a wire whisk works well for this) until creamy. Add minced garlic, pepper, Lite Salt and grated cucumbers. Mix well and store in refrigerator. Serve chilled.

Servings:
6

Serving Size:
1/4 cup

Nutritional analysis per serving:
Calories: 54
Fat: trace
Cholesterol: 1 mg
Protein: 5 gm
Carbohydrate: 8 gm
Sodium: 155 mg

APPETIZERS & BEVERAGES

Hot Crabmeat Appetizer

Madelyn Koontz, R.D.

One of the greatest treasures in our area is our Dungeness Crab. Crabbing is a great sport of all ages and I like to use some of our "catch" in this delicious dip-type appetizer.

1 (8 oz.) pkg. fat-free cream cheese
1 c. flaked crabmeat
2 T. finely-chopped onion
1 T. nonfat milk
2 tsp. cream-style horseradish
1/4 tsp. Lite Salt
1/8 tsp. pepper
1/4 c. sliced almonds

Combine softened cream cheese and remaining ingredients except almonds. Mix well. Spoon mixture into small casserole dish and sprinkle with almonds. Bake at 350° for 15 to 20 minutes, or until warm in the center. Serve on low-fat crackers.

Servings:
16

Serving Size:
2 tablespoons

Nutritional analysis per serving:
Calories: 30
Fat: 4 gm
Cholesterol: 8 mg
Protein: 4 gm
Carbohydrate: 1 gm
Sodium: 131 mg

Salmon Paté

Sonja L. Connor, R.D.

An appetizer which is an excellent use for left-over cooked salmon. Prepare it when the salmon is on hand and store in the freezer. Cracked Pepper Water Crackers (a new cracker we have recently found) or thin slices of French bread are excellent to serve as dippers.

1 (15 oz.) can, drained, or 1 3/4 c. cooked salmon
1 T. fat-free mayonnaise
2 cloves garlic, minced
1/4 tsp. Tabasco sauce
1 to 2 tsp. dill weed
1/4 tsp. Lite Salt (omit if using canned salmon)
1/4 c. chopped green onion
2 tsp. fresh-squeezed lemon juice
1 T. chopped parsley

If using canned salmon, remove skin and bones. Combine all ingredients and mix thoroughly with a fork (not a food processor). Cover and chill in refrigerator.

Servings:
8

Serving Size:
1/4 cup

Nutritional analysis per serving:
Calories:	86
Fat:	4 gm
Cholesterol:	23 mg
Protein:	11 gm
Carbohydrate:	1 gm
Sodium:	309 mg

APPETIZERS & BEVERAGES

This is a picture of Sonja's great uncle, James French's general store in Hoisington, Kansas in the early 1920's. Notice the large box of Kellogg's Toasted Corn Flakes on the shelf in the top right of the picture.

TASTEFULLY OREGON

Shrimp Dill Dip

Janis Bryant, R.D.

This dip can be prepared in 15 minutes. It is delicious served with low-fat crackers or fresh vegetables. This version makes a fairly large amount, but can easily be cut in half.

- 2 c. nonfat sour cream
- 1/2 c. fat-free or light mayonnaise
- 1/2 c. chopped green onions
- 1/2 tsp. garlic powder
- 1/2 tsp. Worcestershire sauce
- 1 tsp. dill weed
- 6 oz. cooked salad shrimpmeat

Combine all ingredients except shrimp in bowl, and mix thoroughly. (Chill if dip is not served immediately.) Add shrimp just prior to serving. Blend carefully until well mixed.

Servings:
12

Serving Size:
1/4 cup

Nutritional analysis per serving:
- Calories: 47
- Fat: trace grams
- Cholesterol: 28 mg
- Protein: 6 gm
- Carbohydrate: 6 gm
- Sodium: 174 mg

APPETIZERS & BEVERAGES

"Smoked" Salmon Ball

Jendy Newman, R.D.

A family favorite for parties and special occasions.

8 oz. Neufchatel (light cream cheese)
1 (14 3/4 oz.) can salmon, or 1 1/2 c. baked salmon
1/4 to 1/2 tsp. liquid smoke (opt.)
1/4 c. chopped fresh parsley
1/4 c. finely-chopped pecans

Blend salmon, cheese and liquid smoke, if using, with mixer until smooth. Form into two balls, sprinkle with chopped nuts and roll in parsley flakes. If saving one to freeze for later use, wait until thawed to roll in parsley flakes. Serve with low-fat crackers or bread.

Servings:
16

Serving Size:
1/16 of recipe

Nutritional analysis per serving:
  Calories: 76
  Fat: 5 gm
  Cholesterol: 18 mg
  Protein: 6 gm
  Carbohydrate: <1 gm
  Sodium: 209 mg

Breakfast Smoothie

Renee Giroux, R.D.

A delicious drink for any hour of the day that takes less than 5 minutes to prepare.

2 c. orange juice
1 banana
1 c. plain nonfat yogurt
1 c. crushed ice or ice cubes

Combine all ingredients in blender and blend 1 minute.

Servings:
4

Serving Size:
1 cup

Nutritional analysis per serving:
Calories: 117
Fat: trace grams
Cholesterol: 1 mg
Protein: 5 gm
Carbohydrate: 24 gm
Sodium: 50 mg

APPETIZERS & BEVERAGES

Favorite Gin Fizz

Joyce Gustafson, R.D.

It is hard to believe how easy this version is to prepare.

1 (6 oz.) can frozen lemonade concentrate, thawed
3/4 c. egg substitute
2 tsp. powdered sugar
3/4 c. nonfat milk
1/2 c. gin
6 ice cubes

Combine all the ingredients in blender and mix. Serve and enjoy.

Servings:
  5 to 6

Serving Size:
  1/2 cup

Nutritional analysis per serving:
  Calories: 161
  Fat: 1 gm
  Cholesterol: 1 mg
  Protein: 6 gm
  Carbohydrate: 19 gm
  Sodium: 87 mg

TASTEFULLY OREGON

1950's view of Gustafson family's drug store in SE Portland, OR. Note the milk delivery wagon. Do you remember when milk used to be delivered to your front door?

APPETIZERS & BEVERAGES

Hot Apple Cider
Ann Reid, R.D.

I like to put the heated cider in a crock-pot on a low temperature. It can be served over a period of several hours; the aroma is wonderful!

7 c. unsweetened apple juice
2 c. orange juice
1/2 c. honey
10 to 15 whole cloves
1 apple, peeled & sliced into wedges
1 orange, sliced into wedges

Combine juices, honey and apple wedges in a heavy kettle. Insert 1 to 2 cloves into each orange wedge and add to juices. Bring to a boil. Reduce heat and simmer 15 minutes. Remove from heat and let stand 5 minutes.

Servings:
8

Serving Size:
1 cup

Nutritional analysis per serving:
Calories: 211
Fat: trace grams
Cholesterol: 0 mg
Protein: <1 gm
Carbohydrate: 53 gm
Sodium: 8 mg

Hot Spice Tea

Madelyn Koontz, R.D.

A very tasty hot drink.

- 1 (8 oz.) jar sugar-free Tang powder
- 3 oz. presweetened lemon-flavored instant tea powder
- 1 1/2 tsp. ground cloves
- 1 1/2 tsp. ground cinnamon

Mix dry ingredients thoroughly and store in a container with a tight lid. To serve, add 1 to 2 teaspoons per cup of boiling water.

Servings:
64

Serving Size:
1 teaspoon/1 cup

Nutritional analysis per serving:
Calories:	7
Fat:	trace grams
Cholesterol:	trace mg
Protein:	trace gm
Carbohydrate:	2 gm
Sodium:	1 mg

APPETIZERS & BEVERAGES

Lemon Velvet

Anne Goetze, R.D.

A delicious anytime drink for children of any age. It's also fun to freeze in paper cups with a stick inserted to make Lemonsicles.

1 (8 oz.) ctn. nonfat lemon yogurt
1 (6 oz.) ctn. orange juice concentrate, thawed
2 1/2 c. nonfat milk
1 tsp. vanilla

Place ingredients in blender. Blend until frothy and serve. Store in the refrigerator and shake before serving.

Servings: 10

Serving Size: 1/2 cup

Nutritional analysis per serving:
Calories: 71
Fat: trace grams
Cholesterol: 2 mg
Protein: 4 gm
Carbohydrate: 14 gm
Sodium: 42 mg

Peachy Soy Cooler

Kathy Schwab, R.D.

This beverage would be appropriate for someone with lactose intolerance or a milk allergy.

1 c. 1% or nonfat vanilla-flavored soy milk
2 lg. fresh peaches, peeled & sliced, or 1 c. canned unsweetened peaches, drained
2 ice cubes

Combine all ingredients and blend in a blender until smooth.

Servings:
2

Serving Size:
1 cup

Nutritional analysis per serving:
Calories:	76
Fat:	2 gm
Cholesterol:	0 mg
Protein:	4 gm
Carbohydrate:	12 gm
Sodium:	15 mg

APPETIZERS & BEVERAGES

Special Citrus Iced Tea

Sonja Connor, R.D.

A delicious warm weather drink. Serve over ice with a sprig of mint. I like to use the decaffeinated tea, but any tea works well.

- 8 Celestial Seasonings herbal Iced Delight tea bags, or 12 decaffeinated *Constant Comment* tea bags (or any decaffeinated black tea)
- 12 lg. fresh mint leaves
- 1/2 c. sugar
- 4 c. boiling water
- 1 (6 oz.) can frozen orange juice concentrate, thawed
- 1 (6 oz.) can frozen lemonade concentrate, thawed
- 12 c. cold water
- Small sprigs of fresh mint, as garnish

Place tea bags, mint leaves and sugar in large bowl, pitcher or glass jar. Pour boiling water over them and steep 10 to 15 minutes. Remove tea bags and mint leaves. Add orange juice and lemonade concentrates and cold water. Stir to mix. Refrigerate and serve very cold.

Servings:
10 to 12

Serving Size:
1 1/2 cups

Nutritional analysis per serving:
Calories: 88
Fat: Trace gm
Cholesterol: 0 mg
Protein: < 1 gm
Carbohydrate: 22 gm
Sodium: 12 mg

TASTEFULLY OREGON

Summertime Strawberry Smoothie
Emma Steen, R.D.

As many Oregonians do, my family picks berries every summer. This assures getting the berries at the peak of their wonderful flavor -- truly eating at its best. I also make preserves and individually freeze some whole berries for this delightful drink.

1 c. nonfat milk
1 c. low-fat vanilla ice cream (I use any brand that contains 2.5 gm fat per 1/2 c.)
1 c. nonfat plain yogurt
10 to 12 fresh or individually frozen strawberries
2 to 3 tsp. sugar
4 to 5 ice cubes

Place ingredients in blender in order given (the ice cubes must be on top to avoid damaging the blade of the blender). Mix until smooth. Pour into glasses or mugs and serve immediately. A nice garnish is a fresh strawberry placed on the edge of the glass, when fresh strawberries are available.

Servings:
4

Serving Size:
1 cup

Nutritional analysis per serving:
Calories: 142
Fat: 2 gm
Cholesterol: 5 mg
Protein: 8 gm
Carbohydrate: 26 gm
Sodium: 104 mg

APPETIZERS & BEVERAGES

The Oregonian

SATURDAY, JUNE 17, 1978

In the tradition of many Oregonians, Emma Steen picks strawberries with children: Michael, 3 years, Michelle, 11 years, and David, 9 (in background). The berry carrier was made by the children's grandfather and used at their strawberry fields on land that is now King City near Tigard, Oregon.

TASTEFULLY OREGON

Tofrutti Smoothie

Kathy Schwab, R.D.

For a thicker shake, use a frozen banana and eliminate ice cubes.

1 c. soft tofu, drained
1 med. banana
1/2 c. orange juice
1 c. fresh or frozen strawberries
1/4 tsp. almond extract
1 to 2 ice cubes

Combine all ingredients in a blender and blend until smooth.

Servings:
  3

Serving Size:
  1 cup

Nutritional analysis per serving:
  Calories: 134
  Fat: 4 gm
  Cholesterol: 0 mg
  Protein: 8 gm
  Carbohydrate: 19 gm
  Sodium: 8 mg

APPETIZERS & BEVERAGES

Wedding Punch
Juanita Dodd, R.D.

This is a delightful mixture of fruit juices. Double the recipe and freeze into cubes or an ice ring for the punch bowl, if desired.

1 (12 oz.) can lemonade concentrate, thawed
1 (12 oz.) can pineapple juice concentrate, thawed
8 c. water
1 lg. btl. (2 liter) lemon-lime carbonated drink (regular or sugar-free)

Mix all ingredients. Add carbonated drink just before serving.

Servings:
 15

Serving Size:
 1 cup

Nutritional analysis per serving (with regular carbonated drink):
- Calories: 137
- Fat: trace grams
- Cholesterol: 0 mg
- Protein: trace grams
- Carbohydrate: 35 gm
- Sodium: 21 mg

TASTEFULLY OREGON

Notes

Breads & Muffins

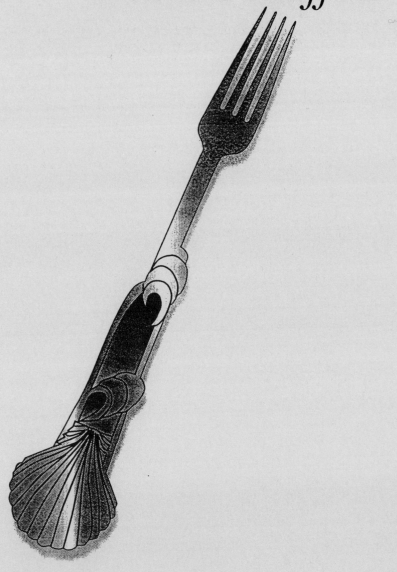

Tastefully Oregon

Hunger Pangs

Hunger pangs? We all experience them once in a while. Actually, we should welcome them. They are a signal that our bodies are ready to replenish their resources with needed food. They are a sign of a "healthy appetite." Too often we drink or eat for reasons other than the physiological ones (thirst and hunger) and the pounds keep creeping on. If this is the case:

- Take your time.. Don't rush toward food. Before you start eating try to visualize the body size you aspire to have. Try a drink of water or juice or a low fat snack to last until the next meal. If the only choices at a party are calorie and fat laden foods, stand with your back to the table.

- Enjoy each mouthful of food, eat SLOWLY and create a pleasant atmosphere around the food or the meal. Food nourishes the soul as well as the body.

- Avoid eating standing up or on-the-run. Designate a favorite place to eat; keep it for meals and even snacks.

- If you still feel hungry after finishing a meal wait a while, 20 minutes if possible. This time lapse often helps one realize that these "pangs" have vanished.

- Before your next meal, remember that "hunger pangs" are often "thirst pangs." Drink water.

This section includes recipes that can help you deal with these "hunger pangs."

BREADS & MUFFINS

Apple Cranberry Muffins

Sher Miller, D.T.R.

A moist and delicious muffin. Raisins are less expensive in place of the cranberries, but if you are a cranberry lover you won't want to leave them out!

3 T. oil
1/2 c. brown sugar
1/4 c. egg substitute
1 3/4 c. whole wheat flour
1/2 tsp. Lite Salt
2 tsp. baking powder
1 tsp. cinnamon
1 c. nonfat milk
1 c. chopped, peeled apple
1/2 c. dried cranberries (or raisins)
1/4 c. chopped almonds

Preheat oven to 425°. Beat together oil, egg substitute and brown sugar in a large mixing bowl until creamy. In a separate bowl, combine whole wheat flour, Lite Salt, baking powder and cinnamon. Add the combined dry ingredients, milk, apple, cranberries and almonds to the creamed mixture; mix just until moistened. Lightly oil muffin tins or line with paper liners and fill with batter until 3/4 full. Bake for about 15 minutes.

Servings:
12

Serving Size:
1 muffin

Nutritional analysis per serving:
Calories: 164
Fat: 5 gm
Cholesterol: trace mg
Protein: 4 gm
Carbohydrate: 27 gm
Sodium: 151 mg

TASTEFULLY OREGON

Blueberry Bran Muffins
Jodi Donnelly Perry, R.D.

2 2/3 c. *All-Bran cereal*
1 1/2 c. nonfat milk
4 egg whites
1 T. vanilla
2 c. flour
2/3 c. brown sugar
2 T. baking powder
3/4 tsp. baking soda
1 1/2 tsp. cinnamon
2 c. fresh blueberries

Preheat oven to 325°. Combine bran cereal, milk, egg whites and vanilla; let stand 5 minutes. Stir together flour, brown sugar, baking powder, baking soda and cinnamon in large bowl. Add blueberries and stir carefully. Spoon into paper-lined muffin tins. Bake for 30 minutes.

Servings:
  16 muffins

Serving Size:
  1 muffin

Nutritional analysis per serving:
  Calories: 142
  Fat: <1 gm
  Cholesterol: trace mg
  Protein: 5 gm
  Carbohydrate: 33 gm
  Sodium: 412 mg

BREADS & MUFFINS

Cereal Bran Muffins

Emma Steen, R.D.

These are best served on the day baked. The texture is more compact than traditional muffins. Note the single gram fat per muffin! An excellent source of dietary fiber.

- 3/4 c. white flour & 3/4 c. whole wheat flour, or 1 1/2 c. white flour
- 2 tsp. baking powder
- 1/2 tsp. baking soda
- 1/2 tsp. cinnamon
- 1 1/2 c. *100% Bran cereal* or *All-Bran cereal*
- 1 1/4 c. skim milk
- 1/3 c. firmly-packed brown sugar
- 2 egg whites
- 1/2 c. plain low-fat yogurt
- 1/2 c. raisins

Preheat oven to 400°. Mix first 4 ingredients in a large bowl. Mix cereal, milk and sugar in another bowl, let stand 5 minutes. Stir in egg whites and yogurt. Add to flour mixture, stirring just until moistened. Fold in raisins. Spoon batter into muffin tin sprayed with non-stick cooking spray. Bake 18 to 20 minutes, until golden brown.

Servings:
12

Serving Size:
1 muffin

Nutritional analysis per serving:
Calories: 127
Fat: <1 gm
Cholesterol: <1 mg
Protein: 5 gm
Carbohydrate: 29 gm
Sodium: 224 mg

TASTEFULLY OREGON

Dorothy's Muffins
Anne Goetze, R.D., L.D.

A friend and co-worker gave me this recipe. It's from her neighbor, Dorothy, and has become a favorite of her family and mine. A food processor can save time with the grating. These muffins are definitely worth a little extra work!

1 c. flour
1 c. oat bran
2 tsp. baking soda
1 tsp. baking powder
1/2 tsp. Lite Salt
2 tsp. cinnamon
1 c. brown sugar
1 1/2 c. grated
  carrots, unpeeled
2 lg. tart, unpeeled
  apples, grated
1/2 c. raisins or
  dried cranberries
1/4 c. oil
1/2 c. skim milk
4 egg whites,
  slightly beaten
1 tsp. vanilla

Preheat oven to 375°. In a large mixing bowl, combine first 6 ingredients. Stir in brown sugar, carrots, apples, raisins or cranberries. Add remaining ingredients and stir just until moistened. Spoon into muffin tins which have been sprayed with nonstick spray, or lined with papers. Bake for 18 to 20 minutes, or until nicely browned.

Servings:
  15 muffins

Serving Size:
  1 muffin

Nutritional analysis per serving:
  Calories: 159
  Fat: 4 gm
  Cholesterol: trace mg
  Protein: 4 gm
  Carbohydrate: 30 gm
  Sodium: 264 mg

BREADS & MUFFINS

Fresh Apple Muffins

Jodie Donnelly, R.D.

1/3 c. oil
1/2 c. sugar
2 egg whites
1 1/2 c. nonfat milk
1 tsp. vanilla
2 c. finely-chopped unpeeled apple (2 med.)
2 c. whole wheat flour
4 tsp. baking powder
3/4 tsp. Lite Salt
1 to 1 1/2 tsp. cinnamon

Preheat oven to 400°. Stir together oil, sugar, egg whites, milk, vanilla and chopped apples. In a separate bowl, mix together the dry ingredients. Add liquid mixture to dry ingredients, stirring only enough to moisten the flour. Spray muffin tins with nonstick spray and fill 2/3 full with batter. Bake for 15 minutes, or until wooden pick inserted in the center comes out clean.

Servings:
24

Serving Size:
1 muffin

Nutritional analysis per serving:
Calories: 92
Fat: 3 gm
Cholesterol: trace mg
Protein: 2 gm
Carbohydrate: 14 gm
Sodium: 129 mg

TASTEFULLY OREGON

Pumpkin Apple Muffins
Denise Cedar, R.D.

A tasty muffin which is also good on the second day. It also works well as a cooking project with children.

2 1/2 c. whole wheat flour (or use part white flour)
1 1/4 c. sugar
1 1/2 tsp. cinnamon
1 1/2 tsp. ginger
3/4 tsp. nutmeg
1/2 tsp. cloves
1 tsp. baking soda
4 egg whites
1 scant c. canned pumpkin (or half of a 16 oz. can)
1/3 c. oil
2 c. chopped green apple

Preheat oven to 350°. Combine all dry ingredients. In a separate bowl, combine egg whites, pumpkin, oil and chopped apples. Add these to the dry ingredients and stir only until moistened. Spoon into muffin tins which have been sprayed with nonstick cooking spray, or lined with papers. Bake for 20 minutes, or until a wooden pick inserted in the center comes out clean.

Servings:
18

Serving Size:
1 muffin

Nutritional analysis per serving:
Calories:	160
Fat:	4 gm
Cholesterol:	0 mg
Protein:	3 gm
Carbohydrate:	28 gm
Sodium:	84 mg

BREADS & MUFFINS

Raisin Bran Muffins
Pam Turman, R.D.

This is a very easy way to increase fiber in your diet. I like to serve these muffins warm. They make a delicious bread for any meal, or as a snack.

10 c. Raisin Bran
3 c. sugar
3 c. white flour
2 c. whole wheat flour
5 tsp. baking soda
2 tsp. Lite Salt
1/2 tsp. nutmeg
1 c. egg substitute
1/2 c. oil
1/2 c. apple juice
1 qt. buttermilk

Mix together cereal, sugar, flours, baking soda, Lite Salt and nutmeg. Add egg substitute, oil, apple juice and buttermilk; mix just until dry ingredients are moistened. Put in container with tight lid.

May be stored in the refrigerator for 5 to 6 weeks and baked as needed. Line muffin tins with paper liners, or spray with nonstick spray. Bake at 375° for 20 to 25 minutes, or until done when tested with a wooden pick.

Servings:
  60

Serving Size:
  1 muffin

Nutritional analysis per serving:
  Calories: 131
  Fat: 2 gm
  Cholesterol: <1 mg
  Protein: 3 gm
  Carbohydrate: 26 gm
  Sodium: 218 mg

Banana Bran Bread

Connie Bondi, R. D.

This chewy, nutty-flavored bread can also be baked as muffins. They keep and freeze well, too.

1/4 c. margarine
1/2 c. brown sugar
2 egg whites, beaten
2 c. *Fiber 1, All-Bran* or *Bran Buds* cereal
1 1/2 c. mashed very ripe banana (use 3 or 4)
1 tsp. vanilla extract
1 1/2 c. flour (a combination of white and whole wheat flour tastes super)
2 tsp. baking powder
1/2 tsp. baking soda

Preheat oven to 350°. Cream margarine and sugar until light and fluffy. Add egg whites and mix well. Stir in cereal, mashed banana and vanilla; mix well to combine. In a separate bowl, combine dry ingredients and add to above mixture, stirring lightly until moistened. Bake in 9x5-inch loaf pan, which has been sprayed with nonstick spray, for 1 hour. Can also be spooned into prepared muffin tins and baked for 15 to 20 minutes.

Servings:
1 loaf (16 slices) or 16 muffins

Serving Size:
1 slice bread

Nutritional analysis per serving:
Calories: 132
Fat: 3 gm
Cholesterol: 0 mg
Protein: 4 gm
Carbohydrate: 26 gm
Sodium: 264 mg

BREADS & MUFFINS

Blueberry Coffee Cake

Juanita Dodd, R. D.

*This is a delicious low-fat breakfast bread - full of berries.
Recipe may be doubled and baked in a 9x13-inch pan with good results.*

1 1/2 c. sugar
4 egg whites
1 T. melted margarine
1/2 c. nonfat milk
2 c. flour
2 tsp. baking powder
1/4 tsp. Lite Salt
2 c. blueberries
   (fresh, or thawed
   frozen berries)

Preheat oven to 350°. Beat sugar and egg whites just until foamy. Add margarine and milk. Sift or mix together flour, baking powder and Lite Salt. Combine wet and dry ingredients and mix well. Gently add blueberries and barely mix. Bake in an 8-inch square pan sprayed with nonstick cooking spray for 40 to 45 minutes, or until done.

Servings:
  9

Serving Size:
  2 1/2-inch by 2 1/2-inch piece

Nutritional analysis per serving:
  Calories: 272
  Fat: 2 gm
  Cholesterol: trace mg
  Protein: 5 gm
  Carbohydrate: 60 gm
  Sodium: 188 mg

TASTEFULLY OREGON

Cherry Banana Bread
Cindy Francois, R.D.

A low-fat banana bread with many variations. Instead of cherry pie filling, you can use the same amount of cranberries, pumpkin or applesauce, or leave out altogether and add more bananas. The fruit makes this bread very moist.

4 c. Reduced-Fat Bisquick
1 c. egg substitute
4 ripe bananas, mashed
1 (20 oz.) can light cherry pie filling
1 c. sugar
1 T. oil
1 tsp. vanilla

Preheat oven to 350°. Mix all ingredients together in a large mixing bowl. Spray bundt pan with nonstick cooking spray. Pour batter into pan and bake for 50 to 60 minutes, until wooden pick inserted in center comes out clean. Let cool before cutting.

Servings:
24

Serving Size:
1 slice

Nutritional analysis per serving:
Calories:	163
Fat:	2 gm
Cholesterol:	trace mg
Protein:	3 gm
Carbohydrate:	30 gm
Sodium:	263 mg

BREADS & MUFFINS

Cindy's husband's great aunt, Kathy Herring, and other workers are sorting prunes in the early 1900's in Dundee, Oregon. (Courtesy of Marion Brumback's <u>Stories of Old Dundee</u>)

TASTEFULLY OREGON

Cherry Bran Bread

Cheryl Bittle, R.D.; Ruth Hayden, R.D.

A great holiday bread.

1 c. white flour
3/4 c. whole wheat flour
1 T. baking powder
1/2 tsp. Lite Salt
1/2 tsp. nutmeg
1/2 c. sugar
1 c. oat bran
1 1/4 c. skim milk
2 egg whites
1 T. oil
1/2 c. chopped nuts
1 c. maraschino cherries, well drained & finely chopped

TOPPING:
1 tsp. margarine
1/4 c. sugar
2 T. finely-chopped nuts
2 to 3 T. maraschino cherries, well drained and finely chopped

Preheat oven to 350°. Stir together flours, baking powder, Lite Salt, nutmeg and sugar. In a separate bowl, combine oat bran and milk. Let it stand 10 minutes. Beat egg whites and oil into bran and milk. Stir in flour mixture. Fold nuts and cherries into batter. Pour batter into 9x5-inch loaf pan which has been sprayed with nonstick spray.

Topping: Heat margarine in small fry pan until bubbly. Remove from heat. Stir in sugar, nuts and cherries. Sprinkle over batter. Bake 1 hour, or until a wooden pick inserted in center comes out clean. Cool 10 minutes and remove from pan to cooling rack.

Servings:
  16 slices

Serving Size:
  1 slice

Nutritional analysis per serving:
  Calories: 166
  Fat: 5 gm
  Cholesterol: trace mg
  Protein: 4 gm
  Carbohydrate: 30 gm
  Sodium: 291 mg

BREADS & MUFFINS

Date Nut Bread

Linda Devereux, R.D.

This is my favorite quick bread recipe. The sweet taste comes from dates and raisins - not sugar.

4 oz. chopped dates
1 c. raisins
1 1/2 c. boiling water
2 c. whole wheat flour
1 tsp. baking soda
1 tsp. baking powder
1/4 tsp. Lite Salt
2 egg whites, slightly beaten
1 tsp. vanilla
1/2 c. chopped walnuts

Combine dates and raisins in small bowl. Pour boiling water over mixture. Set aside to cool slightly. Preheat oven to 350°. Stir together dry ingredients. Stir egg whites and vanilla into cooled date mixture. Add date mixture and nuts to flour mixture; stir until well blended. Spread evenly into a 9x5-inch loaf pan which has been sprayed with nonstick cooking spray. Bake for 40 to 50 minutes, or until wooden pick inserted in the center comes out clean. Cool on wire rack 10 minutes. Remove from pan. (I like to cool overnight, at room temperature, before slicing.)

Servings:
  16

Serving Size:
  1 slice

Nutritional analysis per serving:
  Calories: 125
  Fat: 3 gm
  Cholesterol: 0 mg
  Protein: 3 gm
  Carbohydrate: 24 gm
  Sodium: 109 mg

TASTEFULLY OREGON

French Breakfast Puffs

Juanita Dodd, R.D.

1/3 c. margarine, softened
1/2 c. sugar
2 egg whites
1 1/2 c. flour
1 1/2 tsp. baking powder
1/2 tsp. Lite Salt
1/4 tsp. nutmeg
1/2 c. nonfat milk

TOPPING:
1 tsp. cinnamon
1/2 c. sugar

Preheat oven to 350°. Spray muffin tins with nonstick cooking spray. Mix margarine, 1/2 cup sugar and egg whites thoroughly together. Sift flour, baking powder, Lite Salt and nutmeg. Stir dry ingredients into margarine/sugar alternately with milk. Fill prepared muffin tins 2/3 full. Bake 20 to 25 minutes. (While they are baking, mix cinnamon and remaining 1/2 cup sugar for topping.) When Breakfast Puffs are lightly browned, carefully remove from pan while warm, and roll in cinnamon-sugar mixture.

Servings:
12 puffs

Serving Size:
1 puff

Nutritional analysis per serving:
Calories: 174
Fat: 5 gm
Cholesterol: trace mg
Protein: 3 gm
Carbohydrate: 30 gm
Sodium: 181 mg

BREADS & MUFFINS

Old World Bread

Merri Lynn Coleman, R.D.

*You will like this easy-to-prepare bread.
It is delicious when toasted and freezes well.*

1 T. oil
1/2 c. sugar
2 egg whites
1/2 c. unsweetened applesauce
2 c. buttermilk
1/2 tsp. baking soda
1 1/2 T. caraway seed
1/2 c. raisins
1/2 c. *Grape-Nuts* cereal
2 1/2 c. white flour
1 c. whole wheat flour
1/2 c. wheat germ
1 T. baking powder

Preheat oven to 350°. Spray 10-inch tube or bundt pan with nonstick cooking spray and then lightly flour it. Mix oil and sugar together. Add egg whites and applesauce; stir. Combine buttermilk, baking soda, caraway seeds, raisins and cereal. Add to sugar/applesauce mixture and stir well. Combine flours, wheat germ and baking powder. Stir dry ingredients into rest of mixture and spoon batter into prepared pan. Bake 1 to 1 1/4 hours. Cool in pan for 10 minutes, and then remove from pan and cool on rack. Slice when cool.

Servings:
16

Serving Size:
1 slice

Nutritional analysis per serving:
Calories: 188
Fat: 2 gm
Cholesterol: 1 mg
Protein: 6 gm
Carbohydrate: 38 gm
Sodium: 182 mg

TASTEFULLY OREGON

Overnight Raisin Bread

James Fox, R.D.

I invented this recipe while looking for a breakfast bread with no eggs or dairy products. It is very easy to make and great for someone looking for a high-fiber, everyday, very low-fat recipe.

- 1 c. *100% Bran cereal*
- 1 c. brown sugar
- 1 c. raisins
- 1 c. soy milk (nonfat milk works if that is what you have on hand)
- 1 T. corn syrup
- 1 c. whole wheat flour (pastry flour makes it more tender, but regular flour works well)
- 2 tsp. baking powder

The day before eating: Mix bran, sugar, raisins, milk and corn syrup. Cover and let sit in refrigerator overnight. In the morning, reheat oven to 325°. Blend flour and baking powder together and add to bran mixture. Pour batter into a 9x5-inch loaf pan that has been sprayed with nonstick cooking spray. Bake for 50 minutes, or until wooden pick inserted in the center comes out clean. Slice and serve warm.

Servings:
16

Serving Size:
1 slice

Nutritional analysis per serving:

Calories:	107
Fat:	<1 gm
Cholesterol:	0 mg
Protein:	2 gm
Carbohydrate:	26 gm
Sodium:	98 mg

BREADS & MUFFINS

Pumpkin Cornbread

Connie Bondi, R.D.

Super moist and different cornbread. Great with soups and salads!

3/4 c. white flour
1 tsp. baking powder
1/2 tsp. baking soda
1/2 tsp. nutmeg
1/2 tsp. cinnamon
1/8 tsp. ground cloves
1/4 tsp. Lite Salt
1/2 c. yellow cornmeal
3 T. margarine
3 T. brown sugar
4 egg whites, or 1/2 c. egg substitute
1/2 c. canned pumpkin
1/2 c. nonfat milk

Preheat oven to 350°. Spray an 8-inch square pan with nonstick cooking spray. Combine dry ingredients and set aside. In a large bowl, cream margarine; add sugar, egg whites or egg substitute and pumpkin. Stir until smooth. Add flour mixture alternately with milk, stirring gently. Pour into prepared pan and bake about 25 minutes, or until pick inserted in center comes out clean.

Servings:
8

Serving Size:
2-inch by 4-inch piece

Nutritional analysis per serving:
Calories: 139
Fat: 5 gm
Cholesterol: trace mg
Protein: 4 gm
Carbohydrate: 20 gm
Sodium: 237 mg

TASTEFULLY OREGON

Rieska
(Finnish Flat Bread)
Eeva Gray, R.D.

My mother makes this easy Finnish favorite with many variations. She uses rye, barley or graham flour, depending on what she has on hand. The whole grain makes a high-fiber, almost fat-free complement to a hearty soup or stew.

- 1 c. whole wheat flour
- 2 tsp. baking soda
- 1 c. rolled oats, old-fashioned or quick
- 1 c. light rye flour or white flour
- 1/2 tsp. Lite Salt
- 1 T. sugar
- 2 c. buttermilk
- About 1/2 c. whole wheat flour for preparing dough, divided

Preheat oven to 425°. In a large bowl, mix first 6 dry ingredients together. Add buttermilk and stir to make a dough the consistency of cooked oatmeal. Sprinkle 1/4 cup whole wheat flour on a cookie sheet. Divide dough in half and place both pieces on the cookie sheet. Sprinkle flour over the "sticky" top of the dough. Press dough flat with palm of hand, adding flour if necessary, to make 2 round flat loaves (each about 7 inches in diameter). Leave excess flour on top of loaves. Bake 18 to 22 minutes, or until lightly golden. Cover warm loaves with kitchen towels or waxed paper to keep moist. Cut into wedges; serve warm.

Servings:
16 (8 servings per loaf)

Serving Size:
1/8 of a loaf

Nutritional analysis per serving:
Calories: 96
Fat: 1 gm
Cholesterol: 1 mg
Protein: 4 gm
Carbohydrate: 19 gm
Sodium: 225 mg

BREADS & MUFFINS

Whole Wheat Walnut Bread with Raisins
Maureen McCarthy, R.D.

This is delicious sliced and eaten as is; also it is great toasted. It is a good snack for children of all ages. The recipe cuts in half easily if you don't want to make 2 loaves, but we like it so much that I generally make it this way.

4 1/2 c. whole wheat flour
3/4 to 1 c. sugar
1 1/2 tsp. baking soda
1/2 c. chopped walnuts
3 c. buttermilk, or 1 c. skim milk powder + 3 T. vinegar + 2 3/4 c. water
1 1/2 c. raisins

Preheat oven to 350°. Mix all ingredients together in a medium-sized bowl. Spray 2 loaf pans, 9x5-inches each, with nonstick cooking spray. Pour batter into pans and bake for 50 minutes, or until a wooden pick inserted in center comes out clean. Let sit in pans for 10 minutes to cool; remove bread and cool on wire racks. Slice and serve.

Servings:
 32 (each loaf makes 16 slices)

Serving Size:
 1 slice

Nutritional analysis per serving:
 Calories: 117
 Fat: 2 gm
 Cholesterol: <1 mg
 Protein: 4 gm
 Carbohydrate: 24 gm
 Sodium: 86 mg

TASTEFULLY OREGON

Zucchini-Pineapple Raisin Bread
Emma Steen, R.D.

A tasty way to make use of an abundant zucchini crop. I have modified this recipe by omitting the yolks, decreasing sugar and oil, and increasing fiber a bit by adding part whole wheat flour. Since this recipe makes two loaves, I often freeze one to use later for a handy treat.

3 egg whites
2/3 c. oil
2 tsp. vanilla
1 1/2 c. sugar
2 c. coarsely-shredded zucchini
1 (8 oz.) can crushed juice-packed pineapple, drained
2 c. white flour
1 c. whole wheat flour
1/2 tsp. Lite Salt
2 tsp. baking soda
1/2 tsp. baking powder
1 1/2 tsp. cinnamon
3/4 tsp. nutmeg
3/4 c. raisins
1/4 c. chopped hazelnuts or walnuts

Heat oven to 350°. Beat egg whites; add oil, vanilla and sugar. Continue beating mixture until light and foamy. Stir in shredded zucchini and drained pineapple.

Combine flours, Lite Salt, baking soda, baking powder, cinnamon, nutmeg, raisins and nuts. Stir gently into zucchini mixture, just until blended. Divide batter between two lightly-oiled and floured loaf pans, 9x5-inches each. Bake 50 to 60 minutes, or until wooden pick inserted in center comes out clean. Cool loaves 10 minutes in pans and then remove from pans and cool on rack.

Servings:
32 slices (each loaf makes 16 slices)

Serving Size:
1 slice

Nutritional analysis per serving:
Calories:	142
Fat:	5 gm
Cholesterol:	0 mg
Protein:	2 gm
Carbohydrate:	22 gm
Sodium:	83 mg

BREADS & MUFFINS

Emma Steen's daughter, Michelle, develops food preparation skills. These served her well later as a U.S. Peace Corps Volunteer, West Africa 1994 - 1996.

Iced Cinnamon Rolls

Doris Pavlukovich, R.D.

If you'd rather not make this from scratch, you might try using the frozen bread dough.

2 T. active dry yeast
1/2 c. warm water
1/4 c. margarine
2 c. nonfat milk, scalded
6 c. white flour
2 c. whole wheat flour
1/4 c. applesauce
1/2 c. sugar
1 c. mashed potatoes (instant works well)
1/2 c. egg substitute or 4 egg whites, slightly beaten
1 tsp. Lite Salt
1 c. raisins (place in very hot water for 2 to 3 minutes, then drain)

Soften yeast in warm water. Let sit 10 minutes. In a separate large bowl, add margarine to scalded milk until melted, then cool to lukewarm. Stir in 2 cups white flour, 2 cups whole wheat flour, applesauce, sugar, mashed potatoes, egg substitute or whites, Lite Salt and dissolved yeast. In a separate bowl, combine 1 cup flour with drained raisins and mix lightly with a fork. Stir until dough. Slowly add remaining flour as needed to make a soft dough. Cover with a clean towel and let rise in a warm place in your kitchen until double in size.

Continued on following page.

BREADS & MUFFINS

Continued from preceding page.

FILLING:
2 tsp. cinnamon
2 T. granulated sugar
2 T. brown sugar

ICING:
2 c. sifted powdered sugar
1/2 tsp. vanilla
2 to 4 T. hot water

Divide dough in half and roll into a 1/2-inch-thick rectangle. Combine cinnamon and both sugars and sprinkle on top of dough. Starting with the long side, roll up jelly-roll style; press edges to seal. Cut into 1-inch slices. Place cut-side down on nonstick baking sheets that have been sprayed with nonstick cooking spray. Cover with a clean towel and let rise again until double in size. Bake at 350° for about 15 to 20 minutes. Cool rolls on racks.

Prepare icing by blending sugar and vanilla. Stir in hot water, 1 tablespoon at a time, until icing is thin consistency. Drizzle each roll with icing.

Servings:
24

Serving Size:
1 roll

Nutritional analysis per serving:
Calories: 263
Fat: 3 gm
Cholesterol: <1 mg
Protein: 7 gm
Carbohydrate: 53 gm
Sodium: 117 mg

TASTEFULLY OREGON

Oatmeal Raisin Rolls
Trudee Nims, R.D.

What can smell better than warm yeast rolls? These are definitely worth the effort.

2 1/2 c. whole wheat flour
1 c. rolled oats
1 c. unprocessed wheat bran
1 c. raisins
2 pkg. active dry yeast
1 tsp. Lite Salt
2 c. water
1/2 c. honey
1 T. margarine
1 3/4 c. white flour

Combine 1 cup whole wheat flour, oats, bran, raisins, yeast and Lite Salt. Heat water, honey and margarine until lukewarm and add to flour mixture. Mix well. Stir in remaining whole wheat flour and enough white flour to make a moderately stiff dough (about 1 3/4 cups). Knead 6 to 8 minutes. Shape into a ball. Cover and let rise until double in size (about 40 minutes in a warm kitchen). Punch down and halve dough. Cover and let rest 10 minutes. Shape each half into 12 rolls (24 rolls total). Place on baking sheets which have been sprayed with non-stick cooking spray. Cover and let rise until nearly double (about 45 minutes). Preheat oven to 350° and bake for 15 to 25 minutes.

Servings:
24 rolls

Serving Size:
1 roll

Nutritional analysis per serving:
Calories: 139
Fat: 1 gm
Cholesterol: 0 mg
Protein: 4 gm
Carbohydrate: 31 gm
Sodium: 54 mg

BREADS & MUFFINS

Quick Wheat Bread

Connie Bondi, R.D.

Super-easy and tasty. You can add other grains, seeds or raisins as desired. A good choice for those who like to bake bread, but have little time.

1 1/2 to 2 c. whole wheat flour
1 1/2 to 2 c. white flour
1 T. dry yeast
2 T. sugar
1/2 tsp. Lite Salt
1 T. margarine
2 egg whites, or
   1/4 c. egg substitute
1 c. very warm water

Combine 1 cup whole wheat flour, 1/2 cup white flour, yeast, sugar and Lite Salt in large mixer bowl. Add water and mix well. Add margarine and egg whites or egg substitute. Beat 3 minutes, stir in additional 1/2 to 1 cup whole wheat flour and additional 1 to 1 1/2 cups white flour. Knead, or use dough hook on mixer, until a nice, soft dough results. Shape into loaf shape and place in 9x5-inch loaf pan that has been sprayed with nonstick cooking spray. Cover and let rise about 1 to 1 1/4 hours. Bake at 350° for 35 to 45 minutes, or until done.

Servings:
16

Serving Size:
1 slice

Nutritional analysis per serving:
Calories:	97
Fat:	1 gm
Cholesterol:	0 mg
Protein:	3 gm
Carbohydrate:	19 gm
Sodium:	51 mg

TASTEFULLY OREGON

Notes

Breakfasts Brunches & Lunches

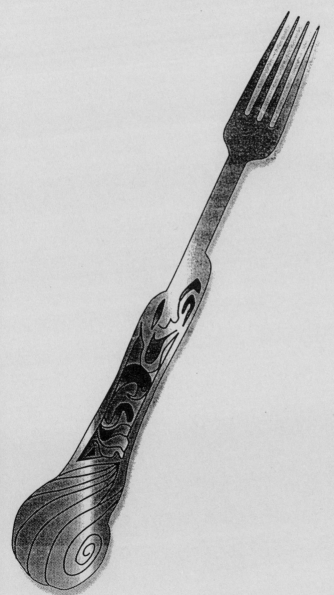

Tastefully Oregon

Calcium--Friend Of Bones, Teeth And Health

While calcium is paramount for the health of growing children and women it is no less important for men. An adequate calcium intake will ensure strong bones and good teeth and prevent osteoporosis. Calcium may even play a role in the prevention of high blood pressure.

As many as 24 million women and men have some degree of osteoporosis. Osteoporosis is a crippling bone disease that develops slowly. So slowly that it often takes years before you realize you have it.

There's no cure for osteoporosis, but you can take steps towards preventing it. The time to prevent it is **now!** During the teens, 20's and 30's, bones can be made stronger and denser. This is your once-in-a-lifetime chance to build up your bone deposits. After about age 35 you can help your body maintain bone deposits through diet and exercise.

Breakfasts, brunches and lunches present great opportunities to add calcium to the diet. Here are a few examples:
- Add low fat or fat free yogurt and fruit to pancakes.
- Eat an orange with your cereal and nonfat milk.
- Spread low fat or fat free cream or ricotta cheese on a bagel.
- Use nonfat yogurt in dips, salad dressings and salads.
- Add nonfat yogurt or low fat cottage cheese as a topping on a baked potato.

BREAKFASTS, BRUNCHES & LUNCHES

Bulgur and Apples
Charlotte Hennessy, R.D.

A unique breakfast or brunch dish.

- 2 c. water
- 1/8 to 1/4 c. brown sugar (depending on the sweetness of the apples)
- 1/8 tsp. Lite Salt
- 1/3 c. nonfat milk powder
- 1/2 tsp. cinnamon
- 1/2 tsp. ground ginger
- 1/3 c. raisins
- 1 c. bulgur
- 2 c. chopped tart apples

Bring water to a boil. Stir in brown sugar, Lite Salt, milk powder, cinnamon, ginger, raisins and bulgur. Remove from heat, cover and let stand in warm place for 30 minutes. Meanwhile, stir and cook apples in a nonstick pan until just tender. Stir apples into cooked bulgur mixture and reheat in microwave about 5 minutes.

Servings:
4

Serving Size:
1 cup

Nutritional analysis per serving:
Calories:	226
Fat:	<1 gm
Cholesterol:	1 mg
Protein:	7 gm
Carbohydrate:	52 gm
Sodium:	78 mg

TASTEFULLY OREGON

Familia

Maureen McCarthy, R.D.

A ready-to-go cereal. This is my daily breakfast staple; a recipe received from a college friend over 20 years ago! Sometimes I put it in an attractive container decorated with a ribbon to give away for gifts.

- 4 c. old-fashioned rolled oats
- 1/2 c. wheat germ, plain or roasted
- 2 c. oat bran or wheat bran
- 2 c. graham cracker crumbs (about 22 crackers)
- 1 c. golden raisins
- 1 c. chopped pitted dates
- 1 c. chopped dried apricots or other dried fruit
- 1/2 c. chopped walnuts, or 1/2 c. sesame seeds

Mix all ingredients in a large mixing bowl. Store at room temperature in a tightly covered 3-quart container. Serve with cold or warm milk as desired.

Servings:
18

Serving Size:
1/2 cup

Nutritional analysis per serving:
Calories:	238
Fat:	5 gm
Cholesterol:	0 mg
Protein:	7 gm
Carbohydrate:	45 gm
Sodium:	84 mg

BREAKFASTS, BRUNCHES & LUNCHES

Vispipuuko "Whipped Pudding"
Kati Delaurier, R.D.

This is a Finnish tradition for breakfast. In the market place, it is cut in squares and served in a bowl with milk and sugar. It also makes a great fruit whip for dessert.

3 c. cranberry juice cocktail
1/4 to 1/2 c. sugar
1/3 c. regular cream of wheat (not instant)

Pour juice into saucepan; add sugar and heat mixture to boiling. Add cream of wheat slowly, stirring constantly. Reduce heat to low and cook 15 minutes. Stir frequently to prevent sticking. Mixture will be thinner than typical cooked cereal. Pour mixture into mixing bowl; allow to cool to room temperature. Place mixing bowl into a larger bowl of ice water. Beat cranberry mixture with electric beater until pink and fluffy, about 10 to 15 minutes. Change water if ice melts. Serve warm or chilled with milk and a sprinkle of sugar.

Servings:
15

Serving Size:
1/2 cup

Nutritional analysis per serving:
Calories:	62
Fat:	trace gm
Cholesterol:	0 gm
Protein:	trace gm
Carbohydrate:	15 gm
Sodium:	1 mg

TASTEFULLY OREGON

Dutch Babies
Pam Turman, R.D.

*These make a special breakfast treat.
Fill with fresh fruit just before serving.*

6 tsp. margarine
1 c. egg substitute
1 c. nonfat milk
1 c. flour

Preheat oven to 450°. Divide margarine among 3 pie plates (8 inches each). Set plates in oven, then mix batter quickly while margarine melts. Put egg substitute in blender and blend at high speed for 1 minute. With motor running, gradually pour in milk, then slowly add flour. Continue blending for 30 seconds. Remove pans from oven and pour batter into hot melted margarine. Return to oven and bake until puffy and well-browned, 20 to 25 minutes. Check after 15 minutes.

Servings:
6

Serving Size:
1/2 Dutch Baby

Nutritional analysis per serving:
Calories:	141
Fat:	4 gm
Cholesterol:	<1 mg
Protein:	7 gm
Carbohydrate:	19 gm
Sodium:	127 mg

BREAKFASTS, BRUNCHES & LUNCHES

Fruity French Toast
James Fox, R.D.

This is a little different twist to French toast. The flavor is great.

1 banana
1/3 c. orange juice
1/2 c. egg substitute
1 c. crushed pineapple, well drained
1/2 tsp. cinnamon
8 slices French bread

Blend together banana, juice, egg substitute, pineapple and cinnamon. Put this mixture in shallow bowl and soak sliced bread in it for about 1 minute. Heat grill to 350° or medium-high. Heavily spray grill with nonstick cooking spray. Grill both sides of each bread slice until golden brown (each side takes about 5 minutes), turning carefully. Serve hot with a dusting of powdered sugar or warm syrup.

Servings:
4

Serving Size:
2 slices

Nutritional analysis per serving:
Calories:	292
Fat:	3 gm
Cholesterol:	trace mg
Protein:	11 gm
Carbohydrate:	56 gm
Sodium:	483 mg

TASTEFULLY OREGON

Gingerbread Pancakes Topped with Lemon Sauce

Julie Corpron, R.D.

We love this Lemon Sauce but the pancakes are also delicious topped with vanilla yogurt and sliced fruit (especially bananas).

LEMON SAUCE:
- 1 c. sugar
- 2 T. cornstarch
- 2 c. water
- 1 T. margarine
- Grated rind of 1 lemon
- 1/4 c. fresh-squeezed lemon juice
- 1 drop yellow food coloring (opt.)

PANCAKES:
- 4 c. *Whole Wheat and Honey Pancake Mix*
- 2 tsp. ground ginger
- 1 tsp. cinnamon
- 1/2 tsp. nutmeg
- 1/4 tsp. ground cloves
- 1 T. molasses
- 3 1/2 c. water

Sauce: Combine the sugar and cornstarch in a small saucepan. Gradually whisk in the water and bring to a boil. Continue stirring and cook until thickened (about 5 minutes) over medium heat. Add margarine, lemon rind and juice. Remove from heat (add food coloring if desired) and stir well.

Pancakes: Combine pancake mix and spices in medium bowl. In separate bowl, blend molasses with 1 cup water. Pour molasses mixture and remaining 2 1/2 cups water over the dry ingredients; mix well. Add more water if a thinner consistency is desired. Spray hot griddle with nonstick cooking spray. Cook pancakes until golden on both sides. Serve immediately.

Servings:
9

Serving Size:
3 pancakes (4 inches each) and about 1/4 cup sauce

Nutritional analysis per serving:
Calories:	329
Fat:	2 gm
Cholesterol:	0 mg
Protein:	8 gm
Carbohydrate:	71 gm

BREAKFASTS, BRUNCHES & LUNCHES

Wheat Hearts Pancakes
Roxie Snyder, R.D.

I found this recipe years ago, and it's a family favorite. We try other pancakes, but none are as good as these with the Wheat Hearts Cereal!

1/2 c. egg substitute
2 c. buttermilk
2 T. oil
1 c. flour
1 c. uncooked *Wheat Hearts Cereal*
2 T. sugar
2 tsp. baking powder
1 tsp. baking soda

Beat together egg substitute, buttermilk and oil with a wire whisk. Add remaining ingredients and blend well. Bake on a hot griddle sprayed with nonstick cooking spray.

Servings:
7 to 8

Serving Size:
2 pancakes
(5 inches each)

Nutritional analysis per serving:
Calories: 241
Fat: 5 gm
Cholesterol: 2 mg
Protein: 8 gm
Carbohydrate: 40 gm
Sodium: 419 mg

TASTEFULLY OREGON

Baked Chicken Sandwich

Joyce Gustafson, R.D.

This party dish comes from a family who serves it at all "Ten-Star" occasions such as baptism of a grandchild, a special birthday lunch, or Mother's Day brunch. It should be assembled the day before and refrigerated overnight to be baked just before serving. Fresh fruit goes very nicely with it.

12 to 16 slices white bread, crusts removed (generally takes 12 slices)

2 T. chopped onion
1/4 lb. sliced fresh mushrooms (1 1/2 c.)
2 c. chopped cooked chicken*
1/4 c. sliced ripe olives, drained
1/3 c. fat-free mayonnaise
5 hard-cooked egg whites, cut in half & thinly sliced

1 (10 1/2 oz.) can Campbell's *Healthy Request* cream of chicken soup
1/2 c. fat-free sour cream
2 T. dry sherry (**not** cooking sherry) (opt.)

Spray a 9x13-inch baking dish with nonstick cooking spray. Trim sides of 6 to 8 slices of bread so they fit across bottom of dish nicely. Put into dish as first layer (bottom of dish should be covered with bread). In nonstick skillet, sauté onions and mushrooms, stirring frequently. In large mixing bowl, mix onions and mushrooms, including liquid, with chicken, olives and mayonnaise. Carefully fold in hard-cooked egg whites so they won't break up. Spread all of this mixture over the bread in this dish. Add remaining 6 to 8 bread slices on top of chicken mixture. In a small bowl, combine cream of chicken soup, sour cream and sherry, if using. Spread over bread. Cover with foil and refrigerate overnight.

Continued on following page.

BREAKFASTS, BRUNCHES & LUNCHES

Continued from preceding page.

3/4 c. grated low-fat Cheddar cheese
Paprika
Chopped parsley, for garnish

One hour and 45 minutes before eating, remove dish from refrigerator and let sit for 1 hour to bring up to room temperature. Preheat oven to 325°. Remove cover of casserole and spread evenly with grated cheese. Sprinkle with paprika. Bake for 40 minutes uncovered. Check to be sure center is heated through and remove from oven; sprinkle with chopped parsley. Let sit for about 30 minutes and cut into 10 squares. Serve warm.

*Cook skinned breasts in microwave for about 10 minutes or use canned.

Servings:
  10

Serving Size:
  4 1/2-inch by 2 1/2-inch piece

Nutritional analysis per serving:
  Calories: 246
  Fat: 5 gm
  Cholesterol: 43 mg
  Protein: 23 gm
  Carbohydrate: 26 gm
  Sodium: 563 mg

TASTEFULLY OREGON

Puffy Chile Relleno Casserole*

Brenda Ponichtera, R.D.

I like this recipe for brunch but it is also good for dinner. Serve it with sliced oranges and grapefruit sections.

3 (7 oz.) cans whole green chiles
8 (6") flour tortillas*, cut into 1" strips
1 lb. grated low-fat Cheddar or Mozzarella cheese
3 c. egg substitute
3/4 c. nonfat milk
1/2 tsp. pepper
1/2 tsp. cumin
1/2 tsp. garlic powder
1 tsp. paprika
Salsa (opt.)
Nonfat plain yogurt (opt.)

Preheat oven to 350°. Drain chilies and remove seeds. Spray a 9x13-inch pan with nonstick cooking spray. Lay half the chiles in the pan. Top with half the tortilla strips and then half the cheese. Repeat another layer using remaining chilies, tortillas and cheese. Beat egg substitute, milk, pepper, cumin and garlic powder; pour over casserole. Sprinkle with paprika. Bake, uncovered, for 40 minutes or until puffy and set in the center. Let stand 10 minutes before serving. Serve with salsa and top with yogurt if desired.

*Buy tortillas with 1 gram of fat or less.

Servings:
8

Serving Size:
1/8th recipe

Nutritional analysis per serving (salsa and yogurt not included):
Calories: 326
Fat: 11 gm
Cholesterol: 30 mg
Protein: 29 gm
Carbohydrate: 25 gm
Sodium: 655 mg

*Reproduced with permission from Quick and Healthy Recipes and Ideas by Brenda J. Ponichtera, R.D. Published by ScaleDown.

BREAKFASTS, BRUNCHES & LUNCHES

Garbanzo Spread
Bob Wilson, D.T.R.

This spread lasts 2 weeks in the refrigerator and freezes well. Use it in sandwiches or as a dip. (Our tester said it would help end "brown bag boredom!")

2 T. sesame seeds
1 T. olive oil
1 lg. onion, finely diced
5 cloves garlic, minced
3 T. basil leaves
1 1/2 tsp. oregano leaves
2 1/2 T. cumin
1/8 tsp. Mrs. Dash-Extra Spicy
1/8 tsp. Lite Salt
1/4 tsp. pepper
2 (16 oz.) cans garbanzo beans, drained & rinsed
2 to 3 T. water
Juice of 2 lemons
5 med. carrots, shredded
1 1/2 c. chopped fresh parsley

Sauté sesame seeds in olive oil until almost brown. Add onions and garlic; cook until just soft. Add seasonings and set aside. In a large food processor, blend garbanzo beans, water and lemon juice until thick and creamy. Add onion and garlic mixture; blend well. Mix carrots and chopped parsley. Add 2/3 of this mixture to garbanzo beans. Blend until smooth. Stir in remaining carrots and parsley by hand so that vegetables remain chunky.

Curry option: Omit Mrs. Dash, change cumin to 1 tablespoon and add 1 teaspoon ground ginger and 1 1/2 tablespoons curry powder.

Servings:
  24

Serving Size:
  1/4 cup

Nutritional analysis per serving:
  Calories: 71
  Fat: 2 gm
  Cholesterol: 0 mg
  Protein: 3 gm
  Carbohydrate: 12 gm
  Sodium: 128 mg

TASTEFULLY OREGON

Hummous

Kathy Schwab, R.D.

This spread can serve as a dip with fresh vegetables, toasted pita triangles or crackers, or be used as a sandwich spread.

- 1 (15 oz.) can garbanzo beans, drained & rinsed
- 3 to 4 T. fresh-squeezed lemon juice, to taste
- 1/2 tsp. soy sauce
- 1 to 2 cloves garlic, minced
- 3 T. tahini (sesame butter)*
- Dash of cayenne pepper
- 1/8 to 1/4 c. water (or use liquid from beans)
- 1/8 tsp. paprika
- 1 T. chopped fresh parsley

Combine beans, lemon juice, soy sauce, garlic, tahini and cayenne in a food processor and blend until smooth. Add water to make it the consistency you like. Garnish with paprika and chopped parsley.

*Tahini is sesame seed butter which can be purchased in most supermarkets in the specialty foods section.

Servings:
6

Serving Size:
1/4 cup

Nutritional analysis per serving:
Calories:	133
Fat:	5 gm
Cholesterol:	0 mg
Protein:	5 gm
Carbohydrate:	18 gm
Sodium:	146 mg

BREAKFASTS, BRUNCHES & LUNCHES

Gyros

Luanna Squires Diller, R.D.

12 oz. lean beef steak (sirloin or round)
2 tsp. olive oil
3 T. fresh-squeezed lemon juice
3 T. red or white wine vinegar
1 tsp. minced garlic
1/4 tsp. sugar
1 tsp. oregano leaves
1/8 tsp. Lite Salt
1/4 tsp. pepper
1 med. red onion, thinly sliced
3 med. tomatoes, sliced into 1/2" wedges

Tzatziki (see Appetizers & Beverages section) or Cucumber Yogurt *Dressing* (see Salads & Salad Dressings section)

8 pita breads (soft, thick type)*

Servings:
8

Serving Size:
1 gyro sandwich

Several hours ahead or night before serving, slice beef in thin strips. (This is easiest if partially frozen.) In medium bowl, mix together olive oil, lemon juice, vinegar, garlic, sugar, oregano, Lite salt and pepper. Add beef; toss to coat all pieces. Marinate at least 2 hours; overnight is best.

Cook beef by either broiling, grilling or frying with no added fat in nonstick skillet; set aside. Warm pitas in nonstick skillet, lightly toasting each side. Place 1 to 2 ounces of beef on center of pita. Add a few onion slices and tomato wedges. Drizzle about 2 tablespoons *Tzatziki* or *Cucumber Yogurt Dressing* on each sandwich. Roll both sides over filling; wrap in a square piece of tinfoil with 1 end open.

*Pita bread that I prefer can be found at Greek deli restaurants.

Nutritional analysis per serving:
Calories: 287
Fat: 5 gm
Cholesterol: 30 mg
Protein: 19 gm
Carbohydrate: 43 gm
Sodium: 443 mg

TASTEFULLY OREGON

Hearty Meatball Submarine Sandwiches
Ann Reid, R.D.

Wonderful tomato sauce with meat balls spooned into a Hoagie Roll. Makes a very hearty lunch or dinner.

- **1 lb. very lean ground beef (9% fat)**
- **2 (8 oz.) cans unsalted tomato sauce**
- 1/4 c. plain bread crumbs
- 1/4 c. minced onion
- 1 clove garlic, minced
- 2 tsp. olive oil
- 1 1/2 c. julienne-cut green bell peppers (thin 1 1/2" strips)
- 1 c. slivered onion
- 2 T. unsalted tomato paste
- 1/2 tsp. basil leaves
- 6 (2 1/2 oz.) submarine rolls

Preheat oven to 350°. Combine ground beef, 1/4 cup tomato sauce, bread crumbs, onion and garlic in bowl; stir well. Shape into 54 (1-inch) meatballs. Place on rack coated with nonstick cooking spray. Place rack in roasting pan. Bake 25 minutes, or until done. Coat nonstick skillet with nonstick cooking spray and add oil. Place over medium heat until hot. Add pepper strips and onion; sauté 5 minutes, stirring occasionally. Add remaining tomato sauce, tomato paste and basil. Simmer, uncovered, 5 minutes. Add meatballs; stir to coat. Heat thoroughly for 3 minutes. If there is time, I like to put this sauce in a crock-pot and simmer for awhile. The meatballs stay together and the flavors blend so well.

To serve, heat rolls in oven; spoon 9 meatballs into each roll; divide sauce evenly.

Continued on following page.

BREAKFASTS, BRUNCHES & LUNCHES

Continued from preceding page.

Servings:
 6

Serving Size:
 1 sandwich

Nutritional analysis per serving:
 Calories: 401
 Fat: 11 gm
 Cholesterol: 28 mg
 Protein: 24 gm
 Carbohydrate: 51 gm
 Sodium: 506 mg

TASTEFULLY OREGON

Thai Salad Rolls
Kelly Streit, R.D.

Ethnic adventures can be found in a brown bag!

- 2 oz. bean threads (1 c. cooked)
- 1/2 c. grated carrots
- 1 c. shredded cabbage
- 3/4 c. chopped celery
- 1 c. bean sprouts
- 1/2 c. chopped fresh cilantro
- 1 1/2 tsp. sesame oil
- 1 tsp. hot pepper sesame oil
- 1/4 c. seasoned rice vinegar
- 1 tsp. chopped garlic
- 1/2 tsp. freshly grated ginger
- 1 T. hoisin sauce*
- 1 T. peanut butter
- 2 T. *lite* soy sauce
- 8 whole wheat flour tortillas
- 12 fresh spinach leaves

Prepare bean threads according to package directions in unsalted water. Rinse with cold water; drain well. In large mixing bowl, combine carrots, cabbage, celery, bean sprouts, cilantro and noodles. In blender, mix together the oils, rice vinegar, garlic, ginger, hoisin sauce, peanut butter and soy sauce. Pour sauce over mixed vegetables; toss well to coat. Refrigerate 30 minutes.

When ready to serve, heat tortillas in microwave for 15 seconds, or until heated through. Lay spinach leaves on top of tortilla, then place 1/2 cup salad mixture in center of tortilla. Fold the sides of tortilla toward the center. Roll up tortilla, starting from bottom.

*Available in Oriental section of most supermarkets or in Oriental specialty stores.

Servings:
8

Serving Size:
1 filled tortilla

Nutritional analysis per serving:
Calories:	134
Fat:	3 gm
Cholesterol:	0 mg
Protein:	4 gm
Carbohydrate:	28 gm
Sodium:	375 mg

BREAKFASTS, BRUNCHES & LUNCHES

Middle Eastern Salad Rolls
Kelly Streit, R.D.

This is one of my old-standby fillings for tortillas or pita bread. Makes a great lunch or dinner on a busy day. I like to add a little chopped lettuce with the filling for a little extra crunch.

1 (15 oz.) can garbanzo beans, drained & rinsed
2 to 3 T. fresh squeezed lemon juice
1 T. sesame tahini*
3/4 c. chopped red onion
1/2 c. grated carrots, divided
3 T. chopped fresh parsley or 1 T. dried parsley
5 T. chopped fresh basil leaves or 1 1/2 T. basil leaves
3/4 tsp. oregano leaves
1 T. ground cumin
1 tsp. chopped garlic
1/8 to 1/4 tsp. cayenne pepper
1 to 2 T. water
8 (8") flour tortillas

In a food processor or blender, combine garbanzo beans, lemon juice, tahini, onions, 1/4 cup carrots, spices and water; blend until smooth. Remove from food processor and mix in remaining 1/4 cup carrots. Heat tortillas in the microwave on HIGH for 15 seconds or until heated through. Place 1/4 cup of the spread in the center of the tortilla. Fold the sides of the tortilla towards the center. Roll the tortilla, starting from the bottom.

*Tahini is sometimes labeled "sesame seed butter" and is usually available in supermarkets in the specialty food section.

Servings:
8

Serving Size:
1/4 cup mix in 1 tortilla

Nutritional analysis per serving:
Calories: 233
Fat: 5 gm
Cholesterol: 0 mg
Protein: 8 gm
Carbohydrate: 40 gm
Sodium: 387 mg

73

TASTEFULLY OREGON

Notes

Soups, Stews & Chili

Tastefully Oregon

Exercise + Healthy Food = Quality Life Style

Whether you are a distance runner, a mountain climber or an avid walker, nutrition plays a critical role in your performance and your health. By choosing a variety of high carbohydrate foods, balanced with adequate protein sources and plenty of fluid, you will equip yourself with an edge-winning diet.

- Select foods high in complex carbohydrates such as breads, cereals, legumes, crackers, and pastas. They are the preferred fuel for the exercising muscle. A general guideline is to choose at least six servings a day of carbohydrate-rich foods.

- Drink fluids regularly. Dehydration impairs athletic performance even at minimal levels. To experiment with the amount of fluid you need to remain hydrated, weigh yourself before and after you exercise. For every pound you lose, drink 2 cups of fluid (alcohol not included).

- Forget the fads. Get back to the basics. Select foods from all food groups and avoid nutrition gimmicks and "myth information."

- Eat regularly and choose from a variety of sources. Don't skip meals or get onto food jags. Variety is the key.

- Eat enough food to maintain body weight and avoid drastic weight changes. Yo-yo dieting is tough on your body's metabolism and psyche.

This section contains a variety of carbohydrate-rich dishes.

SOUPS, STEWS & CHILI

Asopao
(Puerto Rican Rice and Chicken)
Nancy Becker, R.D.

This is a thick chicken and rice stew. My family loves it.

2 lb. chicken thighs and breasts, skinned (about 2 breast halves & 4 thighs)
1 lg. onion, chopped
3 cloves garlic, minced
1 (28 oz.) can tomatoes
1 bay leaf
4 c. water
1 1/2 tsp. oregano leaves
1/2 tsp. ground cumin
1 1/2 tsp. Lite Salt
Black pepper, to taste
3 to 6 drops Tabasco sauce
1 c. uncooked white rice

Put all ingredients except rice into a large pot and bring to a boil. Lower the heat to medium and cook, covered, for 20 minutes. Add the rice, bring to a boil again and simmer 20 minutes more, or until rice is cooked. Serve in bowls with cornbread and salad as side dishes. It needs to be eaten immediately or the rice will absorb most of the liquid and it becomes very thick.

Servings:
6

Serving Size:
1/6th of recipe

Nutritional analysis per serving:
Calories: 328
Fat: 11 gm
Cholesterol: 76 mg
Protein: 24 gm
Carbohydrate: 34 gm
Sodium: 571 mg

TASTEFULLY OREGON

Butternut Ginger Soup

Heidi Hadlett, R.D.

This recipe was created after purchasing a butternut squash at the local farmer's market. The salesman raved about his wife's squash and bean soup. However, he could provide few details ("it has squash and beans"). This is my version.

- 1 T. oil
- 1 c. coarsely-chopped celery
- 1 c. coarsely-chopped onion
- 1 T. flour
- 1 (14 1/2 oz.) can chicken broth
- 2 c. water
- 2 c. fresh butternut squash, peeled & cut in 1" pieces
- 1 (15 oz.) can butter beans, undrained
- 1/2 to 1 tsp. grated fresh ginger
- 1 to 2 tsp. curry powder
- Tabasco sauce, to taste (lately I've been sautéing a chili pepper with onions & omitting the Tabasco sauce)
- 6 T. plain nonfat yogurt, for garnish

Heat oil in large soup pot. Sauté celery and onion over medium-high heat about 5 minutes. Add flour and blend. Slowly add chicken stock, stirring to blend. Add squash. Simmer 20 to 30 minutes or until squash is tender. Mash some of the squash to thicken the soup. Add butter beans and stir. Add ginger, curry powder and Tabasco sauce. Garnish each serving with a dollop of yogurt.

Serving:
  6

Serving Size:
  1 cup

Nutritional analysis per serving:
  Calories: 142
  Fat: 3 gm
  Cholesterol: trace mg
  Protein: 8 gm
  Carbohydrate: 21 gm
  Sodium: 496 mg

SOUPS, STEWS & CHILI

First Prize Western Lentil Soup
Juanita Dodd, R.D.

2 c. dried lentils
4 c. water
2 oz. lean ham, cut up somewhat
1 med. onion, chopped
1/2 c. diced carrots
1/2 c. diced celery
1/4 tsp. Lite Salt
1/4 tsp. pepper

Combine ingredients in a soup pot; bring to a boil, reduce heat, cover, and boil gently for about 3 hours. Add water as needed. (If desired, press soup through a sieve to remove skins.) Serve hot.

Servings:
4

Serving Size:
1 1/4 cups

Nutritional analysis per serving:
Calories: 362
Fat: 2 gm
Cholesterol: 7 mg
Protein: 30 gm
Carbohydrate: 60 gm
Sodium: 307 mg

TASTEFULLY OREGON

Garden Split Pea Soup
Kathy Schwab, R.D.

2 c. green split peas, rinsed & drained
7 c. water
1 stalk celery, diced
1 lg. carrot, diced
1 lg. potato, peeled & diced
1 lg. onion, chopped
3/4 tsp. Lite Salt
3/4 tsp. marjoram
3/4 tsp. thyme leaves

In a soup pot, combine split peas and water. Bring to a boil, reduce heat and simmer, covered, for 30 minutes. Add remaining ingredients and simmer 1 hour, stirring occasionally. May be puréed in a blender or food processor, if desired.

Servings:
10

Serving Size:
1 cup

Nutritional analysis per serving:
Calories: 156
Fat: < 1 gm
Cholesterol: 0 mg
Protein: 10 gm
Carbohydrate: 29 gm
Sodium: 101 mg

SOUPS, STEWS & CHILI

Grandpa's Beef and Barley Soup
Nancy Becker, R.D.

This soup has an incredibly meaty flavor yet it uses only a small amount of beef. It is very hearty and gets better as the week goes by. My father, who is retired, freezes it in small containers for lunches at home.

1 T. oil
1 lb. very lean beef, cut into 1" cubes (I buy top round steak well trimmed)
3 c. chopped fresh mushrooms
2 c. chopped onion
1 yellow bell pepper, finely chopped (about 3/4 c.)
1 red bell pepper, finely chopped
1 tomato, chopped
2 stalks celery, finely chopped
2 c. pearl barley
3 (14 1/2 oz.) cans beef broth
1/4 tsp. freshly-ground pepper
8 c. water, or more

Heat oil in a large soup or stock pot; brown meat in batches until well browned. (This helps to give a really good flavor, so don't rush this process.) Add mushrooms and onions and continue to cook until onions are soft and mushrooms are cooked. Add remaining vegetables and barley, and beef broth. Stir around a few times; add pepper and water. Bring to a boil, cover, then reduce heat and cook until it looks like soup. (Cooking time is approximately 1 1/2 hours.) Some types of pearl barley expand more than others. Add more water if the soup looks too thick for your taste.

Servings:
13

Serving Size:
1 1/2 cups

Nutritional analysis per serving:
Calories:	197
Fat:	3 gm
Cholesterol:	22 mg
Protein:	15 gm
Carbohydrate:	29 gm
Sodium:	297 mg

Hearty Spinach Meatball Soup

Clinical Dietitians, Tuality Hospital

This is one of the most popular soups in our cafeteria.

TURKEY MEATBALLS:
1 lb. lean ground turkey
12 c. dry bread crumbs
1/4 c. finely-chopped onion
1/4 c. egg substitute
  or 2 egg whites
1 T. water
1 T. Worcestershire sauce
1 tsp. Italian seasoning

SPINACH SOUP:
3 (14 1/2 oz.) cans
  *Swanson's Natural
  Goodness 1/3 Less
  Salt chicken broth*
1 c. water
1 c. sliced celery
1/2 c. chopped onions
1 T. chopped fresh parsley
1 1/2 c. sliced carrots
1/4 to 1/2 tsp. pepper
1 (10 oz.) pkg. frozen
  spinach
4 c. canned unsalted
  whole tomatoes
1 1/2 c. macaroni

To make meatballs: Preheat oven to 350°. Combine all meatball ingredients. Roll into 3/4-inch meatballs with hands. Place on nonstick baking sheet. Bake for 15 to 20 minutes. Drain off any fat. Set aside to add to soup.

To make soup: While meatballs are baking, bring chicken stock to boil. Add celery, onion, parsley, carrots, Lite Salt and pepper. Reduce heat to simmer and cook until vegetables are tender (about 1/2 hour). Add frozen spinach and meatballs and simmer until both are fully cooked (about 20 minutes). Add macaroni to soup and simmer an additional 20 minutes until macaroni is tender.

Continued on following page.

SOUPS, STEWS & CHILI

Continued from preceding page.

Servings:
8

Serving Size:
1 cup with 5 to 6 meatballs

Nutritional analysis per serving:
Calories: 284
Fat: 8 gm
Cholesterol: 47 mg
Protein: 17 gm
Carbohydrate: 33 gm
Sodium: 636 mg

TASTEFULLY OREGON

Hearty Vegetable and Lentil Soup
Heidi Hadlett, R.D.

This recipe was created the old-fashioned way, making do with what was available. Served with cornbread it makes a simple, but hearty meal. Leftovers are good served cold as a dip.

1 c. chopped celery (2 stalks)
1 c. sliced carrots (2 whole)
1 sm. onion, chopped
1 clove garlic, minced
1 T. oil
1 c. uncooked lentils
6 c. water
1 (8 oz.) can tomato sauce
1 (10 oz.) pkg. frozen chopped spinach, thawed & drained
1/2 c. ketchup
1/2 tsp. vegetable or beef bouillon granules

In a large nonstick pot, sauté celery, carrot, onion and garlic in oil about 5 minutes. Add lentils, water and tomato sauce. Bring to a boil and reduce heat to simmer. Cover and cook 30 minutes. Add spinach, ketchup and vegetable or beef bouillon granules. Cook about 20 minutes longer or until lentils are tender.

Servings:
  8

Serving Size:
  1 cup

Nutritional analysis per serving:
  Calories: 140
  Fat: 2 gm
  Cholesterol: trace mg
  Protein: 8 gm
  Carbohydrate: 24 gm
  Sodium: 471 mg

SOUPS, STEWS & CHILI

Lentil Soup
Charlotte Hennessy, R.D.

*One of the best lentil soups around!
It is also very attractive; the tomatoes add a rich color.*

- 2 c. dried lentils (1 lb.)
- 8 c. water
- 1 (28 oz.) can tomatoes
- 1 c. diced or grated carrot
- 1 c. chopped onion
- 1 clove garlic, minced
- 1/2 c. catsup
- 1 tsp. Worcestershire sauce
- 1 tsp. Lite Salt
- 2 bay leaves
- 2 T. chopped fresh parsley or 1 tsp. dry parsley flakes
- 1/2 tsp. savory
- 1/2 tsp. oregano leaves
- 1/2 lb. low-fat turkey sausage, diced

Bring lentils and water to a boil and simmer about 20 minutes. Add remaining ingredients and simmer on low heat for 30 minutes to 1 hour.

Servings:
  12

Serving Size:
  1 cup

Nutritional analysis per serving:
Calories:	192
Fat:	2 gm
Cholesterol:	13 mg
Protein:	15 gm
Carbohydrate:	31 gm
Sodium:	528 mg

TASTEFULLY OREGON

Mexicali Stew
Kathrine Cramer, R.D.

*This stew is wonderful served over cornbread.
If "mild" is more your style, reduce the chili peppers by half.*

- 1/2 lb. very lean beef, cut in 1" pieces (I use top round steak, well trimmed)
- 1 yellow onion, chopped
- 2 cloves garlic, minced
- 2 (14 1/2 oz.) cans *no-salt-added* stewed tomatoes (*S & W* has one available)
- 1 T. chili powder
- 2 tsp. oregano leaves
- 2 tsp. ground cumin
- 1/4 tsp. ground pepper
- 1 (15 oz.) can garbanzo beans, drained & rinsed
- 2 lg. carrots, cut in 1/2" pieces
- 1 (4 oz.) can chopped green chili peppers
- 1 (10 oz.) pkg. frozen whole kernel corn, thawed
- 1 T. grated fresh Parmesan cheese
- 2 T. snipped fresh parsley

Spray a large kettle with nonstick cooking spray. Cook beef, onion and garlic until tender. Stir often and add a little water if needed to keep from sticking. Stir in tomatoes, chili powder, oregano, cumin and pepper. Bring to a boil, then reduce heat and simmer, covered, for 1 hour. Stir in garbanzo beans, carrots and chili peppers. Simmer, covered, for an additional 30 minutes. Stir in corn and cook, covered, for 15 minutes more. Serve in bowls sprinkled with Parmesan and parsley.

Servings:
   6

Serving Size:
   about 1 1/2 cups

Nutritional analysis per serving:
Calories:	243
Fat:	5 gm
Cholesterol:	22 mg
Protein:	17 gm
Carbohydrate:	36 gm
Sodium:	462 mg

SOUPS, STEWS & CHILI

Moroccan Vegetable Stew

Kathy Schwab.R.D.

It takes about 20 minutes to assemble this very nice and colorful dish. I like to serve it over couscous pilaf.

1 (28 oz.) can chopped tomatoes
1 (4 oz.) can chopped mild green chiles
1 lg. onion, halved and cut into thin wedges
2 med. carrots, cut into 1" chunks
1 med. sweet potato, peeled & cut into 1" chunks
1 tsp. ground cumin
1/2 tsp. ground coriander
1/4 tsp. Lite Salt
3 med. zucchini, quartered lengthwise & cut into 1" chunks
1 med. red or green bell pepper, chopped
1 (15 oz.) can garbanzo beans, drained & rinsed

In large oven-proof stock pot, combine tomatoes, green chiles, onion, carrots, sweet potato, cumin and coriander. Bring to a boil, reduce heat and simmer, covered for 15 minutes. Add remaining ingredients and stir to combine. Cover and bake at 350° for 30 to 40 minutes, until vegetables are tender.

Servings:
6

Serving Size:
1/6th of recipe

Nutritional analysis per serving:
Calories: 172
Fat: 1 gm
Cholesterol: 0 mg
Protein: 7 gm
Carbohydrate: 36 gm
Sodium: 489 mg

TASTEFULLY OREGON

Navy Bean Soup
Lancia Fish, R.D.

This delicious soup freezes very well.

4 c. dried navy beans*
12 c. water
3 celery stalks, grated
3 sm. carrots, grated
1 med. onion, chopped
1 c. lean ham cubes
1 tsp. Lite Salt
1 tsp. white pepper

Soak beans* in water (with water level at least 1-inch above beans) 8 to 10 hours in a large soup pot. Drain, then add water, celery, carrots, onion, ham, Lite Salt and white pepper. Bring to a boil, cover and simmer for about 2 hours.,

*See *On-The-Mark Black Bean Soup* for quick methods of cooking dried beans.

Servings:
  14

Serving Size:
  1 cup

Nutritional analysis per serving:
  Calories: 195
  Fat: 1 gm
  Cholesterol: 5 mg
  Protein: 13 gm
  Carbohydrate: 35 gm
  Sodium: 242 mg

SOUPS, STEWS & CHILI

On-The-Mark Black Bean Soup
Marilyn Marker, R.D.

2 c. dried black beans or 3 (15 oz.) cans black beans

Quick: Soak dried beans overnight or for 4 hours, then simmer 1 1/2 hours.

Quicker: Cook dried beans in a pressure cooker for 1 1/2 hours with 1 teaspoon oil to prevent foaming.

Quickest: Use canned beans (3 times amount of the dried beans). Drain and rinse beans before adding to the rest of soup. Add water to obtain desired thickness for soup. Reduce salt if using salted variety.

1 c. chopped onion
2 cloves garlic, minced
1 T. olive oil
1 stalk celery, chopped
1 lg. carrot, chopped
1 c. chopped green bell pepper
2 tsp. Lite Salt (reduce if using canned beans)
1 tsp. cumin
1 tsp. coriander
2 c. water
2 tsp. salt-free chicken bouillon granules

Choose method of cooking dried beans or use 6 cups canned beans. Sauté onion and garlic in oil until tender. Add remaining vegetables and spice. Add water to steam vegetables. When tender add to the cooked beans. Simmer over low heat for an hour or so.

Continued on following page.

Continued from preceding page.

2 T. fresh-squeezed lemon juice or wine vinegar
6 T. plain nonfat yogurt
6 T. mild or hot salsa

Before serving add lemon juice or wine vinegar. Ladle into bowls and top with a tablespoon of yogurt and salsa.

Servings:
5

Serving Size:
1 cup

Nutritional analysis per serving:
Calories: 341
Fat: 4 gm
Cholesterol: trace mg
Protein: 19 gm
Carbohydrate: 60 gm
Sodium: 479 mg

SOUPS, STEWS & CHILI

Quick Minestrone Soup
Linda Devereux, R.D.

A "homemade" soup in less than an hour! This one is very easy and flavorful.

8 oz. very lean ground beef (9% fat) or turkey
4 c. beef broth
1 (6 oz.) can unsalted tomato paste
1 sm. onion, chopped
2 stalks celery, chopped
1/2 c. uncooked macaroni or fettucini noodles
1 med. unpeeled potato, cut into chunks
1 (16 oz.) can *no-salt-added* **tomatoes, including juice**
1 1/2 tsp. basil leaves
1 1/2 tsp. dried parsley
1/2 tsp. garlic powder
1 bay leaf
1/2 tsp. pepper
1/4 tsp. thyme
1/4 tsp. oregano leaves

Brown ground meat in nonstick pan, stirring constantly. Drain off any fat and add remaining ingredients in medium-sized saucepan. Simmer about 20 minutes or until macaroni and potatoes are tender. (Do not overcook.) Remove bay leaf before serving.

Servings:
 8

Serving Size:
 1/8th recipe

Nutritional analysis per serving:
Calories: 136
Fat: 3 gm
Cholesterol: 10 mg
Protein: 10 gm
Carbohydrate: 17 gm
Sodium: 478 mg

TASTEFULLY OREGON

Rice and Bean Soup
Sandra Kelly, R.D.

When I have cooked rice on hand I think of making this quick and easy soup which my family loves. I frequently substitute chopped cooked chicken in place of the shrimp. The taste changes slightly, but the soup is still excellent.

1 T. oil
1 c. chopped onion
1/2 c. chopped celery
1 clove garlic, minced
2 T. flour
1/2 c. water
1 tsp. chili powder
1/2 tsp. ground cumin
1 (14 1/2 oz.) can *no-salt-added* whole tomatoes, undrained & chopped
1 (14 1/2 oz.) can chicken broth (Swanson's *1/3 less salt Chicken Broth* is a good lower salt choice)
3/4 lb. uncooked sm. shrimp, peeled & deveined
1 (15 1/2 oz.) can *S & W reduced-salt* kidney beans, drained & rinsed
1 T. fresh-squeezed lime juice
1 c. cooked long grain rice

Fresh cilantro, for garnish
Lime slices, for garnish

Heat oil in a large pot over medium heat. Add onion, celery and garlic. Sauté for 5 minutes. Sprinkle with flour; stir well and cook an additional minute. Add water, chili powder, cumin, tomatoes with juice and chicken broth. Bring to a boil; cover, reduce heat and simmer for 10 minutes.

Add shrimp and beans to soup and stir well. Cook, uncovered, 5 minutes or until shrimp turn pink. Remove from heat, and stir in lime juice. Add rice. Garnish with cilantro and lime slices.

Continued on following page.

SOUPS, STEWS & CHILI

Continued from preceding page.

Servings:
5

Serving Size:
1/5th of recipe

Nutritional analysis per serving:
Calories: 253
Fat: 4 gm
Cholesterol: 97 mg
Protein: 18 gm
Carbohydrate: 37 gm
Sodium: 541 mg

TASTEFULLY OREGON

Soupe au Pistou (Bean and Basil Soup)

Sabine Artaud-Wild, R.D.

I brought this recipe from my native Provence in France and shared it with my colleagues working on the "New American Diet". It is a simple peasant's and fisherman's fare, which fits into "heart healthy" guidelines without modification except for a decrease in the amounts of oil originally suggested.

1 c. chopped potatoes
2 c. chopped carrots
2 c. chopped onions
12 c. water
2 c. fresh green beans
1 c. uncooked macaroni
1/2 tsp. Lite Salt
1/4 c. tomato paste
3 cloves garlic, minced
2 T. fresh basil or
   2 tsp. dried leaves
1/4 c. fresh grated Parmesan cheese
1 T. olive oil
1 (16 oz.) can white beans, drained & rinsed

Boil potatoes, carrots and onion in water until almost cooked. Add green beans, macaroni noodles and Lite Salt. Cook until tender. In a separate bowl, combine tomato paste, garlic, basil and cheese. Slowly beat in the oil. Add about 2 cups of hot soup (prepared above) slowly; beat vigorously upon addition. Pour mixture back into soup pot and mix well. Add white beans. Serve hot.

Continued on following page.

SOUPS, STEWS & CHILI

Continued from preceding page.

Servings:
10

Serving Size:
1 cup

Nutritional analysis per serving:
Calories: 168
Fat: 3 gm
Cholesterol: 2 mg
Protein 7 gm
Carbohydrate: 30 gm
Sodium: 189 mg

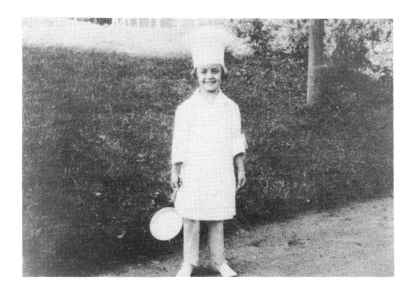

Sabine had an interest in cooking at a very young age! She is pictured as a French Pastry Chef on her way to a costume party.

TASTEFULLY OREGON

Split Pea and Herb Soup
Tanya Boynay, R.D.

This soup is great with whole grain rolls and a large salad.

- 2 c. dried green split peas
- 8 c. water
- 2 cloves garlic, minced
- 1 med. onion, chopped
- 1 c. cubed lean ham, well-trimmed
- 1 c. chopped celery
- 1 c. chopped carrots
- 1/2 tsp. pepper
- 1 1/2 tsp. thyme leaves
- 1 1/2 tsp. rosemary
- 2 bay leaves

Using a large pot, heat split peas, water, garlic and onion to boiling 1 to 2 minutes. Remove from heat and let stand 1 hour. Add ham, celery, carrots, pepper, thyme, rosemary and bay leaves. Heat to boiling, then reduce heat to low. Cover and simmer 2 to 3 hours.

Servings:
  10

Serving Size:
  1 cup

Nutritional analysis per serving:

Calories:	166
Fat:	1 gm
Cholesterol:	7 mg
Protein:	13 gm
Carbohydrate:	27 gm
Sodium:	227 mg

SOUPS, STEWS & CHILI

Summertime Gazpacho
(A Cold Soup)
Joyce Gustafson, R.D.

Hot day? This cold soup, loaded with fresh vegetables, is delicious with crunchy bread and fresh fruit.

1 (26 oz.) can cream of tomato soup
3 1/4 c. cold water
1/4 c. wine vinegar
1/2 tsp. garlic powder or to your taste
Pinch of cayenne pepper
1/2 c. sliced avocado
1 1/2 c. chopped fresh tomato
1/4 c. sliced black olives, drained
1 c. chopped cucumber
1/4 c. chopped green onions

Mix soup, water, vinegar, garlic powder and cayenne together. A wire whisk works well to blend it well. Add remaining ingredients and chill at least 4 hours. Serve cold.

Servings:
10

Serving Size:
1 cup

Nutritional analysis per serving:
Calories:	75
Fat:	3 gm
Cholesterol:	0 mg
Protein:	2 gm
Carbohydrate:	13 gm
Sodium:	546 mg

TASTEFULLY OREGON

Tomato Florentine Soup

Christie Digman, R.D.

By popular demand we requested the recipe after this soup was served at a meeting of dietitians! Some suggestions are included to lower the sodium, if you are interested.

- 1 c. chopped onion
- 5 to 6 cloves garlic, minced
- 8 c. chicken broth, divided (*Swanson's Natural Goodness* has 1/3 less sodium)
- 1 1/2 tsp. oregano leaves)
- 1 tsp. thyme leaves
- 1 1/2 tsp. basil leaves
- 1/2 tsp. black pepper
- 1/4 c. red wine
- 2 (14 1/2 oz.) cans chopped tomatoes, undrained (we suggest using *no-salt-added canned tomatoes* to keep the sodium low)
- 1 (12 oz.) can unsalted tomato paste
- 1/2 c. water
- 1 (10 oz.) pkg. frozen chopped spinach, thawed
- 1 T. balsamic vinegar

- 2 T. grated Parmesan cheese, for garnish

Spray a large soup pot with nonstick spray and warm over medium heat. Add onion, garlic and 1/4 cup of the broth. Stir and cook until onions are limp. Stir in oregano, thyme, basil, pepper and red wine. Add remaining broth, chopped tomatoes, tomato paste, water and thawed spinach which has been drained and squeezed dry. Mix and bring soup to a simmer; cook for about 10 minutes. Add balsamic vinegar and serve immediately after adding vinegar. Spoon grated Parmesan cheese on top of each bowl when serving.

Continued on following page.

SOUPS, STEWS & CHILI

Continued from preceding page.

Servings:
14

Serving Size:
1 cup

Nutritional analysis per serving:
Calories: 70
Fat: 1 gm
Cholesterol: trace mg
Protein: 3 gm
Carbohydrate: 11 gm
Sodium: 420 mg

The Home Economics Tea Room Kitchen 1918 at Oregon Agricultural College. Many of our state's dietitians learned how to make delicious treats for entertaining in this kitchen. Notice the 8 lemon pies on the menu for a party. (Courtesy of Oregon State University Archives, Harriet's Collection #848).

TASTEFULLY OREGON

Vegetable Barley Soup
Kathy Schwab, R.D.

As with most soups, the flavor improves if made ahead and reheated. It is an excellent recipe which takes 10 to 15 minutes to assemble. The cook can be off doing other things while it cooks.

1 lg. onion, chopped
2 cloves garlic, minced
1 T. margarine
1 lb. fresh mushrooms, sliced
1/2 tsp. Lite Salt
6 c. water
1/2 c. pearl barley
2 T. *Lite* soy sauce
1/2 tsp. thyme leaves
1/2 tsp. marjoram leaves
3 T. white wine (opt.)
1 med. carrot, diced
1 (15 oz.) can Cannellini beans, drained & rinsed, or use butter beans
1/2 c. frozen whole kernel corn
1/4 tsp. black pepper

In a soup pot, sauté onions and garlic in margarine until soft. Add mushrooms and Lite Salt and cook until tender. Add water, barley, soy sauce, herbs, wine and carrots. Bring to a boil, then reduce heat and simmer, covered, until barley is tender, about 1 1/2 hours. Add beans, corn and pepper. Cook 10 to 20 minutes longer.

Servings:
12

Serving Size:
1 cup

Nutritional analysis per serving:
Calories: 86
Fat: 1 gm
Cholesterol: 0 mg
Protein: 4 gm
Carbohydrate: 16 gm
Sodium: 293 mg

SOUPS, STEWS & CHILI

Zesty Black Bean Soup
Tanya Boynay, R.D.

This is a large recipe that can be easily cut in half. It has excellent flavor which we really enjoy on cool, winter evenings. I like to serve it with fresh baked foccacia bread.

4 c. dried black beans or 6 (15 oz.) cans black beans (*S & W* has a 50% reduced-salt version)
4 (14 1/2 oz.) cans chicken broth
8 c. water
1 bunch celery with leaves, chopped
1 lb. carrots, chopped (3 1/2 c.)
2 lg. onions, chopped
2 to 4 garlic cloves, minced
Grated zest (rind) of 1 lg. lemon
Juice of 1 lemon
1 tsp. Lite Salt (omit if using canned beans)
1/2 tsp. pepper

If using dried beans: Soak beans overnight in large bowl with enough water to cover beans by 2 inches. Drain. Put beans in a large 12-quart pot and combine with chicken broth, water, celery, carrots, onions, garlic and lemon zest. Reserve rest of the lemon for later. Bring to boil over high heat. Reduce heat to low and simmer, uncovered, until liquid is just below surface of beans and ingredients are very tender, about 2 1/2 to 3 hours (if using canned beans simmer for about 1 hour). Using a hand mixer, purée soup to a smooth or slightly lumpy consistency. Stir in lemon juice, Lite Salt and pepper and cook over medium heat. Stir constantly until heated through.

Servings:
16

Serving Size:
1 cup

Nutritional analysis per serving:
Calories:	207
Fat:	2 gm
Cholesterol:	1 mg
Protein:	15 gm
Carbohydrate:	35 gm
Sodium:	567 mg

TASTEFULLY OREGON

Zucchini Tomato Soup
Ruth Hayden, R.D.

Great on a cool day. It also is very quick and easy to prepare. This soup is very tasty and light so I often double it so there is plenty for second helpings.

1/4 c. chopped onion
1 clove garlic, chopped
4 c. sliced zucchini
1/2 c. beef broth
1/4 tsp. basil leaves
2 lg. tomatoes, cut in quarters
1/2 tsp. pepper

4 tsp. grated Parmesan cheese
4 tsp. *real bacon bits* or *Bacon Bits* (opt.)

Combine all ingredients in a saucepan (except Parmesan cheese and *bacon bits*). Simmer about 20 minutes or until zucchini is fork-tender. Purée in blender or food processor. Sprinkle each serving with 1 teaspoon Parmesan cheese and bacon bits, if using. Serve hot.

Servings:
4

Serving Size:
1 cup

Nutritional analysis per serving:
Calories: 54
Fat: 1 gm
Cholesterol: 2 mg
Protein: 4 gm
Carbohydrate: 9 gm
Sodium: 150 mg

SOUPS, STEWS & CHILI

Champion Chili
Nancy Oberschmidt, R.D.

This is an adaptation of a recipe from a favorite magazine many years ago. The bulgur makes it look meatier than it is and helps to reduce the fat. (Our testers loved it and said it got even better the second day!)

1 lb. dried black turtle beans
14 c. water, divided
1 tsp. oil
1 lg. onion, chopped
1 green bell pepper, chopped
1 stalk celery, chopped
1 med. carrot, chopped
1 lb. very lean ground beef (9% fat)
2 cloves garlic, minced
1 c. boiling water
1 c. uncooked bulgur (cracked wheat)
1 sm. jalapeño pepper, minced
1 (14 1/2 oz.) can peeled, diced tomatoes
1 (7 oz.) can diced green chilies
1 (15 oz.) can *no-salt-added* tomato sauce
1 (12 oz.) can light beer
2 T. mild chili powder
1 T. ground cumin
1 bay leaf
1/2 tsp. Tabasco
1/2 tsp. Lite Salt

Wash beans and discard water. Place beans in 8 cups of water and boil for 5 minutes; then soak for 1 hour. Drain off soaking water, add 6 cups water and boil gently for 1 hour. Heat oil in skillet and sauté vegetables slightly. Add beef and garlic and stir until meat is cooked and vegetables are tender. In a separate bowl, add 1 cup boiling water to bulgur and set aside. Add remaining ingredients and cooked beans to meat/vegetable mixture. Add soaked bulgur and cook chili gently for 1 hour.

Continued on following page.

Continued from preceding page.

Servings:
  10

Serving Size:
  1/10th of recipe

Nutritional analysis per serving:
  Calories: 328
  Fat: 6 gm
  Cholesterol: 17 mg
  Protein: 23 gm
  Carbohydrate: 47 gm
  Sodium: 430 mg

SOUPS, STEWS & CHILI

Chicken Chili

Cathy Petersen, D.T.R.

This saucy chili has good flavor and is very easy to fix. It was rated wonderful at 4 separate testing sessions and it only takes 15 minutes to assemble.

- 2 lb. ground chicken or turkey breast
- 2 (14 1/2 oz.) cans unsalted stewed tomatoes (*S & W* has one available*)
- 1 (10 3/4 oz.) can tomato purée
- 1 sm. onion, chopped
- 1 T. crushed bottled or fresh garlic
- 2 to 4 T. chili powder
- 1 T. ground cumin
- 1/8 tsp. pepper
- 1 (15 1/4 oz.) can kidney beans, drained & rinsed (*S & W* has 50% less salt*)

Brown ground chicken or turkey in a nonstick skillet. Stir while browning and break into pieces. Add a small amount of water if needed to keep chicken from sticking to skillet. Drain off any fat that accumulates. Add remaining ingredients and simmer 35 to 40 minutes.

*Lower salt products are suggested to reduce the sodium content.

Servings:
  6

Serving Size:
  1 1/2 cups

Nutritional analysis per serving:
  Calories: 313
  Fat: 5 gm
  Cholesterol: 77 mg
  Protein: 39 gm
  Carbohydrate: 36 gm
  Sodium: 594 mg

TASTEFULLY OREGON

Chili Molé

Kathy Schwab, R.D.

A rich, dark chili that is just delicious. I like to serve it with cornbread.

- 1 (15 oz.) can pinto beans
- 1 (15 oz.) can kidney beans (*S & W* has a 50% reduced-salt version)
- 1 (15 oz.) can black beans, drained (*S & W* has a 50% reduced-salt version)
- 1 lg. onion, coarsely chopped
- 3 cloves garlic, minced
- 1 T. oil
- 2 (14 1/2 oz.) cans *no-salt-added* tomatoes, chopped
- 1 c. water
- 1 c. salsa, fresh or commercial
- 2 T. cocoa powder
- 1 1/4 tsp. cumin
- 1 1/4 tsp. oregano leaves
- Dash ground nutmeg
- Dash ground allspice
- 1/4 tsp. cayenne pepper

Drain and rinse all the canned beans and set aside. Sauté onion and garlic in oil (adding a little water, if needed) until soft. Add remaining ingredients and bring to a boil. Reduce heat and simmer, covered, for 20 minutes. Uncover and simmer an additional 10 minutes.

Servings:
6

Serving Size:
1 3/4 cups

Nutritional analysis per serving:
Calories:	261
Fat:	3 gm
Cholesterol:	0 mg
Protein:	14 gm
Carbohydrate:	50 gm
Sodium:	587 mg

SOUPS, STEWS & CHILI

Quick and Easy Black Bean Chili
Connie Evers, R.D.

Quick, easy, tasty and filling -- what more could you ask for?

1 med. onion, chopped
1 lb. very lean ground beef (9% fat)
2 (15 oz.) cans black beans, undrained
1 (15 oz.) can tomato sauce
1 (6 oz.) can unsalted tomato paste
1 c. water
2 T. chili powder

Heat a nonstick cooking pot and brown onion and ground beef. Stir frequently and add a little water if needed to keep from sticking. Drain off any fat that appears. Add remaining ingredients and simmer for about 30 minutes. Serve and enjoy.

Servings:
8

Serving Size:
1 cup

Nutritional analysis per serving:
Calories:	250
Fat:	5 gm
Cholesterol:	32 mg
Protein:	21 gm
Carbohydrate:	32 gm
Sodium:	601 mg

TASTEFULLY OREGON

White Bean Chili with Hot Peppers
Sandra Kelly, R.D.

This delicious chili can be as hot as you want it! Vary amounts of jalapeños, chili powder and cayenne to suit your taste buds.

1 c. chopped onion (1 lg.)
1/4 c. dry sherry
1 c. chopped green bell peppers (2 med.)
2 fresh jalapeño peppers, chopped
1 sm. eggplant, finely diced
2 c. vegetable broth or water
3 c. cooked white beans or 2 (15 1/2 oz.) cans white beans, drained & rinsed
4 lg. tomatoes, chopped
2 tsp. chili powder
1 tsp. ground coriander
1 tsp. ground cumin
1 tsp. Lite Salt or *Mrs. Dash* salt substitute
1/4 tsp. cayenne pepper

1 c. plain nonfat yogurt, for garnish

Sauté onions in the sherry until soft and translucent. Add the chopped bell pepper, jalapeños and eggplant. Stir well to coat with cooking liquid. Simmer this mixture until eggplant is soft, adding vegetable broth or water if eggplant starts to stick. Add remaining vegetable broth (or water), white beans, tomatoes, chili powder, coriander, cumin, Lite Salt and cayenne and bring to a boil. Lower heat and simmer 1 hour. Taste and add additional cayenne if desired. Serve hot with a heaping tablespoon of yogurt on top of each bowl of chili.

Servings:
8

Serving Size:
1 cup

Nutritional analysis per serving:
Calories: 177
Fat: 1 gm
Cholesterol: < 1 mg
Protein: 11 gm
Carbohydrate: 31 gm
Sodium: 375 mg

Salads & Salad Dressings

Tastefully Oregon

Five A Day Is The Way

What is the most attractive display in food stores?
Undoubtedly it's the fresh produce section--those colorful and plentiful fruits and vegetables.

Five A Day--that is, eat at least five servings of fruits and vegetables a day is advice that comes from health promoting organizations. Why the push to increase produce intake? More and more research shows that people who regularly consume fruits and vegetables have fewer cancers, heart disease, strokes and colon diseases.

On The Way To Five A Day

- Include fresh fruits and vegetables with each meal.
- Frequent salad bars and choose lots of raw vegetables, but beware of toppings (croutons, nuts, seeds, olives) and rich dressings.
- Sneak vegetables into dishes such as spaghetti sauce, soups, stews and meatloaf.
- Use cooking liquid from vegetables to make sauces, soups and stews.
- Have fresh vegetables cleaned and ready to eat (prepackaged baby carrots are very handy). Add a low fat dip for a special treat.
- Top pizza with broccoli, spinach or other vegetables.
- Make a colorful salad with a variety of melons and berries.
- Make a frosty drink by blending 1 cup of melon, berries or banana and 1 cup of ice. A touch of sugar will sweeten it or add a little lemon juice for a tart flavor.
- Grill a kabob of vegetables using a basting sauce for added flavor.
- Top vanilla frozen yogurt with fresh berries.
- Keep an attractive bowl of colorful fruit on the table.

SALADS & SALAD DRESSINGS

Blue Ribbon Potato Salad
Cindy Francois, R.D.

This delicious salad has a light oil and vinegar dressing and can be served warm or cold (I prefer cold). The flavors blend well if made the day before serving.

6 c. cubed red potatoes, unpeeled
6 T. chopped green onions
1/4 c. red wine vinegar
1 T. olive oil
3 T. chopped chives
3/4 tsp. Lite Salt
3/4 tsp. pepper
3/4 tsp. sugar

Bring cubed potatoes to a boil and simmer for about 10 minutes or until potatoes are tender, but not mushy. Drain well. Add chopped green onions while potatoes are still warm. In a separate bowl, mix vinegar, oil, chives, Lite Salt, pepper and sugar. Add to potato and onion mixture. Cover well and refrigerate until ready to serve.

Servings:
6

Serving Size:
1 cup

Nutritional analysis per serving:
Calories: 162
Fat: 2 gm
Cholesterol: 0 mg
Protein: 3 gm
Carbohydrate: 33 gm
Sodium: 145 mg

TASTEFULLY OREGON

Chilled Potato and Green Bean Salad

Terese Scollard, R.D.

The flavors blend well if made a day ahead and refrigerated overnight. Diced, cooked and chilled chicken, turkey, salmon or tuna can be added to make it a main-dish salad.

- 1 1/2 lb. (3 lg.) red or white potatoes, steamed & quartered
- 12 oz. (1 1/2 c.) fresh or frozen whole green beans, steamed & chilled
- 3 hard-cooked egg whites, quartered
- 1/2 c. chopped fresh parsley
- 1/2 c. diced red bell pepper
- 1/2 tsp. Lite Salt
- 3/4 c. fat-free Italian salad dressing

Steam potatoes and green beans in separate pans just until done. Cool and cut into bite-size pieces. (Potatoes look attractive if left unpeeled.) Add hard-cooked egg whites, parsley, red pepper and Lite Salt. Gently blend in salad dressing. Do not overmix.

Servings:
6

Serving Size:
1 cup

Nutritional analysis per serving:
Calories:	138
Fat:	trace gm
Cholesterol:	0 mg
Protein:	5 gm
Carbohydrate:	30 gm
Sodium:	491 mg

SALADS & SALAD DRESSINGS

Camp Cooking 1920 was taught at Oregon State College to both Home Ec majors and Forestry students. Note the white aprons! (Courtesy of Oregon State University Archives, Harriet's Collection #978)

TASTEFULLY OREGON

Hot Potato Salad
Nuha Rice, R.D.

6 med. red potatoes, unpeeled & cut into 1" cubes
2 T. olive oil
2 T. rice vinegar
1 T. sugar
1/4 tsp. dry mustard
1/4 tsp. black pepper
1/3 c. finely-chopped red onion
1/4 c. diced red bell pepper
1/8 tsp. paprika
2 T. chopped fresh parsley

Cover potatoes with water, bring to a boil, reduce heat, and cook 12 to 14 minutes or until potatoes are just tender. Drain and set aside. Combine olive oil with vinegar, sugar, dry mustard and pepper. Mix in pepper, onions, bell pepper and paprika. Pour over drained warm potatoes and serve immediately. Sprinkle top with chopped parsley.

Servings:
6

Serving Size:
1 cup

Nutritional analysis per serving:
Calories	172
Fat:	5 gm
Cholesterol:	0 mg
Protein:	3 gm
Carbohydrate:	31 gm
Sodium:	7 mg

SALADS & SALAD DRESSINGS

Bean Salad Supreme
Madelyn Koontz, R.D.

Great salad for a potluck; can use other bean combinations--I have just suggested my favorites. It is best to make this several hours before serving, or marinate overnight. This is a large salad, but can easily be cut in half, if desired.

- 1 (16 oz.) can cut green beans
- 1 (16 oz.) can red kidney beans
- 1 (16 oz.) can garbanzo beans
- 1 (16 oz.) can yellow wax beans
- 1 (16 oz.) can pinto beans
- 1 (2 3/4 oz.) can sliced black olives
- 1 (6 oz.) jar artichoke hearts
- 1 red onion, thinly sliced
- 1/2 c. minced green bell pepper
- 10 to 12 med. fresh mushrooms, sliced

Drain and rinse all beans, olives and artichoke hearts; combine with onions, green pepper and mushrooms. Combine marinade ingredients, mix well until sugar is dissolved (if marinating overnight, add parsley and basil on the day you are serving salad so won't lose fresh look).

Continued on following page.

Continued from preceding page.

MARINADE:
1/4 c. chopped fresh parsley
1/4 c. chopped fresh basil (can use 1 1/2 T. dried, but I really prefer fresh)
1 tsp. garlic powder
1/2 tsp. oregano leaves
1/2 c. sugar
1/4 c. olive or vegetable oil
1/3 c. red wine vinegar
1/4 c. red dinner wine

Pour marinade over bean mixture. Cover and refrigerate several hours or overnight.

Servings:
12

Serving Size:
1 cup

Nutritional analysis per serving:
Calories: 213
Fat: 6 gm
Cholesterol: 0 mg
Protein: 8 gm
Carbohydrate: 33 gm
Sodium: 418 mg

SALADS & SALAD DRESSINGS

Black and White Bean Salad

Sandra G. Kelly, R.D.

This is a wonderful summer potluck salad and always gets rave reviews. It is also a nice option for vegetarian dinner guests. For quick version use canned beans.

1 c. (7 oz.) dry black beans or 2 (15 oz.) cans black beans, drained & rinsed
1 c. (7 oz.) dry Great Northern beans or 1 (15 oz.) can white beans, drained & rinsed
1 c. sliced green onions
1 c. diced red bell pepper (2 med.)
1 c. diced green bell pepper (2 med.)
2 med. tomatoes, chopped
3 T. red wine vinegar
2 T. chicken broth
1 T. olive oil
1 tsp. Lite Salt
1 clove garlic, minced
1/2 tsp. freshly-ground black pepper

If using dry beans: Sort and wash beans. Place in separate large pans. Cover with water 3 inches above beans. Bring both pots of beans to boil; boil 5 minutes. Remove from heat. Cover; let stand 1 hour. Drain. Cover beans with water; bring to boil. Reduce heat; simmer 1 hour or until beans are tender. Drain; rinse with cold water. Drain again. Then continue as directed below.

If using canned beans: Combine beans, onion, red and green peppers and tomatoes in a serving bowl. In separate small bowl, combine vinegar, chicken broth, olive oil, Lite Salt, garlic and pepper. Stir with wire whisk until well blended. Pour over bean mixture; toss gently. Cover; marinate in refrigerator at least 4 hours.

Servings:
8

Serving Size:
1 cup

Nutritional analysis per serving:
Calories: 198
Fat: 3 gm
Cholesterol: 0 mg
Protein: 12 gm
Carbohydrate: 34 gm
Sodium: 157 mg (using dried)
421 mg (using canned beans)

TASTEFULLY OREGON

Fiesta Salad with Black-Eyed Peas
Kimra Warren Hawk, R.D.

This salad can be made the night before serving, which really helps some of my busy days!

2 (16 oz.) cans black-eyed peas, drained & rinsed
1 1/2 c. frozen corn, thawed & drained
1 c. finely-diced carrots
1 c. finely-diced celery
1 finely-diced red bell pepper
2 minced green onions
1/3 c. seasoned rice vinegar
1/2 c. cilantro leaves, if desired

Mix all ingredients except cilantro, and refrigerate. If using, add cilantro just before serving, so it keeps looking fresh.

Servings:
8

Serving Size:
1 cup

Nutritional analysis per serving:
Calories: 136
Fat: <1 gm
Cholesterol: 0 mg
Protein: 7 gm
Carbohydrate: 27 gm
Sodium: 444 mg

SALADS & SALAD DRESSINGS

Heart of Texas Black-Eyed Pea Salad

Gretchen Rose Newmark, R.D.

This dish is very quick and easy to prepare, and is low in fat and high in fiber. The longer it sits, the better it tastes. It can be eaten as a meatless main course or served as a side dish. I adapted it from a fashionable restaurant in Ft. Worth, Texas--I have changed it a little over the years as my tastes have changed.

2 (16 oz.) cans black-eyed peas, drained & rinsed, or 3 1/2 c. cooked black-eyed peas
1 mild, sweet red onion, chopped
1 lg. green bell pepper, chopped
1/4 c. finely-chopped parsley
1 c. nonfat Italian or vinaigrette dressing

Mix the first 4 ingredients. Add salad dressing. Allow salad to sit for 2 or more hours before serving, if possible. This salad can be served cold or at room temperature.

Servings:
  8

Serving Size:
  Generous 1/2 cup

Nutritional analysis per serving:
  Calories: 102
  Fat: <1 gm
  Cholesterol: 0 mg
  Protein: 6 gm
  Carbohydrate: 20 gm
  Sodium: 517 mg

TASTEFULLY OREGON

Navy Bean and Tomato Salad with Balsamic Vinaigrette

Madelyn Koontz, R.D.

This hearty bean salad can be very colorful depending upon the varieties of beans chosen.

1/3 c. orange juice
1/4 c. balsamic vinegar
1 T. olive oil
1 T. fresh chopped basil or 1/2 tsp. basil leaves
Pinch of freshly-ground black pepper

5 c. cooked beans (navy, lima, black or white) or 3 (15 oz.) cans, drained & rinsed
4 lg. tomatoes, sliced thin
8 lg. lettuce leaves

In a small bowl, mix together juice, vinegar, oil, basil and pepper. Add beans and chill. When ready to serve, line salad plates with lettuce leaves. Arrange tomatoes over lettuce and mound bean mixture on top. Garnish with basil sprigs.

Servings:
 8

Serving Size:
 1 cup approximately

Nutritional analysis per serving:
Calories:	197
Fat:	3 gm
Cholesterol:	0 mg
Protein:	11 gm
Carbohydrate:	35 gm
Sodium:	8 mg

SALADS & SALAD DRESSINGS

White Bean and Garlic Salad

Kathy Schwab, R.D.

1 head garlic that contains at least 8 cloves
2 (15 oz.) cans cannellini beans, drained & rinsed
1/2 c. finely-chopped red onion
3 green onions, cut into 2" lengths & slivered
1 T. olive oil
1/8 tsp. black pepper

Roast garlic by placing a whole, unpeeled head of garlic in a preheated 350° oven for 1 hour, or until soft and browned. Cool. Remove 8 cloves and press or mince them. Combine the pressed garlic with the rest of the ingredients. Serve cool or at room temperature.

Servings:
  5

Serving Size:
  1 cup

Nutritional analysis per serving:
  Calories: 253
  Fat: 3 gm
  Cholesterol: 0 mg
  Protein: 14 gm
  Carbohydrate: 44 gm
  Sodium: 11 mg

TASTEFULLY OREGON

Apple and Greens with Garlic Dijon Dressing

Sonja Connor, R.D.

I received this recipe, along with a rope of garlic, a jar of Dijon mustard and a bottle of wine from a friend as a Christmas gift. It gives a different twist to a green salad and has been immensely popular.

GARLIC-DIJON DRESSING:
- 2 T. fresh-squeezed lemon juice
- 2 T. rice vinegar
- 1 tsp. Dijon mustard
- 2 T. olive oil
- 1/4 tsp. fresh ground black pepper
- 1 to 3 cloves garlic, minced

SALAD:
- 8 c. torn greens (romaine, red lettuce, etc.)
- 2 lg. Delicious apples, unpeeled & chopped
- 1/2 c. sliced red onion
- 1 1/2 c. chopped yellow or red bell pepper
- 1/4 c. chopped filberts or almonds

- 3 T. fresh grated Parmesan cheese

Combine dressing ingredients and mix well with a wire whisk until smooth. Set aside while salad is assembled.

Place torn greens in a salad bowl. Add apples, onions, peppers and nuts. Toss gently with dressing and sprinkle top with grated Parmesan cheese.

Continued on following page.

SALADS & SALAD DRESSINGS

Continued from preceding page.

Servings:
  12

Serving Size:
  1 cup

Nutritional analysis
per serving:
  Calories: 77
  Fat: 5 gm
  Cholesterol: 1 mg
  Protein: 2 gm
  Carbohydrate: 9 gm
  Sodium: 45 mg

The Beaver Inn is the diner Sonja's mother and aunt owned and ran during the 1950's and early 1960's. It was located across from the high school, home of the Beavers, in Scott City, Kansas, a community of 4,000 on the plains of western Kansas.

TASTEFULLY OREGON

Chicken Salad with Grapes and Almonds

Emma Steen, R.D.

This salad is a delightful combination of tastes and textures.

- 3 c. cooked chicken, cut in chunks (cook 5 breast halves)
- 2 T. orange juice
- 2 T. white vinegar
- 1 tsp. Lite Salt
- 3 c. cooked rice (1 c. uncooked)
- 1 1/2 c. seedless grapes (for color use both green & red)
- 1 1/2 c. sliced celery
- 1 1/2 c. pineapple tidbits, drained
- 1/2 c. toasted almonds, sliced (see note)
- 3/4 c. nonfat mayonnaise
- 3/4 c. nonfat plain yogurt

In a medium bowl, combine chicken, orange juice, vinegar and Lite Salt; set aside. In a large bowl, combine cooked rice, grapes, celery, pineapple, almonds, mayonnaise and yogurt. Add chicken mixture to rice mixture and mix well. Refrigerate 6 to 8 hours to allow flavors to blend.

Note: To toast almonds, spread on baking sheet and bake in 350° oven 5 to 6 minutes or until brown.

Servings:
  10

Serving Size:
  1 cup

Nutritional analysis per serving:
Calories:	219
Fat:	4 gm
Cholesterol:	33 mg
Protein:	16 gm
Carbohydrate:	29 gm
Sodium:	372 mg

SALADS & SALAD DRESSINGS

Fresh Mushroom Salad
Connie J. Bondi, R.D.

A different and tasty salad!

2 c. sliced mushrooms or whole sm. mushrooms
1/2 c. sliced green onions, white part only
5 sun-dried tomato halves, not oil packed
2 T. chopped fresh parsley
1 T. chopped fresh basil
1 sm. clove garlic, minced
2 T. raspberry vinegar or rice vinegar
1 T. fresh lemon juice
2 tsp. olive oil

Combine mushrooms, green onions, tomatoes, parsley, basil and garlic in medium bowl. Set aside. In small covered container, combine vinegar, lemon juice and olive oil, and shake well. Pour over vegetables and toss to combine. Cover and refrigerate for at least 30 minutes, but overnight is better. Serve on lettuce leaves arranged on a platter.

Servings:
4

Serving Size:
1/2 cup

Nutritional analysis per serving:
Calories:	48
Fat:	3 gm
Cholesterol:	0 mg
Protein:	2 gm
Carbohydrate:	6 gm
Sodium:	74 mg

TASTEFULLY OREGON

Marinated Vegetable Salad
Kathy Schwab, R.D.

6 c. assorted vegetables (cauliflower, broccoli, carrots, green beans, etc.)
1/2 c. low-calorie *Bernstein's Reduced-Calorie Italian With Cheese* salad dressing
Black pepper

Cut vegetables into similar-size pieces. Steam or microwave vegetables until crisp-tender (about 3 to 4 minutes). It works to cook them together, although broccoli does not take as long as the other vegetables suggested, so put it in after the others have cooked for 2 minutes.

When vegetables are done, drain well and cool slightly. Toss with salad dressing and pepper and chill at least 1 hour or overnight. Drain before serving.

Servings:
  4

Serving Size:
  1 cup

Nutritional analysis per serving:
  Calories: 121
  Fat: 6 gm
  Cholesterol: 4 mg
  Protein: 3 gm
  Carbohydrate: 17 gm
  Sodium: 335 mg

SALADS & SALAD DRESSINGS

Rice and Vegetable Salad

Jodie Donnelly Perry, R.D.

- 2 c. cooked brown rice
- 1 c. shredded carrots
- 1 c. shredded, unpeeled zucchini
- 2 T. finely-chopped onion
- 2 T. fresh lemon juice
- 4 tsp. oil
- 1/2 tsp. thyme leaves
- 1/4 tsp. Lite Salt
- 1 T. dried parsley flakes or chopped fresh parsley or cilantro
- 1/8 tsp. black pepper

In medium bowl, combine rice, carrots, zucchini and onions. Toss. In small bowl, combine remaining ingredients. Pour over rice mixture and toss to blend. Chill. Serve cold.

Servings:
4

Serving Size:
1 cup

Nutritional analysis per serving:
Calories:	170
Fat:	6 gm
Cholesterol:	0 mg
Protein:	3 gm
Carbohydrate:	28 gm
Sodium:	86 mg

TASTEFULLY OREGON

Summer's Best Salad

Pat Turman, R.D.

This is a colorful low-calorie salad that keeps well in the refrigerator for several days. A change of pace in salads.

- 2 med. zucchini, sliced (4 c.)
- 1 c. chopped green onions
- 2 c. chopped celery
- 1 1/2 c. chopped green bell pepper
- 1 T. fresh basil leaves
- 1 tsp. tarragon leaves
- 1 1/2 tsp. Lite Salt
- 1/2 tsp. black pepper
- 2 c. chopped med. tomatoes
- 1/4 to 1/3 c. red wine vinegar

Combine all ingredients except vinegar. Steam until crisp-tender or microwave for 2 to 3 minutes. Be careful not to overcook vegetables. Drain off any water that may have accumulated. Add vinegar to vegetables and toss well. Chill.

Servings:
6

Serving Size:
1 cup

Nutritional analysis per serving:
Calories:	48
Fat:	trace
Cholesterol:	0 mg
Protein:	2 gm
Carbohydrate:	11 gm
Sodium:	321 mg

SALADS & SALAD DRESSINGS

Bing Cherry Salad

Susan Briggs, R.D.

1 (16 1/2 oz.) can pitted bing cherries or 1 3/4 c. fresh or frozen pitted bing cherries
1 (20 oz.) can pineapple chunks or tidbits canned in pineapple juice
1 (.06 oz.) pkg. sugar-free cherry gelatin
1/2 c. chopped walnuts
6 oz. fat-free cream cheese, cut into sm. pieces (opt.)
12 oz. diet cola
3 T. fat-free or light mayonnaise (opt.)

Servings:
9

Serving Size:
3-inch square

Drain cherries and pineapple, reserving juice. Add water to juice to make 2 1/2 cups, and heat in a saucepan. Add gelatin and stir to dissolve. Cool slightly. Add cola. Stir well. Add cherries and pineapple. Chill until thick, but not set. Fold in nuts and cream cheese, if using. Pour into 8-cup mold or 9-inch square pan and chill until set. If desired, garnish with a teaspoon of light or fat-free mayonnaise on each serving.

Nutritional analysis per serving:
Calories:	110
Fat:	4 gm
Cholesterol:	0 mg
Protein:	2 gm
Carbohydrate:	18 gm
Sodium:	9 mg

TASTEFULLY OREGON

Lemon Supreme Salad
Joyce Gustafson, R.D.

A wonderful recipe from a friend's mom; I always liked to go to their home as the food was great! This molded salad has some of the fresh vegetables in the salad, with the rest on top, so it is very pretty.

- 1 (8 oz.) can crushed pineapple, drained (save the juice)
- Boiling water
- 1 (.06 sugar-free or 6 oz. regular) pkg. lemon Jell-O
- 1 c. *light* Cool Whip, thawed
- 1/4 c. chopped walnuts
- 1 c. chopped red or green bell pepper
- 1 c. chopped celery
- 6 green onions, chopped, including the green part
- 1 c. fat-free mayonnaise or Miracle Whip

Drain pineapple, reserving juice. Add water to juice to make 2 1/2 cups, and heat in a saucepan. Add lemon Jell-O and stir to dissolve. Cool until syrupy. Add thawed Cool Whip, drained pineapple and nuts. Mix chopped vegetables together and add 2/3 of the mixture to the molded salad, saving the rest for garnish. Mix well and pour into a 9x13-inch glass dish and chill. When salad is set, ice with mayonnaise or Miracle Whip, cover top with remaining chopped vegetables as a garnish. Cover well with plastic wrap and chill until serving time. Cut into squares and serve on lettuce.

Servings:
  12

Serving Size:
  3 x 3 1/4 inches

Nutritional analysis per serving:
Calories:	115
Fat:	7 gm
Cholesterol:	7 mg
Protein:	<1 gm
Carbohydrate:	11 gm
Sodium:	187 mg

SALADS & SALAD DRESSINGS

Oregon Raspberry Salad
Helen Proctor, R.D.

Excellent with poultry. Also can be a great dessert!

1 (.06 oz.) pkg. sugar-free raspberry gelatin
2 c. boiling water
2 (10 oz.) pkg. frozen unsweetened raspberries
1 1/2 c. unsweetened applesauce
2 c. nonfat sour cream
2 c. mini marshmallows

Dissolve gelatin in boiling water and cool to lukewarm. Add frozen berries and applesauce. Mix and pour into pan approximately 7x11 inches. Refrigerate overnight or until set firm. Mix sour cream and marshmallows. Spread over salad and chill several hours. Cut into squares and serve on lettuce leaves.

Servings:
12

Serving Size:
2 1/2-inch square

Nutritional analysis per serving:
Calories: 90
Fat: trace gm
Cholesterol: 0 mg
Protein: 4 gm
Carbohydrate: 20 gm
Sodium: 68 mg

Chicken Ravioli Salad with Fruit

Joyce Gustafson, R.D.

Great for a summer dinner or a special luncheon salad. My husband was most disappointed recently when, after some "humming and stirring" in the kitchen to prepare this, I took the whole thing away for a potluck. Luckily for me, there was enough left for him to have some for dinner.

- 3 chicken breasts, skinned & boned
- 8 oz. cheese ravioli, cooked, drained & cooled (choose smallest ones you can find)
- 2 c. seedless grapes
- 1 c. snow peas, cut into 1/3's
- 12 spinach leaves, torn up (about 3 c.)
- 3 celery stalks, chopped
- 1 (6 oz.) jar artichoke hearts (not marinated), cut in half
- 2 kiwis, peeled & sliced
- 1/2 cucumber, cut in half & sliced
- 1/2 c. raisins
- 1 green onion, chopped

Several hours before serving or the day before: Cook chicken breasts (microwaving in a little water does this very quickly), cool and chop into bite-size pieces. Cook ravioli according to package directions in unsalted water; drain well and cool.

Continued on following page.

SALADS & SALAD DRESSINGS

Continued from preceding page.

DRESSING:
2/3 c. light or fat-free mayonnaise
1/4 c. fresh grated Parmesan cheese
1/3 c. fresh-squeezed lemon juice
White pepper, to taste

Spinach leaves & mandarin oranges, for garnish, if desired

Two and a half hours before serving: Combine all the salad and dressing ingredients separately. Pour dressing over salad and toss lightly. Cover and refrigerate. Serve over a bed of spinach leaves, and garnish with mandarin oranges, if desired.

Servings:
 8

Serving Size:
 1 1/2 cups

Nutritional analysis per serving:
 Calories: 310
 Fat: 8 gm
 Cholesterol: 83 mg
 Protein: 20 gm
 Carbohydrate: 40 gm
 Sodium: 607 mg

TASTEFULLY OREGON

Colorful Vegetable and Pasta Salad

Luanna Squires Diller, R.D.

A colorful salad. Terrific for potlucks or picnics.

SALAD:
- 1 (16 oz.) pkg. *California Blend* frozen vegetables, cooked to tender-crisp & well drained
- 3 c. vegetable-flavored pasta spirals, cooked firm, drained & rinsed in cold water
- 1 c. chopped celery
- 1/2 c. chopped onion
- 4 tomatoes, cut in wedges
- 1 c. chopped green bell pepper
- 1/2 c. sliced black olives
- 1/2 c. sliced green olives

DRESSING:
- 1 (1 oz.) pkt. *Hidden Valley Ranch* original salad dressing mix
- 1/2 c. *Marukan* Seasoned Rice Vinegar
- 1/4 c. water

Combine all salad ingredients in a large bowl. In a small bowl, combine dressing mix, rice vinegar and water. Stir with a small wire whisk until dressing is dissolved. Pour over salad ingredients and toss gently. Refrigerate several hours or overnight before serving.

Servings:
14

Serving Size:
1 cup

Nutritional analysis per serving:
Calories:	116
Fat:	2 gm
Cholesterol:	0 mg
Protein:	4 gm
Carbohydrate:	22 gm
Sodium:	354 mg

SALADS & SALAD DRESSINGS

Macaroni Salad
Gloria Dickman, D.T.R.

This salad is always a crowd pleaser.

8 oz. uncooked salad macaroni (1 1/2 c.)
1 c. chopped onion
3/4 c. grated carrot
4 sm. sweet pickles, chopped
1 (3.8 oz.) can sliced black olives, drained
2/3 c. fat-free mayonnaise or 1/3 c. *light* mayonnaise & 1/3 c. nonfat plain yogurt
3 to 4 T. fresh-squeezed lemon juice, to taste

Cook macaroni according to package directions in unsalted water. Drain and rinse with cold water. Add onions, carrots, pickles and black olives; mix. Blend mayonnaise and lemon juice and add to salad. Mix well, cover and refrigerate until chilled.

Servings:
7

Serving Size:
1 cup

Nutritional analysis per serving:

Calories:	181
Fat:	2 gm
Cholesterol:	0 mg
Protein:	5 gm
Carbohydrate:	36 gm
Sodium:	465 mg

TASTEFULLY OREGON

Somen Oriental Salad
Jane Wong, R.D.

This is a large-sized, beautiful salad; it would be great for a potluck. If you make this salad ahead of time, be sure to put the noodles in a colander, rinse them with cold water to separate the noodles and drain well before adding any of the dressing.

1 (16 oz.) pkg. Somen (Japanese noodles*)
1 T. toasted sesame seeds
3 T. sugar
1/4 c. soy sauce
2 T. sesame oil
1/4 c. + 2 T. rice vinegar
2 c. shredded greens (romaine, iceberg, butter lettuce, etc.)
2 tomatoes, chopped (1 1/2 c.)
1 cucumber, peeled & chopped (1 c.)
4 green onions, chopped (3/4 c.)
1 c. frozen peas, thawed & drained
2 c. broccoli or cauliflower, cut into sm. pieces
1 c. grated carrots
3/4 c. egg substitute scrambled in nonstick skillet & thinly sliced
1 c. shrimpmeat or chopped cooked chicken
Several sm. strips dried seaweed (opt.)

Break Somen noodles in half and cook just until tender (2 or 3 minutes). Drain and rinse with cold water. Place noodles in a large bowl and set aside. In a container with a lid, combine sesame seeds, sugar, soy sauce, oil and rice vinegar, and shake well to mix. Pour half of the dressing over the noodles and toss to coat well. Add greens, tomatoes, cucumber, green onions, peas, broccoli or cauliflower, carrots, egg slices, shrimp or chicken and seaweed (if desired). Just before serving, pour remaining dressing over the top and toss. Enjoy!

*Found in most supermarkets in the Oriental food department.

Continued on following page.

SALADS & SALAD DRESSINGS

Continued from preceding page.

Servings:
12

Serving Size:
1 1/2 cups

Nutritional analysis per serving:
Calories: 288
Fat: 4 gm
Cholesterol: 19 mg
Protein: 12 gm
Carbohydrate: 51 gm
Sodium: 532 mg

TASTEFULLY OREGON

Oriental Chicken Salad

Marge Norman, R.D.

My dietitian friend, Peggy, introduced me to this beautiful and festive main-dish salad. It is some work to assemble, but is really worth it as it is something special to serve when entertaining family and friends.

DRESSING:
2 T. minced fresh parsley
2 to 3 cloves garlic, minced
1/2 c. teriyaki sauce (I use low-sodium, if available)
2 T. sesame oil
1 T. oil
2 T. tahini*
2 T. rice vinegar
2 T. dry sherry
1 T. brown sugar
2 tsp. ground coriander
Few drops hot chili oil (opt.)

Several hours before serving, or the day before: Process parsley and garlic in a food processor or blender. Add remaining dressing ingredients and process until smooth. Cook chicken breasts (microwave in a little water does this very quickly), cool and chop into 1-inch pieces. Cook noodles in unsalted water according to package directions; drain well and cool. Separate broccoli into flowerets and cook quickly in the microwave oven, or drop into boiling water, drain, rinse in cold water and drain again. Toast cashew nuts and sesame seeds for a few minutes in oven to brown. Prepare remaining vegetables as directed. Set all ingredients aside or refrigerate, if needed, until ready to assemble salad.

*Sesame seed butter which is available in specialty section of most supermarkets.

Continued on following page.

SALADS & SALAD DRESSINGS

Continued from preceding page.

SALAD:
- 8 chicken breasts, boned & skinned
- 1 (8 oz.) pkg. Chinese noodles or spaghetti noodles
- 1 bunch broccoli, cut into flowerets
- 2 T. toasted cashews
- 1 T. toasted sesame seeds
- 2 red or yellow bell peppers, cut into thin strips
- 1 med. jicama, peeled & cut into thin strips
- 5 scallions, cut into thin strips
- 48 snow peas, trimmed & cut into 1/4" wide lengths
- 6 c. thinly-sliced Napa (Chinese) cabbage

When ready to assemble: Coat chicken with a small amount of dressing just before combining salad ingredients. Assemble salad by layering on a large (16- to 18-inch) serving platter in this order: cabbage, noodles, 1/3 of dressing, chicken, vegetables, 1/3 dressing, cashews and sesame seeds on top. Serve remaining dressing on the side.

Servings:
  10

Serving Size:
  1/10th of recipe (large main-dish serving)

Nutritional analysis per serving:
  Calories: 322
  Fat: 10 gm
  Cholesterol: 52 mg
  Protein: 27 gm
  Carbohydrate: 31 gm
  Sodium: 634 mg

TASTEFULLY OREGON

Berry Vinegar
Connie Bondi, R.D.

This recipe is quick, easy and yummy! It can be used in any salad dressing that calls for vinegar, but is especially good in dressing for fruit salads or greens that have fruit added. It makes nice gifts, too.

4 c. vinegar
1/3 c. sugar
2 c. rinsed berries (strawberries, raspberries, blueberries)
3 cloves garlic, peeled & split

Combine all ingredients in a saucepan and bring to a boil. Simmer 10 minutes. Remove from heat, cover tightly and let "steep" for 2 days.

Strain through cheesecloth or fine sieve into containers with tight-fitting lids. Store in a cool place.

Servings:
1 quart (64 tablespoons)

Serving Size:
1 tablespoon

Nutritional analysis per serving:

Calories:	8
Fat:	trace gm
Cholesterol:	0 mg
Protein:	trace gm
Carbohydrate:	2 gm
Sodium:	trace mg

SALADS & SALAD DRESSINGS

Cucumber Yogurt Dressing (Tzatziki)

Luanna Squires Diller, R.D.

Very quick and easy. This dressing is excellent on Gyros (see Breakfasts, Brunches & Lunches section). I, also, often serve it with salmon, use it as a salad dressing or as a dip with fresh vegetables.

1 lg. cucumber, peeled & seeded
2 cloves garlic, minced
2 (8 oz.) containers plain nonfat yogurt (I like *Nancy's* or *Dannon*)*
1 tsp. white wine vinegar

Drain cucumber on paper towels after seeding. Cut into 1-inch chunks and place in food processor with garlic. Chop fine (can be grated if no processor is available). Place yogurt in small bowl; add vinegar and cucumber/garlic mixture. Mix well and refrigerate at least 1 hour before serving to give the flavors time to blend.

*To thicken for a dip, drain yogurt in cheesecloth overnight before adding cucumber and garlic.

Servings:
   20 (makes 2 1/2 cups)

Serving Size:
   2 tablespoons

Nutritional analysis per serving:
Calories:	15
Fat:	trace gm
Cholesterol:	trace mg
Protein:	1 gm
Carbohydrate:	2 gm
Sodium:	18 mg

TASTEFULLY OREGON

Homemade Ranch-Style Dressing
Cheryl Kirk, R.D.

This version of an old favorite is very low in fat as well as low in salt. It is easy to double the recipe and have plenty on hand so it can be available for a salad dressing, as dip for vegetables or a topping for baked potatoes.

1/4 c. nonfat mayonnaise
3/4 c. nonfat plain yogurt
1 c. buttermilk
1 T. minced onion
1/4 tsp. basil leaves
1/4 tsp. sage
1/4 tsp. thyme leaves
1/4 tsp. garlic powder
1 T. minced parsley

Combine all ingredients. Mix well. Cover and refrigerate.

Servings:
8

Serving Size:
1/4 cup

Nutritional analysis per serving:
Calories: 32
Fat: trace gm
Cholesterol: 1 mg
Protein: 2 gm
Carbohydrate: 5 gm
Sodium: 135 mg

SALADS & SALAD DRESSINGS

Rice Vinegar Dressing

Luanna Squires Diller, R.D.

This dressing can be served with pasta, vegetables, or tossed salads. It's also a great marinade for fish.

- 2/3 c. seasoned rice vinegar (this is rice vinegar with added sugar & salt)
- 1/3 c. water
- 1 T. Dijon mustard
- 1 tsp. crushed basil leaves
- 1/2 to 1 tsp. horseradish

Mix all ingredients in a pint jar. Shake well before using. Keep refrigerated.

Servings:
  8

Serving Size:
  2 tablespoons

Nutritional analysis per serving:
  Calories: 24
  Fat: trace gm
  Cholesterol: 0 mg
  Protein: trace gm
  Carbohydrate: 6 gm
  Sodium: 535 mg

TASTEFULLY OREGON

Yogurt Vinaigrette Salad Dressing

Ruth Carey-Flynn, R.D.

Excellent "all purpose" nonfat dressing for fresh greens.

1 c. nonfat plain yogurt
1/4 c. seasoned rice vinegar
1 to 2 cloves fresh garlic, minced
1/2 to 3/4 tsp. Italian seasoning, or a combination of cumin & curry

Put all ingredients in a pint jar. Close lid and shake well until blended.

Servings:
10

Serving Size:
2 tablespoons

Nutritional analysis per serving:
Calories: 15
Fat: trace gm
Cholesterol: trace mg
Protein: 1 gm
Carbohydrate: 2 gm
Sodium: 19 mg

SALADS & SALAD DRESSINGS

Quick Ranch-Style Dressing
Cheryl Kirk, R.D.

This salad dressing can be used as a dip for vegetables, bagels, low-fat crackers or as a topping for baked potatoes.

1/4 c. fat-free or light mayonnaise
3/4 c. nonfat plain yogurt
1 c. buttermilk
4 tsp. pkg. *Ranch Salad Dressing Mix*

Combine mayonnaise, yogurt, buttermilk and salad dressing dry mix (stir mix well before measuring, to distribute the spices). Combine with a wire whisk or spoon. Cover and refrigerate.

Servings:
8

Serving Size:
1/4 cup

Nutritional analysis per serving:
- Calories: 38
- Fat: trace gm
- Cholesterol: 2 mg
- Protein: 3 gm
- Carbohydrate: 6 gm
- Sodium: 326 mg

TASTEFULLY OREGON

Notes

Side Dishes & Sauces

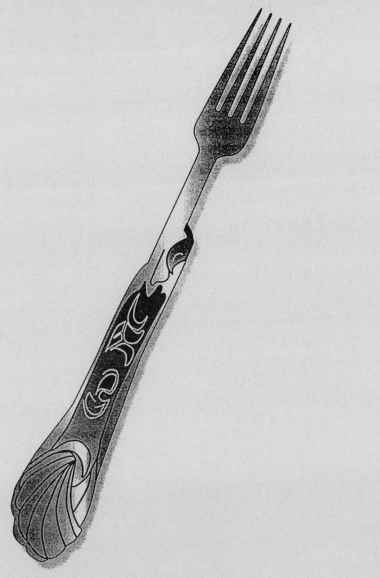

Tastefully Oregon

Should I Take Antioxidants?

- Over the last decade there has been an enormous interest in scientific circles and in the public in the possibility that antioxidant vitamins might help in preventing cancers, heart disease and even aging.

- Antioxidants neutralize free radicals that are the byproducts of many normal functions of the body, preventing damage to the cells and the dangerous oxidation of LDL, the bad (atherogenic) form of blood cholesterol.

- Antioxidant vitamins are found in plant foods: fruits, vegetables, seeds and nuts.

- The main antioxidant vitamins include beta carotene (the precursor of vitamin A), vitamin C and vitamin E.

- The antioxidant puzzle is not yet solved. Studies on the effects of taking supplements have shown conflicting results.

- Not to be ignored are the studies that have pointed out other protective factors in fruits and vegetables such as anti-cancer substances, soluble fiber and saponins. There are probably many more that have not been discovered.

Do What Mother Always Said--"Consume a Variety of Fruits and Vegetables"

SIDE DISHES, SAUCES & CONDIMENTS

Picnic Three-Bean Casserole

Dawn Kinzel, R.D.

This recipe is always a favorite at picnics or potlucks.

1 (16 oz.) can pinto beans, drained & rinsed
1 (16 oz.) can lima beans, drained & rinsed
2 (16 oz.) cans *B&M Brick Oven Baked Beans,* 99% fat-free
1 c. chopped onion
1/2 c. ketchup*
3 T. white vinegar
1 T. liquid smoke (opt.)

Mix all the ingredients in a crock-pot, or large pot which has a tight lid. Cook in crock-pot on low for 4 to 6 hours. If you want to use a conventional oven, preheat to 325° and bake, covered, for 1 1/2 to 2 hours. Add a little water if beans begin to look dry.

*The sodium content can be reduced by using low-sodium ketchup.

Servings:
12

Serving Size:
1/2 cup

Nutritional analysis per serving:
Calories:	196
Fat:	2 mg
Cholesterol:	5 gm
Protein:	10 gm
Carbohydrate:	38 gm
Sodium:	554 mg

TASTEFULLY OREGON

Southwestern Red Beans and Rice

Connie L. Dow, R.D.

My husband's favorite! This dish is quick, easy, low-fat and is also very economical. For a delicious meal add a tossed green salad and hot cornbread.

2 1/2 c. water
1 c. brown rice
1 lg. red onion, chopped
2 cloves garlic, minced
1 T. olive oil
1 (16 oz.) can diced tomatoes
1 (15 1/2 oz.) can kidney beans, drained & rinsed
2 T. chili powder
1 tsp. black pepper
1 tsp. *Mrs. Dash* or other salt-free seasoning
1 T. dried parsley
1/4 tsp. Tabasco sauce

In large saucepan, bring water to a full boil. Add rice and stir; reduce heat, cover and simmer 45 minutes. Remove from heat and let sit 5 to 10 minutes. Meanwhile, in large skillet, sauté onion and garlic in olive oil until tender. Add diced tomatoes, including liquid; stir well. Add seasonings and simmer until thickened, approximately 10 to 15 minutes. Add kidney beans and continue to simmer until rice finishes cooking. When rice has cooked, add to skillet and mix well. Serve immediately.

Servings:
4

Serving Size:
1/4 of recipe

Nutritional analysis per serving:
Calories: 379
Fat: 6 gm
Cholesterol: trace mg
Protein: 14 gm
Carbohydrate: 70 gm
Sodium: 555 mg

SIDE DISHES, SAUCES & CONDIMENTS

Basmati Rice Pilaf

Kathy Schwab, R.D.

1 (14 1/2 oz.) can chicken broth
2/3 c. water
1/2 lg. onion, finely chopped
2 cloves garlic, minced
1 c. uncooked Basmati rice (or long-grain white rice)

In a saucepan, bring about 1/2 cup of chicken broth to a boil. Add onion and garlic, and sauté until onion is soft. Add remaining broth and water and bring to a boil. Add rice, stir, cover and reduce heat to low. Cook for 20 minutes; remove pan from heat and let rest 5 minutes. Fluff with a fork and serve.

Servings:
4

Serving Size:
1/4 of recipe

Nutritional analysis per serving:
Calories: 217
Fat: 1 gm
Cholesterol: 0 mg
Protein: 7 gm
Carbohydrate: 42 gm
Sodium: 217 mg

TASTEFULLY OREGON

Cheesy Rice with Green Chiles

Charlotte Hennessy, R.D.

This is a great way to use leftover rice.

- 3 c. cooked rice
- 1 (4 oz.) can diced green chiles
- 1 c. nonfat sour cream
- 1 c. grated reduced fat sharp Cheddar cheese
- 2 T. chopped green onions

Combine cooked rice, chiles, sour cream, and 1/2 cup of the cheese and place in casserole dish. Sprinkle remaining cheese over the top. Cover and microwave 4 to 8 minutes (use longer time if casserole is heated directly from the refrigerator). Sprinkle green onions over the top and serve.

Servings:
4

Serving Size:
1 cup

Nutritional analysis per serving:

Calories:	250
Fat:	4 gm
Cholesterol:	12 mg
Protein:	12 gm
Carbohydrate:	41 gm
Sodium:	468 mg

SIDE DISHES, SAUCES & CONDIMENTS

Italian Risotto
Emma Steen, R.D.

Risotto is a traditional dish of Northern Italy. A pinch of saffron, if available, can be added just before serving to give authentic Milanese flavor to this creamy rice that is cooked to al denté (rice retains a firm texture).

4 tsp. olive oil, divided
3 cloves garlic, minced
3/4 c. chopped onion
1 1/2 c. sliced mushrooms
1 1/2 c. arborio rice
2 (14 1/2 oz.) cans *Natural Goodness 1/3 Less Salt Chicken Broth*, heated (*it is important that the broth is hot when added to the rice*)

4 tsp. freshly-grated Parmesan cheese (1 tsp. per serving)

In a nonstick 3-quart saucepan, heat 2 teaspoons oil and sauté garlic, onion and mushrooms. Transfer to a bowl and set aside. In the same saucepan, add remaining 2 teaspoons oil and lightly brown the rice. Bring chicken broth to a near boil. Add about half of the hot liquid, keeping the other half hot. Stir rice slightly and cover with tight lid. Cook over low heat for 10 minutes. Add the remaining half of hot broth and cook another 10 minutes. (Mixture should be creamy and somewhat al denté, which means "to the tooth"). Add additional chicken broth as needed. Stir in the browned onions and mushrooms. Serve warm. Pass grated Parmesan cheese to sprinkle over the top.

Servings:
4

Serving Size:
1 cup

Nutritional analysis per serving:
Calories: 375
Fat: 7 gm
Cholesterol: 1 mg
Protein: 10 gm
Carbohydrate: 66 gm
Sodium: 611 mg

TASTEFULLY OREGON

Pimiento Rice

Dolores Einen, R.D.

This is a Basque recipe that our family loves. It is good with fish, poultry or meat entrées. Saffron can be added, if desired. It gives an excellent flavor.

2 tsp. olive oil
1 med. yellow onion, chopped
2 cloves garlic, minced
1 c. uncooked rice
2 c. chicken broth
1 (2 oz.) jar chopped pimientos, drained
1/8 to 1/4 tsp. saffron (opt.)

In a heavy 2-quart saucepan, heat oil and sauté onion and garlic. Cook until onion is transparent. Add rice and brown, stirring constantly. When rice has browned, add chicken broth, pimientos, and saffron, if using. Return to boiling, stir, cover and reduce heat to low. Cook for 20 minutes. Remove from heat and let stand 10 minutes before serving.

Servings:
4

Serving Size:
1 cup

Nutritional analysis per serving:
Calories: 225
Fat: 5 gm
Cholesterol: 3 mg
Protein: 4 gm
Carbohydrate: 41 gm
Sodium: 505 mg

SIDE DISHES, SAUCES & CONDIMENTS

Broccoli-Corn Casserole
Jan Daoust, R.D.

1 T. margarine
1/2 c. crushed corn flakes
2 c. chopped broccoli
3 egg whites, slightly beaten, or 1/2 c. egg substitute
1 (16 oz.) can creamed corn
1/2 tsp. Lite Salt
1/8 tsp. pepper
1 slice bread, crusts removed & cut into sm. cubes

Melt margarine and add to crushed corn flakes. Set aside. Cook broccoli slightly; drain well. In a separate bowl, mix together egg whites or egg substitute, creamed corn, broccoli, Lite Salt, pepper, and bread cubes. Pour into an 8x8-inch baking pan that has been sprayed with nonstick cooking spray. Top with corn-flake crumbs. Bake for 40 minutes, uncovered.

Servings:
  6

Serving Size:
  1/6 of casserole

Nutritional analysis per serving:
  Calories: 119
  Fat: 3 gm
  Cholesterol: trace mg
  Protein: 5 gm
  Carbohydrate: 22 gm
  Sodium: 435 mg

TASTEFULLY OREGON

Mediterranean Vegetables
Nuha Rice, R.D.

- 1 T. olive oil
- 1 1/2 c. thinly-sliced onion
- 1 c. sliced green bell pepper
- 1 tsp. minced garlic
- 1 (16 oz.) can Italian stewed tomatoes, coarsely chopped
- 2 c. cubed, unpeeled eggplant (1 lg.)
- 1 1/2 c. thinly-sliced zucchini
- 1/2 tsp. thyme
- 1 bay leaf
- 1/4 tsp. black pepper

Heat olive oil over medium heat in a large heavy pan (a Dutch oven works well). Add onions, green pepper and garlic. Sauté, stirring occasionally, until onions are transparent (about 5 minutes). Mix in tomatoes, eggplant, zucchini, thyme, bay leaf and pepper. Cover and simmer over medium-low heat, stirring occasionally, until vegetables are tender (about 15 minutes). Remove cover and cook an additional 5 to 10 minutes. Remove bay leaf. Can be served hot or cold.

Servings:
  6

Serving Size:
  1/6 of recipe

Nutritional analysis per serving:

Calories:	76
Fat:	3 gm
Cholesterol:	0 mg
Protein:	2 gm
Carbohydrate:	13 gm
Sodium:	157 mg

SIDE DISHES, SAUCES & CONDIMENTS

Baked French Fries
Kathy Schwab, R.D.

A fun variation of this is to substitute 4 carrots or a large sweet potato or yam for two of the potatoes. Omit paprika and season with a small amount of pepper.

4 med. potatoes, unpeeled
1 T. oil
1/2 tsp. paprika
1/2 tsp. Lite Salt

Preheat oven to 450°. Spray a jellyroll pan with nonstick cooking spray. Cut potatoes into strips, about 1/2-inch thick. Place strips into a plastic bag, add oil and shake until strips are coated. Spread evenly over pan and bake, 30 to 45 minutes, turning occasionally. Sprinkle with paprika and Lite Salt.

Servings:
4

Serving Size:
1/4 of recipe

Nutritional analysis per serving:
Calories:	142
Fat:	4 gm
Cholesterol:	trace mg
Protein:	3 gm
Carbohydrate:	26 gm
Sodium:	146 mg

TASTEFULLY OREGON

Kate Aaloo
(Cut Potatoes)
William E. Connor, M.D.

In 1989, Dr. Connor was selected as one of the two individuals honored nationally with Honorary Membership in the American Dietetic Association. Much of his life's work has involved studying nutrition and researching the relationship of fats and heart health. This is one of his favorite recipes.

1 T. oil
1 whole dried red pepper
1 T. cumin seed
1 T. crushed garlic
1 med. chopped tomato, or 1 (16 oz.) can unsalted tomatoes
3 lg. peeled potatoes, sliced 3/8" thick (5 c.)
1/4 c. chopped fresh cilantro
1 tsp. Lite Salt
1 tsp. ground cumin
1/2 tsp. turmeric
1 tsp. paprika
2 T. water

Heat oil, add whole dried red pepper and cumin seed, and stir well until seeds get a red roasted tint. (This takes only a few minutes.) Quickly add garlic and stir for about 1 minute. Add tomatoes and sliced potatoes. Stir until potatoes are coated with oil. Add cilantro and spices and stir carefully. Reduce heat to low, sprinkle with water, and cover with a tight lid. Continue to cook potatoes about 30 minutes or until done. Add water as needed. Occasionally stir gently, and watch carefully so they will not burn.

Servings:
4

Serving Size:
1 1/4 cups

Nutritional analysis per serving:
Calories:	142
Fat:	4 gm
Cholesterol:	0 mg
Protein:	3 gm
Carbohydrate:	25 gm
Sodium:	288 mg

SIDE DISHES, SAUCES & CONDIMENTS

Roasted Potatoes
Kathy Schwab, R.D.

4 red or russet potatoes, unpeeled & cut into 1" chunks (enough to make 5 c.)
2 tsp. olive oil
3 cloves garlic, minced
2 tsp. rosemary leaves, or 1 tsp. basil leaves & 1 tsp. oregano leaves
1/8 tsp. black pepper
1/2 tsp. Lite Salt

Preheat oven to 375°. Spray a baking sheet with nonstick spray. In a large bowl, combine potato chunks, oil, garlic, rosemary or basil, oregano, pepper and Lite Salt. Toss to coat potatoes well. Spread in a single layer on the prepared baking sheet. Bake until brown and potatoes are cooked through, turning once or twice (it takes about 30 to 40 minutes). Serve while warm.

Servings:
4

Serving Size:
1 cup

Nutritional analysis per serving:
Calories: 158
Fat: 2 gm
Cholesterol: 0 mg
Protein: 3 gm
Carbohydrate: 32 gm
Sodium: 148 mg

TASTEFULLY OREGON

Fruit Sauce
Charlotte Hennessy, R.D.

My family prefers this sauce to syrup for waffles or pancakes. A great way to use frozen berries. I also serve it cold on shortcake.

1 T. cornstarch
1 c. fruit juice*
1/4 to 1/2 c. sugar (depending on the sweetness of the fruit juice)
4 c. fruit (berries, pineapple, peaches, etc.), cut in bite-sized pieces

Mix cornstarch, juice and sugar in a 1 1/2-quart microwavable dish. Cover and cook in a microwave oven, on HIGH, for about 5 minutes or until thickened. (Stir every minute to keep it smooth.) This also could be done in a saucepan on top of the stove. Cool slightly, and gently stir in the fruit. Serve warm or cold.

*Use juice from thawed frozen berries, pineapple juice, apple juice, or blend some fresh fruit.

Servings:
8

Serving Size:
1/2 cup

Nutritional analysis per serving:
Calories:	84
Fat:	trace gm
Cholesterol:	0 mg
Protein:	trace gm
Carbohydrate:	21 gm
Sodium:	1 mg

SIDE DISHES, SAUCES & CONDIMENTS

"Lite" Hollandaise Sauce
Anne Goetze, R.D.

A quick sauce for vegetables adapted from the Oregon Dairy Council's Quick 2 Fix brochure.

2 T. margarine
2 T. flour
1/4 c. egg substitute
1 c. plain nonfat yogurt
1 tsp. fresh-squeezed lemon juice
1/8 tsp. cayenne pepper

Combine margarine and flour in saucepan and heat until melted. Let cool slightly; add egg substitute and mix well. Add yogurt and heat 2 to 3 minutes, stirring frequently. Add lemon juice and cayenne.

Servings:
4

Serving Size:
1/3 cup

Nutritional analysis per serving:
Calories: 113
Fat: 6 gm
Cholesterol: 1 mg
Protein: 6 gm
Carbohydrate: 8 gm
Sodium: 142 mg

TASTEFULLY OREGON

Marinara Sauce
(Tomato Sauce)
Sonja Connor, R.D.

This is wonderful served over fresh pasta or whenever you need a nicely flavored tomato sauce. Double the recipe and keep some in the freezer. I make quarts of this every fall, using the tomatoes from Bill's garden. (It must be my additions to the compost that makes them so big.)

1 clove garlic, minced
1 T. olive oil
2 (16 oz.) cans *no-salt-added* **tomatoes**
2 (8 oz.) cans *no-salt-added* **tomato sauce**
1 tsp. oregano leaves
1 T. chopped or dried parsley

Sauté garlic in olive oil. Add tomatoes and tomato sauce slowly. Stir in oregano and parsley. Bring to a boil and simmer, covered, for 20 minutes to 2 hours. (The longer, the better!) Break up the tomatoes with a potato masher and stir sauce occasionally.

Servings:
4

Serving Size:
1 cup

Nutritional analysis per serving:
Calories: 131
Fat: 4 gm
Cholesterol: 0 mg
Protein: 3 gm
Carbohydrates: 22 gm
Sodium: 193 mg

SIDE DISHES, SAUCES & CONDIMENTS

Fresh Strawberry Chutney

Anne Goetze, R.D.

Our family enjoys this chutney or relish throughout strawberry season with grilled chicken. It is best served the day of preparation.

- 2 T. balsamic vinegar
- 2 T. orange juice
- 1 T. Dijon mustard
- 1 T. honey
- 1/2 tsp. grated orange peel
- 1/4 to 1/2 tsp. red pepper flakes
- 1 pt. fresh strawberries, sliced
- 3 T. raisins
- 3 T. chopped walnuts

In a medium bowl, combine balsamic vinegar, orange juice, mustard, honey, orange peel and red pepper flakes. Add strawberries, raisins and walnuts. Toss gently.

Servings:
14

Serving Size:
2 tablespoons

Nutritional analysis per serving:
Calories:	30
Fat:	1 gm
Cholesterol:	0 mg
Protein:	<1 gm
Carbohydrate:	5 gm
Sodium:	28 mg

Berry Freezer Jam

Joyce Gustafson, R.D.

This gem came from my mom and can be made with any combination of berries, but this is my family's favorite. The color is terrific and it is a "soft set", so works well on pancakes and waffles, as well as on our breakfast toast.

2 pt. raspberries
1 pt. strawberries
1/4 c. rosé wine
1 T. grated orange rind
5 1/2 c. sugar
1/2 c. light corn syrup
2 (1 3/4 oz.) pkg. pectin
1 1/2 c. water

Wash, stem, and put well-drained berries in a large bowl. Mash berries together. Add rosé wine, orange rind, sugar and corn syrup to the berries; mix well and set aside. In a small saucepan, combine pectin and water. Bring to a full boil and boil for 1 minute, stirring constantly (I use small whisk). Pour hot pectin into other ingredients; stir until well mixed and ladle into clean freezer containers. Let stand for 24 hours before freezing.

Servings:
Makes 10 cups
(160 tablespoons)

Serving Size:
1 tablespoon

Nutritional analysis per serving:
Calories:	34
Fat:	trace gm
Cholesterol:	0 mg
Protein:	trace gm
Carbohydrate:	9 gm
Sodium:	3 mg

Vegetarian Main Dishes

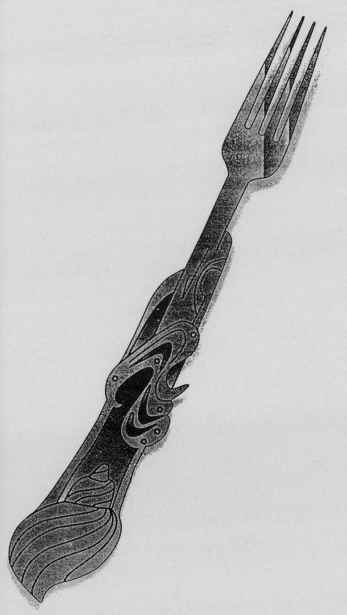

Tastefully Oregon

Vegetarian--Well, Some Of The Time

The recipes in this section offer a variety of tasty dishes that should satisfy both vegetarians and non vegetarians. Try them share them and add them to your collection of healthy recipes. Here are some facts about a vegetarian eating style.

- A growing number of people in the US are choosing a vegetarian or near-vegetarian eating style for ethical, ecological, philosophical or health reasons.

- There are strong indications that a vegetarian diet is a healthy one, reducing the risks of heart disease, certain types of cancer and other diet-related ailments.

- A carefully planned vegetarian diet will provide all necessary nutrients. Grains, beans, tofu, nuts and vegetables are good sources of protein; most of the basic vegetarian foods are rich in vitamins and minerals, free of cholesterol and low in fat.

A Word of Caution

- Milk products can be high in fat, particularly cheese; choose the low fat varieties.
- Egg yolks are high in cholesterol (1 yolk contains 2/3 of the days' recommended level); use egg whites or egg substitute.
- Nuts and regular tofu are high in fat; use nuts sparingly and select *Lite* tofu.
- Because vitamin B-12 is found only in animal foods, strict vegetarians may need to take a supplement.

VEGETARIAN MAIN DISHES

Brown Rice Skillet Medley
Judy Forest, R.D.

This recipe is quick and easy. Serve with bread and fruit. My family likes it meatless, but sometimes I add cooked turkey, chicken or turkey kielbasa if I have it handy.

1 1/4 c. *10-minute Brown Rice*
1 (4 1/2 oz.) can stewed tomatoes, Mexican or Italian flavored
3/4 c. water
1/2 tsp. Lite Salt
Choice of:
   Mexican flavor, use:
     1 tsp. cumin
     1/2 tsp. chili powder
     1/2 tsp. garlic powder
   or Italian flavor, use:
     1/2 tsp. oregano leaves
     1/2 tsp. rosemary leaves
     1/2 tsp. thyme leaves
     1/4 tsp. fennel seeds (opt.)
1 (16 oz.) pkg. frozen loose-pack vegetables (I like the fiesta blend)
1 1/2 c. frozen peas
1 c. cooked turkey or chicken (opt.)

In a 10- or 12-inch nonstick skillet, combine uncooked rice, tomatoes, water, Lite Salt and other seasonings. If using Mexican flavored tomatoes, use cumin, chili powder and garlic powder; if using Italian flavored tomatoes, add oregano, rosemary and thyme. Bring to a boil, cover, reduce heat and simmer 5 minutes. Add vegetables and peas, cover and cook 5 minutes longer and add more water if mixture becomes dry. Add turkey or chicken, if using. Check rice and vegetables for doneness and cook up to 5 minutes more, or until rice is tender.

Continued on following page.

TASTEFULLY OREGON

Continued from preceding page.

Servings:
4

Serving Size:
1 1/4 cups

Nutritional analysis per serving:
    Calories: 249
    Fat: 2 gm
    Cholesterol: 0 mg
    Protein: 9 gm
    Carbohydrate: 48 gm
    Sodium: 538 mg

VEGETARIAN MAIN DISHES

Cajun Red Beans and Rice

Terese Scollard, R.D.

I always serve this quick dish with cornbread. Additional vegetables such as chopped onions and green or red peppers can be added to the beans.

2 (16 oz.) cans red beans, drained & rinsed (I recommend *S&W Lite* which contains 50% less salt)
1 (16 oz.) can Cajun-seasoned stewed tomatoes, chopped
2 T. dried onion flakes
2 T. chopped green chiles
1/4 to 1/2 tsp. Tabasco sauce (depends on how hot you like it!)
1 1/2 c. regular or quick-cooking brown rice

Combine beans and chopped tomatoes in saucepan or crock-pot. Add onion flakes, green chiles and Tabasco sauce. Cook gently, 15 to 20 minutes in saucepan or 1 to 2 hours in crock-pot. Cook rice in unsalted water according to package directions.

To serve: Place rice in large soup bowl or on a plate and add a scoop of beans on top. Pass Tabasco sauce so each person can add as they desire.

Servings:
5

Serving Size:
1 cup rice and 3/4 cup beans

Nutritional analysis per serving:
Calories:	397
Fat:	2 gm
Cholesterol:	0 mg
Protein:	17 gm
Carbohydrate:	83 gm
Sodium:	639 mg

TASTEFULLY OREGON

Lentil Casserole
Beth Vallance, R.D.

The original recipe was obtained from my dietitian friend, Marlene Young, R.D., from Idaho Falls, Idaho. It's easy to prepare and leaves time to do other things while lentils are cooking.

1 3/4 c. dried lentils
2 c. water
2 c. chopped tomatoes
1/3 c. chopped onion
1 clove garlic, crushed
1/8 tsp. marjoram leaves
1/8 tsp. thyme leaves
2 tsp. Lite Salt
1/4 tsp. pepper
2 lg. carrots, chopped (2 c.)
2 stalks celery chopped (3/4 c.)
4 oz. part-skim Mozzarella cheese, grated

Preheat oven to 350°. Combine lentils, water, tomatoes, onion, garlic, marjoram, thyme, Lite Salt and pepper, and place in a 9x13-inch baking dish which has been sprayed with nonstick spray. Bake, covered, for 30 minutes. Add carrots and celery and return to oven and bake, uncovered, for 40 minutes longer. Sprinkle casserole with grated Mozzarella cheese and bake long enough to brown and melt cheese (watch carefully).

Servings:
6

Serving Size:
1/6th of recipe

Nutritional Analysis per serving:
Calories: 274
Fat: 4 gm
Cholesterol: 11 mg
Protein: 22 gm
Carbohydrate: 41 gm
Sodium: 493 mg

VEGETARIAN MAIN DISHES

Mexi Tamale Pie
Robin Stanton, R.D.

This is a great recipe for two people to prepare (one the filling and one the crust) in under 45 minutes, start to finish.

BEAN FILLING:
- 1 T. oil
- 1 sm. onion, chopped
- 3 cloves garlic, minced
- 1 med. green bell pepper, chopped
- 1 med. red bell pepper, chopped
- 1 (8 oz.) can unsalted tomato sauce
- 1 T. chili powder
- 1 T. hot chili peppers, seeds removed & chopped (or 1/2 tsp. red pepper flakes)
- 2 (15 oz.) cans kidney or pimento beans, drained, rinsed & mashed
- 1 c. frozen corn
- 3 T. minced fresh parsley
- Fresh ground pepper

To prepare filling: Heat oil in a large, nonstick skillet. Sauté onion, garlic, green and red peppers until the vegetables are softened. Stir in the tomato sauce, chili powder, chili peppers, mashed beans, corn, parsley and pepper. Simmer the mixture, stirring constantly, until heated through. Spray a large 9x13-inch baking dish with nonstick cooking spray. Spread the bean filling evenly in bottom of the dish.

Continued on following page.

TASTEFULLY OREGON

Continued from preceding page.

CRUST:
1 1/2 c. yellow cornmeal
3 3/4 c. water
1/2 tsp. Lite Salt
3 oz. or 3/4 c. grated low-fat cheese (*Jarlsberg Lite* is a good one)

To prepare crust: Preheat oven to 375°. In a saucepan, combine cornmeal, water and Lite Salt. Stirring constantly, bring to a boil and continue cooking until it thickens slightly. Spoon over top of filling. Bake, uncovered, for about 20 minutes. Remove from oven, sprinkle grated cheese on top and bake an additional 5 minutes.

Servings:
9

Serving Size:
3x4-inch piece

Nutritional Analysis per serving:
Calories:	232
Fat:	3 gm
Cholesterol:	2 mg
Protein:	11 gm
Carbohydrate:	42 gm
Sodium:	454 mg

VEGETARIAN MAIN DISHES

Pasta with Garden Vegetables
Donna Oleksa, R.D.

We call it "tutto" from the original name Conchiglie Con Tutto Giardino--pasta with the whole garden.

1 1/2 c. thinly-sliced carrots
1 c. chopped green onions
1 lg. red onion, coarsely chopped
3/4 c. thinly-sliced radishes
1/2 c. coarsely-chopped Italian parsley
1/4 c. fresh chopped basil, or 1 1/2 T. dried leaves
5 cloves garlic, minced
3 c. chopped tomatoes
3 c. diced zucchini
1 lg. green bell pepper, diced
1 1/2 c. dry white wine or water
1 1/2 tsp. Lite Salt
3/4 tsp. black pepper
1 tsp. sugar
1 T. margarine
1 T. flour
1 c. nonfat milk
1 (6 oz.) can tomato paste

Spray large cooking pot with nonstick cooking spray. Add carrots, green and red onions, radishes, parsley, basil and garlic. Add a very small amount of water to prevent sticking. Sauté the vegetables, stirring often, until they begin to color, about 20 minutes. Reduce heat, cover the saucepan and simmer the vegetables for about 15 minutes. Add tomatoes, zucchini, bell pepper, wine or water, Lite Salt, pepper and sugar. Simmer the sauce, uncovered, for about 45 minutes to 1 hour.

In a small saucepan, melt margarine. Stir in flour until a smooth paste develops. Slowly add milk, stirring it into the paste with a wire whisk. Add tomato paste and whisk the mixture again until it is very smooth. Stir it into the vegetables. Continue simmering the sauce over low heat, stirring often, until it is thickened.

Continued on following page.

TASTEFULLY OREGON

Continued from preceding page.

1 1/2 lb. shell-shaped pasta
1/2 c. fresh grated Parmesan cheese

Cook the pasta in a large kettle of unsalted boiling water until al denté (barely cooked), drain, and pour into a large serving dish. Add vegetable sauce, toss, and sprinkle grated Parmesan over the top. Serve immediately.

Servings:
8

Serving Size:
A generous 2 cups

Nutritional analysis per serving:
Calories: 432
Fat: 5 gm
Cholesterol: 5 mg
Protein: 16 gm
Carbohydrate: 74 gm
Sodium: 562 mg

166

VEGETARIAN MAIN DISHES

Pasta with Black Beans and Tomatoes
Kathy Schwab, R.D.

Leftovers taste great reheated in the microwave.

1 med. onion, coarsely chopped
2 cloves garlic, minced
1 T. oil
1 (15 oz.) can black beans, drained & rinsed (*S&W* 50% reduced salt)
1 (16 oz.) can stewed tomatoes, undrained & coarsely chopped
1 T. chili powder
2 tsp. ground cumin
1 tsp. crushed oregano
4 c. hot, cooked rotini pasta (8 oz. dried)

In a large skillet, sauté onion and garlic in oil until tender. Stir in beans, tomatoes, chili powder, cumin and oregano. Bring to a boil, reduce heat, cover and simmer 15 minutes, stirring occasionally. Remove cover and cook over high heat until liquid is reduced and sauce is thickened to desired consistency. Toss bean mixture with pasta.

Servings:
4

Serving Size:
1 3/4 cups

Nutritional analysis per serving:
Calories: 345
Fat: 5 gm
Cholesterol: 0 mg
Protein: 14 gm
Carbohydrate: 66 gm
Sodium: 572 mg

TASTEFULLY OREGON

Pasta Primavera

Christie Digman, R.D.

My dietetic internship days in Dallas, Texas were filled with okra, hush puppies and catfish. This recipe came to me just in time to satisfy my craving for food that reminded me of home in the Pacific Northwest.

8 oz. angel hair pasta, uncooked
1 T. olive oil
3 cloves garlic, minced
1/2 c. sliced green onions
2 c. sliced broccoli flowerets
1 c. thinly-sliced carrots
1 T. basil leaves
1/2 tsp. Lite Salt
2 c. sliced fresh mushrooms
1/2 tsp. black pepper
1/2 c. Chablis, other dry white wine or water
3 T. grated Parmesan cheese

Cook pasta in unsalted water according to package directions. Drain and keep warm.

Heat oil in a large nonstick skillet. Sauté garlic and onions until onions are softened. Add broccoli, carrots, basil and Lite Salt. Continue cooking for 5 minutes or until vegetables are crisp-tender, stirring often. Add mushrooms, pepper and wine. Cook and stir for 2 minutes or until mushrooms are tender. Gently toss pasta with vegetable mixture and Parmesan cheese. Serve immediately.

Servings:
4

Serving Size:
1 1/2 cups

Nutritional analysis per serving:
Calories: 341
Fat: 6 gm
Cholesterol: 4 mg
Protein: 13 gm
Carbohydrate: 55 gm
Sodium: 257 mg

VEGETARIAN MAIN DISHES

Spinach Lasagna
Anne Goetze, R.D.

This recipe was given to me at a "spice shower" when I was married, and has become a family favorite. I often use homemade sauce, or if time is short, I use prepared spaghetti sauce. The lasagna also freezes well.

2 (10 oz.) pkg. frozen, chopped spinach, thawed & drained
1 (16 oz.) ctn. fat-free ricotta cheese
1/2 c. fresh grated Parmesan cheese
6 egg whites, slightly beaten
1/8 tsp. Lite Salt
1/4 tsp. pepper
1/8 tsp. nutmeg
1 (8 oz.) pkg. lasagna noodles, uncooked
4 c. *Marinara Sauce* (see Side Dishes, Sauces & Condiments section), or 1 (32 oz.) jar spaghetti sauce
8 oz. part-skim Mozzarella cheese, sliced

Preheat oven to 350°. Mix together spinach, ricotta, Parmesan, egg whites, Lite Salt, pepper and nutmeg. Spray a 9x13-inch baking dish with nonstick cooking spray. Layer in this order: uncooked lasagna noodles, sauce and Mozzarella slices. Spread spinach filling and continue with layers of noodles, sauce and cheese. Cover with foil and bake for 1 hour. Cut into squares and serve.

Servings:
  8

Serving Size:
  1/8th of recipe

Nutritional analysis per serving:
  Calories: 388
  Fat: 9 gm
  Cholesterol: 38 mg
  Protein: 26 gm
  Carbohydrate: 40 gm
  Sodium: 532 mg

TASTEFULLY OREGON

Spinach Manicotti
Kathy Schwab, R.D.

An Italian friend ate this and insists it's like her mom's. (Must be the nutmeg!)

4 c. *Marinara Sauce*, see Side Dishes, Sauces & Condiments, or use your favorite recipe or a commercial spaghetti sauce (which may be higher in sodium)
8 oz. manicotti shells (12 pieces) or jumbo shells
1 (15 oz.) ctn. fat-free ricotta cheese
2 egg whites
1/2 tsp. nutmeg
2 T. basil leaves
1/4 tsp. black pepper
2/3 c. fresh grated Parmesan cheese, divided
1 1/2 c. grated part-skim Mozzarella cheese
1 (10 oz.) pkg. frozen chopped spinach, thawed & drained

Prepare *Marinara Sauce* and set aside. Cook manicotti shells in unsalted water according to package directions; drain well. Preheat oven to 350°. Mix ricotta cheese, egg whites, nutmeg, basil, pepper, 1/3 cup Parmesan cheese and all of the Mozzarella cheese, and spinach in a large bowl. Put enough *Marinara Sauce* in 9x13-inch baking dish to cover it 1-inch deep (about 2 cups). Stuff manicotti shells with cheese mixture and arrange in baking dish. Cover with remaining *Marinara Sauce*. Cover pan with foil and bake for 25 minutes. Remove foil, sprinkle with remaining 1/3 cup Parmesan cheese and bake, uncovered, 10 minutes longer.

Servings:
  6

Serving Size:
  2 manicotti shells

Nutritional analysis per serving:
  Calories: 420
  Fat: 12 gm
  Cholesterol: 25 mg
  Protein: 30 mg
  Carbohydrate: 51 gm
  Sodium: 645 mg

VEGETARIAN MAIN DISHES

Szechuan Broccoli

Christie Digman, R.D.

I like to serve this delicious and easy vegetable stir-fry over hot steamed rice.

2 T. soy sauce (use Lite soy sauce if you want to reduce the sodium)
1/4 c. rice or cider vinegar
2 tsp. sugar
2 T. sesame seeds
1 T. oil
1 tsp. crushed red pepper
1 tsp. minced fresh ginger root
3 cloves garlic, minced
10 c. coarsely-chopped broccoli

Combine soy sauce, vinegar and sugar; set aside. Heat large skillet or wok over medium heat. Add sesame seeds; cook and stir 1 to 2 minutes or until browned. Remove seeds and set aside.

Heat oil in skillet or wok and add pepper, ginger and garlic. Stir-fry for 30 seconds. Add broccoli and stir-fry 1 minute. Add soy sauce mixture; stir well. Cover and cook 3 to 4 minutes or until broccoli is just crisp-tender. Sprinkle with sesame seeds and serve immediately.

Servings:
4

Serving Size:
1 3/4 cups

Nutritional analysis per serving:

Calories:	135
Fat:	7 gm
Cholesterol:	0 mg
Protein:	8 gm
Carbohydrate:	17 gm
Sodium:	575 mg

TASTEFULLY OREGON

The Six-Minute Meal
Judy Forest, R.D.

In a hurry? This delicious dish can be prepared in just 6 minutes!

1 lg. (8 oz.) potato
1 c. frozen loose-pack vegetables (I like the fiesta blend)
1/2 c. nonfat or 1% fat cottage cheese
1 T. Parmesan cheese

Cut potato into 8 pieces; place in large cereal bowl. Add frozen vegetables, cover and microwave on HIGH for 6 minutes or until potato is cooked. Combine cottage cheese and Parmesan cheese. Spread over top of cooked potato and vegetable mixture, cover and microwave 15 seconds or until heated through.

Variations:
• Replace vegetables with 1/2 cup spaghetti sauce or salsa.
• Replace cottage and Parmesan cheeses with 2 ounces low-fat turkey kielbasa (smoked turkey sausage) chopped into small pieces.
• Replace cottage and Parmesan cheeses with 2 ounces salad shrimp, imitation crab, or any cooked meat, poultry or seafood.

Servings:
1

Serving Size:
1 recipe

Nutritional analysis per serving:
Calories:	338
Fat:	3 gm
Cholesterol:	6 mg
Protein:	23 gm
Carbohydrate:	57 gm
Sodium:	590 mg

VEGETARIAN MAIN DISHES

Three-Bean and Rice Casserole
Dawn Kinzel, R.D.

I love to make this dish for dinner and serve it with hot bread and salad. Then we have wonderful leftovers for lunch or as a side dish with chicken or fish.

1 T. oil
1 med. onion, chopped
2 c. uncooked long-grain white or brown rice
1 (15 oz.) can kidney or pinto beans*, drained & rinsed
1 (15 oz.) can garbanzo beans*, drained & rinsed
1 (15 oz.) can black beans*, drained & rinsed
1 (14 to 16 oz.) can tomatoes, drained & saved
1 (4 oz.) can chopped green chiles, drained
3 1/2 c. water (use juice from canned tomatoes for part of this)
1 (10 oz.) pkg. frozen green peas
1/2 c. pimento-stuffed green olives

Preheat oven to 375°. Heat oil in an ovenproof pot. Sauté onion over medium heat until tender. Add uncooked rice and stir until opaque. Add drained beans, tomatoes, chiles and water. Stir and bring to a boil. Cover and place in oven. Bake about 45 minutes, until water is absorbed and rice is tender (brown rice takes about 1 1/2 hours). Add peas and olives. Bake an additional 10 to 15 minutes until heated through.

*We recommend *S&W* 50% Less Salt.

Servings:
  6 to 8

Serving Size:
  1 1/2 cups

Nutritional Analysis per serving:
  Calories: 552
  Fat: 6 gm
  Cholesterol: 0 mg
  Protein: 23 gm
  Carbohydrate: 102 gm
  Sodium: 560 mg

TASTEFULLY OREGON

Tofu Baked Beans
James M. Fox, R.D.

A great way to use tofu. Sliced green pepper can be added and seasoning can be varied according to your taste.

- 4 to 5 c. cooked or canned kidney or pinto beans, drained & rinsed (start with 2 1/4 c. beans if using dry)*
- 1 lg. onion, chopped
- 1 clove garlic, minced
- 2 c. tomato sauce
- 1 c. stewed tomatoes
- 2 T. tomato paste
- 2 T. Dijon mustard
- 3 T. blackstrap or dark molasses
- 2 tsp. *Lite* soy sauce
- 1 tsp. basil leaves
- 1 tsp. oregano leaves
- 2 to 5 drops Tabasco sauce, to taste
- 2 lb. tofu, drained & rinsed

Preheat oven to 325°. Combine all ingredients (except tofu) into a 4-quart baking dish. Cut tofu into 1/2-inch cubes and gently fold into the combined ingredients. Bake for 1 1/2 hours.

*If using dry beans, soak overnight; rinse before using. See *On-Your-Mark Black Bean Soup* for speedy method.

Servings:
8

Serving Size:
1/8 of recipe

Nutritional analysis per serving:
Calories: 287
Fat: 7 gm
Cholesterol: 0 mg
Protein: 20 gm
Carbohydrate: 40 gm
Sodium: 543 mg

VEGETARIAN MAIN DISHES

Tofu Patties
Julie Geraci, R.D.

These are crunchy on the outside and soft on the inside. They can be served on hamburger buns or eaten as is. Vegetarians will enjoy this.

1 (12 oz.) pkg. tofu, drained
1/4 c. egg substitute
1/4 c. flour or 1/2 c. cooked rice
1 T. soy sauce
3/4 c. grated low-fat Cheddar cheese
1/4 tsp. minced garlic
1/4 tsp. oregano leaves
1/8 tsp. pepper
1/2 onion, chopped
1 stalk celery, chopped
1/4 c. chopped green bell pepper
1/4 c. sesame seeds
1 tsp. olive oil
1/2 c. chopped mushrooms

Preheat oven to 350°. Put tofu in a fine mesh strainer. Mash with back of spoon to get as much liquid out as possible. Transfer tofu to a bowl and break it up into pieces. Add egg substitute, flour or cooked rice, soy sauce, cheese, garlic, oregano leaves and pepper. Stir to combine. Heat olive oil and sauté onion, celery, green pepper and mushrooms until onion is tender. Combine with the tofu mixture. If mixture is too wet to form patties, add a little more flour. Form into 6 to 8 patties. Put sesame seeds on both sides. Spray a baking sheet with nonstick cooking spray. Place patties on baking sheet. Bake for approximately 30 minutes, until patties are golden brown.

Servings:
6 to 8 patties

Serving Size:
1 patty

Nutritional analysis per serving:
Calories: 164
Fat: 10 gm
Cholesterol: 8 mg
Protein: 12 gm
Carbohydrate: 8 gm
Sodium: 292 mg

TASTEFULLY OREGON

White Beans Provencale
Christie Digman, R.D.

Any leftover beans can be heated and spread on a corn or flour tortilla for a great second-time-around.

- 1 tsp. olive oil
- 2 cloves garlic, minced
- 1/4 to 1/2 tsp. fennel seeds
- 1/2 tsp. thyme leaves
- 2 (16 oz.) cans white Cannellini or Great Northern beans, drained & rinsed
- 1 (14 1/2 oz.) can unsalted stewed tomatoes (*S&W* has one available)
- 1/2 tsp. ground black pepper

Heat oil in medium-size skillet over medium heat. Add garlic, fennel seeds and thyme. Cook a few seconds until fragrant. Add drained beans, tomatoes and pepper. Heat to simmer, and cook slowly until heated through (about 5 minutes).

Servings:
 4

Serving Size:
 1 cup

Nutritional analysis per serving:
Calories:	308
Fat:	2 gm
Cholesterol:	0 mg
Protein:	18 gm
Carbohydrate:	56 gm
Sodium:	447 mg

Seafood Main Dishes

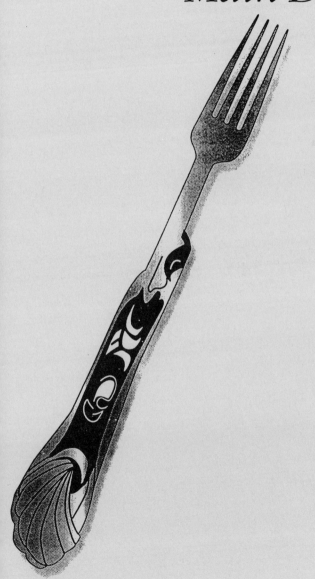

Tastefully Oregon

Omega-3 What?

- Fish and shellfish contain little fat and their fat is rich in omega-3 fatty acids.

- Many studies have shown that omega-3 fatty acids lower the blood levels of fats called triglycerides and make the blood less likely to form clots in narrowed arteries, thus lowering the risk of heart disease.

Seafood Is Fast Food!

- Seafood is the "fast food" par excellence.

- Seafood can be cooked from the frozen state (can you say the same for meats?).

- Seafood must be cooked quickly to keep its moisture and delicate taste.

- Seafood combines well with many added flavors (lemon, dill, thyme, basil, marjoram, ginger, soy sauce, green onion).

- Oregon's lakes, rivers and ocean are rich in fish and shellfish. Discover and enjoy them by using the recipes in this section.

SEAFOOD MAIN DISHES

Bouillabaisse
Sabine Artaud-Wild, R.D.

Serve with French bread to use for dipping in the soup, so all the sauce can be enjoyed! It's a great party dish.

2 lg. onions, thinly sliced
2 leeks, minced
1 T. oil
4 cloves garlic, minced
3 lg. tomatoes, peeled, seeded & diced
5 c. water
3 c. clam juice, or 2 (12 oz.) cans
2 T. chopped fresh parsley
1 bay leaf
1/2 tsp. fennel seeds
1/2 tsp. thyme or basil leaves
1/2 tsp. saffron
2" piece fresh orange peel
1/2 tsp. Lite Salt
1/2 tsp. pepper
2 lb. lean fish bones, trimming, etc. (this adds additional flavor to the stock)

To prepare stock: In a large kettle, cook onions and leeks slowly in oil until tender, but not browned. Stir in the garlic and tomatoes. Cook 5 minutes. Add water, clam juice, herbs, and Lite Salt and pepper. Tie fish bones and trimmings together in a large piece of cheesecloth. Add this bundle to vegetables. Simmer, covered, for 30 minutes. Discard fish bones and trimmings, strain stock or purée it through a food mill. Stock can be refrigerated or frozen at this point.

Continued on following page.

TASTEFULLY OREGON

Continued from preceding page.

2 lb. assorted lean fish and shellfish (more than one kind—bass, snapper, halibut, turbot, cod, scallops, etc.), cut in large pieces

Twenty minutes before serving: Bring the fish stock to a boil. Add fresh fish and shellfish. Bring rapidly back to boiling and cook 5 minutes or until fish flakes easily with a fork. Do not overcook.

Servings:
8

Serving Size:
1 1/2 cups

Nutritional analysis per serving:
Calories:	175
Fat:	4 gm
Cholesterol:	41 mg
Protein:	22 gm
Carbohydrate:	13 gm
Sodium:	376 mg

SEAFOOD MAIN DISHES

Fish Fillets in Red Wine
Chedwah J. Stein, R.D.

I use halibut, but this recipe would have good results with any fish.

- 1 T. olive oil
- 1 c. diced red onion
- 3 T. diced carrot
- 3 T. diced celery
- 1/2 c. chopped mushrooms
- 2 T. flour
- 4 fish fillets (about 6 oz. each) such as snapper, cod or halibut
- 1 c. red wine
- 1/2 tsp. Lite Salt
- 1/2 tsp. pepper

In a large nonstick skillet, heat olive oil and add onion, carrot, celery and mushrooms. Sauté over low heat until tender. Remove from pan and set aside. Lightly flour the fish fillets. Add fillets to pan and brown lightly on each side. Remove from pan. Add red wine to pan, stirring up any browned bits, and boil gently for 1 minute. Return fish and vegetables to pan; add Lite Salt and pepper. Reduce heat, cover, and cook a few minutes, spooning vegetables and wine sauce over fish. It is done when fish flakes easily and flavors are blended.

Servings:
4

Serving Size:
1 fish fillet with sauce

Nutritional analysis per serving:

Calories:	299
Fat:	8 gm
Cholesterol:	54 mg
Protein:	37 gm
Carbohydrate:	10 gm
Sodium:	241 mg

TASTEFULLY OREGON

Fish Gumbo
Nancy Becker, R.D.

This is a large recipe, that can be easily cut in half. This gumbo is really a fish stew that will warm your insides. Don't let the long list of ingredients daunt you—it's really a very easy dish to assemble. Okra is not to everyone's liking; however, I find that it adds a great flavor and texture. Any combination of fish can be used. Gumbo should definitely be served with rice.

8 oz. fresh or frozen okra, trimmed & cut into 1" pieces
1 T. olive oil
1 c. chopped onion
1 c. chopped celery
1 c. chopped green bell pepper
1 c. chopped red bell pepper
2 cloves garlic, minced
1 tsp. ground cumin
1/4 tsp. Tabasco sauce
1/2 tsp. Lite Salt
1/2 tsp. black pepper
1 bay leaf
8 oz. clam juice plus 3 c. water, or 4 c. water
1 (28 oz.) can tomatoes
1 lb. red snapper, cut into 1" pieces
1/2 lb. halibut, cut into 1" pieces
1/2 lb. shrimp (rock shrimp comes without shells so is easy to prepare)
Hot cooked rice

Defrost okra, if using frozen. Dry it off with a towel. Heat olive oil in a big pot. Sauté okra in oil until lightly browned. Add onions, celery, bell peppers, and garlic. Stir and cook for about 5 minutes over medium heat. Add cumin, Tabasco, Lite Salt, pepper, and bay leaf; cook for 1 or 2 minutes more. Add clam juice, water and tomatoes with juice. Cook, uncovered, for 20 minutes, stirring occasionally. Add fish and shrimp and cook gently for 5 more minutes. Serve in bowls over rice.

Continued on following page.

SEAFOOD MAIN DISHES

Continued from preceding page.

Servings:
8

Serving Size:
2 cups

Nutritional analysis per serving:
Calories: 173
Fat: 4 gm
Cholesterol: 72 mg
Protein: 24 gm
Carbohydrate: 11 gm
Sodium: 411 mg

TASTEFULLY OREGON

Lemon-Lime Salmon
Alyce Puppe Waverly, R.D.

After frequently fishing in Alaska, I needed to find "67" ways to prepare salmon. This is one of our favorites, especially when grilled on the barbecue. I like to prepare this ahead of time and marinate the salmon up to 4 hours.

2 lemons
2 limes
2 T. dry mustard
2 cloves garlic, minced
1 tsp. freshly-ground pepper
1/4 tsp. Lite Salt
3 salmon steaks (1 lb. each)

Grate peel from the lemons and limes and put in a small saucepan. Squeeze juice from the same lemons and limes. Add juice, mustard, garlic, pepper, and Lite Salt to the saucepan. Bring to a boil. Remove from heat and transfer marinade to shallow dish. Add salmon and turn so fish is coated with marinade. Cover and refrigerate up to 4 hours.

Grill or broil salmon 4 to 5 minutes per side. Brush occasionally with marinade.

Servings:
6

Serving Size:
1/2 salmon steak

Nutritional analysis per serving:

Calories:	342
Fat:	19 gm
Cholesterol:	120 mg
Protein:	37 gm
Carbohydrate:	5 gm
Sodium:	222 mg

SEAFOOD MAIN DISHES

Mexican-Style Marinated Flounder
Robin Stanton, R.D.

This spicy marinade is excellent for both fish and chicken. The ginger flavor is great!

- 2" piece fresh ginger, grated
- 4 cloves garlic, minced
- 1/4 c. chopped cilantro
- 1/4 c. lime juice
- 1/4 sp. crushed red pepper flakes
- 1 T. olive oil
- 4 fillets flounder (about 2 lb.), or any white fish
- 1/4 tsp. black pepper
- 1/2 tsp. chili powder
- 1 lime for garnish, sliced in thin wedges

In glass baking dish, combine ginger, garlic, cilantro, lime juice and red pepper flakes. Beat with a fork until blended. Add oil and beat again. Place fillets in dish, turning once to coat with marinade. Cover with plastic wrap and put in the refrigerator. Marinate for 30 to 40 minutes, turning occasionally.

When ready to cook: Preheat broiler. Line broiler pan with foil. Arrange fillets on broiler pan. Cook 3 to 6 minutes per side, or until fish is flaked easily with a fork. Sprinkle with pepper and chili powder. Garnish with lime wedges.

Servings:
4

Serving Size:
1 fish fillet

Nutritional analysis per serving:
Calories: 197
Fat: 6 gm
Cholesterol: 78 mg
Protein: 31 gm
Carbohydrate: 6 gm
Sodium: 137 mg

TASTEFULLY OREGON

Orange Roughy with Sun-Dried Tomatoes
Caryl Batdorf, R.D.

The fish and vegetables can be baked in the oven if you do not have parchment paper, but it is easy to use and makes a lovely dinner entrée.

Parchment paper*
4 fillets orange roughy (about 6 oz. each)
1/4 c. chopped sun-dried tomatoes
1/4 c. fresh-squeezed lemon juice
2 T. chopped fresh thyme, or 2 tsp. dried thyme leaves
4 tsp. minced garlic
1/4 tsp. Lite Salt
1/4 tsp. pepper
Oil or melted margarine for brushing paper

Preheat oven to 400°. Cut four 12-inch circles from parchment paper. Fold each circle in half. Unfold paper and place fish next to fold. Combine sun-dried tomatoes, lemon juice, thyme, garlic, Lite Salt and pepper. Distribute evenly over fish. Fold other half of paper over fish and seal edges with tightly-creased overlapping folds. Place on baking sheet and brush with oil or melted margarine. Bake for 8 to 11 minutes, or until packages are browned and puffed up.

*Cooking/baking paper can be purchased in most supermarkets or food specialty store. Do not use waxed paper.

Servings:
  4

Serving Size:
  1 fillet

Nutritional analysis per serving
  Calories: 170
  Fat: 2 gm
  Cholesterol: 44 gm
  Protein: 33 gm
  Carbohydrate: 5 gm
  Sodium: 278

SEAFOOD MAIN DISHES

Shrimp Creole
Ann Reid, R.D.

A microwave dish—easy for busy cooks!

4 c. cooked rice (start with 1 1/4 c. uncooked)
1/2 c. chopped green bell pepper
1/4 c. chopped celery
4 green onions, thinly sliced
1 clove garlic, minced
2 T. margarine
1 (16 oz.) can whole tomatoes, chopped
1 (6 oz.) unsalted tomato paste*
2 T. chopped fresh parsley or 2 tsp. dried
1/2 tsp. Lite Salt
1/4 tsp. crushed red pepper flakes
12 oz. precooked popcorn shrimp

Cook rice in unsalted water according to package directions. Meanwhile, combine green pepper, celery, green onions, garlic and margarine in shallow 2-quart baking dish. Cover with plastic wrap, allowing 1 corner to be uncovered. Microwave on HIGH 3 minutes. Drain tomatoes, reserving 1/2 cup of liquid. Add chopped tomatoes, reserved liquid, tomato paste, parsley, Lite Salt, red pepper flakes and shrimp to vegetable mixture. Cover as before and microwave at MEDIUM HIGH (70% power) for 11 to 13 minutes or until done. Stir at 5-minute intervals. Let stand 5 minutes. Serve over hot cooked rice.

*Some lower salt products are suggested to reduce the sodium content.

Servings:
  4

Serving Size:
  3 ounces shrimp in sauce and 1 cup rice

Nutritional analysis per serving:
Calories:	416
Fat:	8 gm
Cholesterol:	166 mg
Protein:	25 gm
Carbohydrate:	62 gm
Sodium:	593 mg

TASTEFULLY OREGON

Sesame Halibut

Lauren Hatcher, R.D.

Fish is best cooked over barbecue grill, or may be broiled in oven.

- 2 lb. halibut fillets or steaks or other firm-textured fish
- 1/4 c. frozen orange juice concentrate, thawed
- 2 T. ketchup
- 1 T. soy sauce
- 1 T. fresh-squeezed lemon juice
- 1/4 tsp. pepper
- 3/4 tsp. sesame oil
- 1 T. brown sugar
- 1 T. toasted sesame seeds

Two hours before meal time: Rinse fish with cold water. Pat dry with paper towels. Remove and discard any bones or skin, then cut fish into large chunks (about 1 1/2-inch cubes). Place in a bowl. In a small bowl, combine orange juice concentrate, ketchup, soy sauce, lemon juice, pepper, sesame oil and brown sugar. Pour mixture over fish, stir gently to coat fish chunks, cover and marinate in refrigerator for 2 hours, turning once.

When ready to cook: Thread fish chunks on four 14-inch skewers, reserving marinade. Cook over medium-hot barbecue grill or broil in oven, about 15 minutes. Turn once while cooking and baste with reserved marinade. Fish is done when it flakes easily with a fork. Top with toasted sesame seeds.

Continued on following page.

SEAFOOD MAIN DISHES

Continued from preceding page.

Servings:
4

Serving Size:
5 ounces halibut

Nutritional analysis per serving:
Calories: 220
Fat: 4 gm
Cholesterol: 99 mg
Protein: 36 gm
Carbohydrate: 8 gm
Sodium: 502 mg

A fine catch one fall day in 1978 for Lauren, her husband, Paul, and brother, Larry. Lauren's cousin (not pictured), who had taken them fishing, was a commercial fisherman at the time. He said these ling cod were "little ones".

TASTEFULLY OREGON

Steamed Halibut with Black Bean Sauce

Heidi Hadlett, R.D.

This recipe was inspired by a similar dish served at a favorite restaurant. I'm sharing my easy method for steaming, also.

- 1 1/2 lb. halibut fillets, other firm white fish or salmon fillets
- 1 T. oil (I prefer sesame oil)
- 1 T. black bean garlic sauce*
- 1 T. soy sauce
- 1 T. rice vinegar or white wine
- 1 T. brown sugar
- 4 green onions, chopped
- 1 to 2 cloves garlic, minced
- 1 T. finely-minced or grated fresh ginger

Rinse and dry fish thoroughly. Place fish in heat-proof baking dish (I use a 10-inch Pyrex pie dish). Coat fish with oil on both sides. Combine black bean sauce, soy sauce, rice vinegar, green onions, garlic, and ginger; cover fish with sauce.

To steam fish use a wok or other large pan. Place pie rack in wok or steamer; add enough water to reach just below rack. Bring water in wok or steamer to boil. Place container with fish on rack; cover wok or steamer. Steam 10 to 15 minutes, depending on thickness of fish. Steam makes delicious sauce. Serve with hot steamed rice.

*Available in Asian grocery stores.

Servings:
4

Serving Size:
1/4 of recipe

Nutritional analysis per serving:
Calories: 211
Fat: 6 gm
Cholesterol: 90 mg
Protein: 33 gm
Carbohydrate: 6 gm
Sodium: 434 mg

Chicken & Turkey Main Dishes

Tastefully Oregon

Speedy Meals For Speedy Days

- Prepare simple side dishes: carrot sticks, frozen vegetables, bread or dinner rolls, and cut up fruit. Spend most of your time on preparing one easy main dish. Try some of the excellent recipes in this section.

- When you have a minute, prepare larger quantities that can be divided, frozen and used for those hurried days. Once a week make 2 casseroles--one to eat now and one for the freezer.

- Leftover chili or other "thick" soups make great toppers for baked potatoes. Add a salad, bread and fresh fruit to complete the meal.

- For quick healthy chicken nuggets, cut chicken breasts in small pieces and dip in 1/2 cup nonfat yogurt mixed with 2 tablespoons of mustard and rolled in crushed cornflakes. Bake about 15 minutes at 400°F on a nonstick baking sheet.

- Who said dinner has be hot? A cold turkey sandwich, fresh vegetables with low fat dip, fruit and milk are just as nutritious as an elaborately prepared hot meal.

- Buy pre-washed greens for salads, precut stir-fry vegetables, grated low fat cheese, skinless, boneless chicken breasts and fresh cut up fruit. The extra cost is still cheaper than a drive to the fast food outlet.

- Quick ideas for young people are given at the beginning of the section "Especially for Children."

CHICKEN & TURKEY MAIN DISHES

Asian Chicken and Vegetable Kabobs

Kathy Schwab, R.D.

MARINADE:
1/4 c. Lite soy sauce
1 T. sesame oil
2 T. rice vinegar (or lemon juice)
2 tsp. minced garlic
1 T. minced fresh ginger
1 scallion, thinly sliced
1/4 tsp. ground black pepper

KABOBS:
2 chicken breasts, boned & skinned
1 lg. onion
1 red or green bell pepper, cut into 1 1/2" pieces
24 fresh mushrooms, 1 1/2" in diameter
1 zucchini, sliced into 1/2" rounds
8 skewers, for grilling

In a shallow glass bowl, whisk together marinade ingredients. Cut chicken into 1 1/2-inch pieces and add to marinade, stirring to coat. Cover and refrigerate 3 hours or overnight.

If using wooden skewers, soak in water 30 minutes before using. Place onions, peppers, mushrooms and zucchini in large bowl and pour chicken and marinade over, stirring to coat the vegetables. If time allows, let vegetables marinate 15 minutes before cooking. Thread skewers, alternating vegetables and chicken. When ready to barbecue, preheat grill. Cook kabobs over medium-hot coals until chicken is no longer pink in center and juices run clear.

Servings:
4

Serving Size:
2 kabobs

Nutritional analysis per serving (including all of the marinade):
Calories: 163
Fat: 6 gm
Cholesterol: 37 mg
Protein: 17 gm
Carbohydrates: 11 gm
Sodium: 640 mg

189

TASTEFULLY OREGON

Broiled East Indian Chicken

Chedwah J. Stein, R.D.

Choose the family's favorite chicken pieces to marinate and broil for a delicious meal. Couscous or a rice dish are good to serve with it.

1 onion, cut in chunks
4 cloves garlic, peeled
1 1/2" piece ginger, peeled & finely chopped
2 tsp. ground cumin
1 tsp. ground coriander
1/2 tsp. ground cardamom
1 tsp. Lite Salt
1/2 tsp. red pepper flakes
1/4 c. fresh-squeezed lime juice
1 T. oil
3 lb. chicken breasts, thighs, legs, etc., skinned

Blend the onion, garlic, ginger, cumin, coriander, cardamom, Lite Salt, pepper flakes, lime juice and oil in a blender or food processor until puréed. Marinate the chicken pieces in the purée for 2 to 24 hours, covered, in the refrigerator.

Broil chicken on a rack, 4 to 5 inches from the heat, for about 20 to 30 minutes or until done (avoid overcooking and drying it out). Turn as needed while broiling.

Servings:
6

Serving Size:
4 ounces broiled chicken

Nutritional analysis per serving:
Calories: 243
Fat: 10 gm
Cholesterol: 94 mg
Protein: 34 gm
Carbohydrate: 4 gm
Sodium: 256 mg

CHICKEN & TURKEY MAIN DISHES

Chicken with Mustard Sauce

Jennifer Scott, R.D.

6 chicken breasts, boned & skinned
1 c. water
1/2 tsp. Lite Salt (can be eliminated if you wish to reduce the sodium content of the recipe & the flavor is still good)
1/2 tsp. thyme
2 T. margarine
1 green onion, thinly sliced
2 T. flour
1 T. prepared mustard

1/4 c. chopped parsley

In 10-inch skillet over high heat, heat chicken breasts, water, Lite Salt (if using) and thyme to boiling. Reduce heat to low; cover and simmer for 10 minutes or until chicken is fork-tender, turning chicken breasts once. With slotted spoon remove chicken to large warm platter; reserve liquid. In 1-quart saucepan over medium heat, melt margarine; add green onion and cook until tender, stirring constantly. Add flour, mustard and reserved liquid. Stir constantly until sauce is thickened and smooth. Pour sauce over chicken breasts. Garnish with parsley sprigs. Serve with steaming hot rice.

Servings:
6

Serving Size:
1 chicken breast

Nutritional analysis per serving:
Calories: 187
Fat: 7 gm
Cholesterol: 65 mg
Protein: 26 gm
Carbohydrate: 3 gm
Sodium: 227 mg

TASTEFULLY OREGON

Chicken with Caramelized Onion Marmalade

Anne Goetze, R.D.

I found this recipe in a favorite magazine. It originally suggested grilling the chicken, but I found this easier.

ONION MARMALADE:
2 lg. red onions, thinly sliced
3 T. brown sugar
3/4 c. dry red wine
3 T. balsamic vinegar

3 T. Dijon mustard
1 1/2 tsp. fresh-squeezed lemon juice
1/2 tsp. ground pepper
1 tsp. Worcestershire sauce
1 tsp. minced garlic

CHICKEN:
4 chicken breasts, boned & skinned (about 4 oz. each)

Onion Marmalade: Combine onions and brown sugar in nonstick skillet. Cook over moderate heat, stirring often, until onions begin to caramelize and turn golden, 15 to 20 minutes. Stir in wine and vinegar, increase heat to medium-high and bring to boil. Reduce heat; cook, stirring often, until most of liquid has evaporated (15 to 30 minutes).

Preheat oven to 350°. Combine mustard, lemon juice, pepper, Worcestershire sauce and garlic. Place chicken breasts in baking dish and cover with sauce. Bake, uncovered, for about 20 minutes or until juices run clear. Place chicken on platter and top with Onion Marmalade.

Servings:
  4

Serving Size:
  1 chicken breast with sauce

Nutritional analysis per serving:
  Calories: 219
  Fat: 4 gm
  Cholesterol: 63 mg
  Protein: 24 gm
  Carbohydrate: 15 gm
  Sodium: 359 mg

CHICKEN & TURKEY MAIN DISHES

Chicken Cordon Bleu

Linda Devereux, R.D.

This is a lovely dish to serve to guests. It is one of our favorites!

3 T. flour
1 tsp. paprika
4 chicken breasts, boned & skinned
4 (1 oz.) slices very lean ham
4 (1 oz.) slices low-fat Swiss cheese (*Jarlsberg Lite* is a good one)
2 tsp. oil
1/2 chicken bouillon cube
1 c. water

3 c. cooked rice

On waxed paper, mix flour and paprika. Roll up chicken with slice of ham and cheese on each and secure with wooden pick. Coat chicken roll-ups in flour/paprika mixture. In 12-inch skillet, cook chicken in oil until browned on all sides. Add 1/2 bouillon cube and water; heat to boiling. Reduce heat to low. Cover and simmer 30 minutes or until tender. Remove chicken from pan. Serve chicken over hot rice.

Servings:
4

Serving Size:
1 stuffed chicken breast

Nutritional analysis per serving:

Calories:	410
Fat:	11 gm
Cholesterol:	70 mg
Protein:	37 gm
Carbohydrate:	39 gm
Sodium:	646 mg

TASTEFULLY OREGON

Chicken Diane

Jodi Moon, R.D.

Our family's pet name for this dish is "smashed chicken". It's an all-time favorite!

- 3 T. chopped green onions or fresh chives
- Juice of 1 lemon or lime
- 2 T. brandy, cognac or apple juice
- 2 tsp. Dijon mustard
- 1 c. sliced fresh mushrooms
- 1/4 c. chicken broth or water
- 1 T. chopped fresh parsley

- 4 chicken breasts, boned & skinned
- 1/2 tsp. Lite Salt
- 1/8 tsp. black pepper
- 1 T. olive or your favorite salad oil

In nonstick skillet, combine onions/chives, lemon/lime juice, brandy/cognac, mustard and mushrooms. Add chicken broth or water; cook on low to medium heat 15 minutes or until mushrooms are done. Stir frequently, until sauce is smooth and thickened somewhat; keep sauce warm while chicken is cooked.

Place chicken breasts between sheets of waxed paper. Pound slightly with side of a large knife (this is where nickname comes from); sprinkle with Lite Salt and pepper. Heat oil in skillet, then cook chicken over medium-high heat 3 minutes, each side. Do not overcook! Transfer to warm serving platter. Add parsley to sauce and pour over chicken. Serve immediately.

Servings:
4

Serving Size:
1 breast with sauce

Nutritional analysis per serving:

Calories:	203
Fat:	7 gm
Cholesterol:	73 mg
Protein:	28 gm
Carbohydrate:	3 gm
Sodium:	315 mg

CHICKEN & TURKEY MAIN DISHES

Chicken Fajitas
Sandy S. Miller, R.D.

A good "finger-licking" meal. Fajitas are fun to eat.

MARINADE:
2 tsp. chili powder
1 tsp. ground cumin
2 tsp. Worcestershire sauce
1/2 tsp. olive oil
1 T. balsamic vinegar

8 oz. chicken breasts, boned & skinned
8 flour tortillas
1 onion, sliced
1 green bell pepper, sliced

1/2 c. plain nonfat yogurt or low-fat sour cream
1/2 c. chopped tomatoes or fresh salsa

About 1 1/2 hours before eating, combine marinade ingredients. Cut chicken into long, thin strips; marinate an hour or so.

Preheat oven to 300°. Wrap tortillas in foil after sprinkling with a little water, and heat in oven 10 to 15 minutes (or wrap in plastic and heat in microwave for 2 to 3 minutes). Sauté onions and peppers in nonstick skillet until cooked but still crisp. Remove from skillet. Put chicken in skillet; sauté, stirring constantly, browning on both sides, about 2 to 3 minutes. Add onions, pepper and any leftover marinade. Add a little water if mixture is too dry. Remove warm tortillas from oven. Set out yogurt and salsa. Fill tortillas with sautéed chicken and vegetables, yogurt and salsa (dividing evenly among 8 tortillas). Roll up to eat.

Servings:
4

Serving Size:
2 fajitas

Nutritional analysis per serving:
Calories:	278
Fat:	6 gm
Cholesterol:	32 mg
Protein:	19 gm
Carbohydrate:	38 gm
Sodium:	405 mg

TASTEFULLY OREGON

Chicken Meatballs

Cathy Quinn, R.D.

These meatballs can also be used for hors d'oeuvres by shaping into smaller size. The combination of flavors is wonderful!

- 1 1/4 lb. ground chicken or turkey
- 1/2 c. Italian-style bread crumbs
- 1/2 c. nonfat milk
- 1/4 c. fresh grated Parmesan cheese
- 2 cloves garlic, minced
- 1/4 tsp. oregano leaves
- 1/4 tsp. basil leaves
- 2 T. minced parsley
- 1/4 tsp. pepper

Mix all ingredients together until well blended. Form into balls (approximately one tablespoon each). Brown on all sides in nonstick skillet, about 1 minute each. Serve with pasta and *Marinara Sauce* (see *Side Dishes, Sauces & Condiments* section), or use your favorite spaghetti sauce.

Servings:
8 to 10

Serving Size:
2 meatballs

Nutritional analysis per serving:
Calories:	166
Fat:	9 gm
Cholesterol:	61 mg
Protein:	16 gm
Carbohydrate:	7 gm
Sodium:	354 mg

CHICKEN & TURKEY MAIN DISHES

Chicken Paprika
Mary Stansell, R.D.

Good with hot noodles or rice.

1/4 c. flour
1 1/2 tsp. Lite Salt
2 T. paprika
1/4 tsp. black pepper
1/4 tsp. ground ginger
1/4 tsp. basil leaves
1/8 tsp. garlic powder
1/8 tsp. nutmeg
3 lb. chicken pieces, skinned
2 T. oil
1/4 c. sherry
2 tsp. Worcestershire sauce
1 tsp. chicken bouillon granules or 1 bouillon cube
1 c. sliced fresh mushrooms
1 c. nonfat sour cream

Mix flour, Lite Salt, paprika, pepper, ginger, basil, garlic powder and nutmeg in plastic bag. Shake chicken pieces with this mixture to evenly coat. Heat oil in a heavy nonstick skillet. Brown chicken slowly. Combine sherry, Worcestershire sauce, chicken bouillon, mushrooms and sour cream; pour over browned chicken; add cover and simmer 30 to 45 minutes or until tender (or bake, covered, in 350° oven.) Add water as needed.

Servings:
6

Serving Size:
1/6 of recipe

Nutritional analysis per serving:
Calories: 278
Fat: 10 gm
Cholesterol: 89 mg
Protein: 32 gm
Carbohydrates: 11 gm
Sodium: 598 mg

TASTEFULLY OREGON

Chicken and Wild Rice
Doris Pavlukovich, R.D.

This is a favorite back in Minnesota where a lot of wild rice is grown.

1 T. margarine
1 med. onion, chopped
1/2 c. sliced mushrooms
1/2 c. diced celery (or carrots & broccoli to add color)
2 c. cooked & cubed chicken breast
2 c. cooked wild rice or brown rice
1 c. cooked white rice
1/2 of 10 3/4 oz. can cream of mushroom soup
1 c. chicken broth

Chopped fresh parsley, for garnish

Preheat oven to 325°. In a nonstick skillet, melt margarine. Sauté onions, mushrooms and celery, or other vegetables until tender. Combine remaining ingredients and put in a 2-quart casserole dish which has been sprayed with nonstick cooking spray. Bake, uncovered, for 1 hour. Garnish with parsley, if desired.

Servings:
  8

Serving Size:
  1/8 of casserole

Nutritional analysis per serving:
  Calories: 204
  Fat: 8 gm
  Cholesterol: 32 mg
  Protein: 15 gm
  Carbohydrate: 20 gm
  Sodium: 304 mg

CHICKEN & TURKEY MAIN DISHES

Company Chicken
Jill Calamar, R.D.

An easy and elegant company dish. It goes nicely with wild rice.

1 (10 1/2 oz.) can Campbell's *Healthy Request* cream of mushroom soup
1 (4 oz.) can mushrooms, with liquid
1 c. low-fat sour cream
1/2 c. white wine
8 chicken breasts, boned & skinned
1/2 tsp. paprika
1/4 c. chopped fresh parsley

Preheat oven to 325°. Combine mushroom soup, mushrooms, sour cream and wine. Mix well. Arrange chicken in 7x11-inch baking dish. Pour sauce over chicken, spreading evenly. Sprinkle lightly with paprika and parsley. Bake, uncovered, for 1 1/2 hours.

Servings:
  8

Serving Size:
  1 chicken breast with sauce

Nutritional analysis per serving:
  Calories: 218
  Fat: 8 gm
  Cholesterol: 88 mg
  Protein: 29 gm
  Carbohydrate: 5 gm
  Sodium: 286 mg

TASTEFULLY OREGON

Cranberry Curry Chicken
Jackie Sparks, R.D.

Don't limit this colorful dish to the holiday season--its mild curry taste is great anytime of the year. Serve the sauce over brown rice or couscous (which is very easy and quick to prepare).

- 1 tsp. margarine
- 2 T. minced shallots or onion
- 1 T. balsamic or raspberry vinegar
- 4 (4 oz.) chicken breasts, boned & skinned
- 1 c. whole-berry cranberry sauce
- 1 c. peeled & chopped green apple
- 1/4 c. golden raisins
- 2 T. coarsely-chopped walnuts
- 3/4 to 1 tsp. curry powder

Preheat oven to 350°. Spray a 10-inch shallow casserole dish with nonstick cooking spray. Add margarine and shallots. Bake, uncovered, for 5 minutes. Add vinegar to dish; stir. Add chicken breasts, basting tops with vinegar/onion mixture. Bake, uncovered, for 10 minutes. Mix together cranberry sauce, apple, raisins, walnuts and curry. Cover chicken with sauce and bake additional 15 to 20 minutes, or until chicken is cooked and sauce bubbles.

Servings:
4

Serving Size:
1 chicken breast with sauce

Nutritional analysis per serving:
- Calories: 305
- Fat: 6 gm
- Cholesterol: 63 mg
- Protein: 24 gm
- Carbohydrate: 39 gm
- Sodium: 97 mg

CHICKEN & TURKEY MAIN DISHES

Diane's Mexi-Chicken Casserole
Juanita Dodd, R.D.

An easy Mexican-style dish which would be great with guacamole, warm tortillas, tomatoes, salsa and shredded lettuce. It makes a fun casual-type meal.

1 1/2 lb. chicken breast (about 6 breasts, boned & skinned)
12 corn tortillas
2 (10 1/2 oz.) cans Campbell's *Healthy Request* cream of chicken soup
1 c. nonfat milk
1/2 c. salsa
1 c. grated low-fat Cheddar cheese

To cook chicken: Place washed chicken in glass dish and cover with plastic wrap with a few drops of water. Microwave on HIGH about 5 minutes. Drain and cut into cubes.

Preheat oven to 350°. Place chicken cubes in bottom of a 9x13-inch casserole dish which has been sprayed with nonstick cooking spray. Cut tortillas into small pieces and spread over chicken. In a separate bowl, mix soup, milk and salsa and spread over chicken and tortilla pieces. Bake for 45 minutes. Remove from oven and sprinkle cheese over top of casserole and let melt.

Servings:
8

Serving Size:
1/8 of casserole

Nutritional analysis per serving:
Calories: 259
Fat: 7 gm
Cholesterol: 61 mg
Protein: 25 gm
Carbohydrate: 23 gm
Sodium: 506 mg

Herbed Chicken

Juanita Dodd, R.D.

A very tasty dish.

- 1 T. olive oil
- 1 lg. tomato, chopped
- 1 stalk celery, thinly sliced
- 2 T. dried parsley flakes
- 6 cloves garlic, quartered
- 1/2 tsp. Lite Salt
- 1/2 tsp. black pepper
- 1/2 tsp. oregano leaves
- 1/2 tsp. basil leaves
- 1/8 tsp. nutmeg
- 4 chicken breasts, boned & skinned

The day before: In a microwave dish, mix together olive oil, tomato, celery, parsley flakes, garlic, Lite Salt, pepper, oregano, basil and nutmeg. Microwave mixture on HIGH for 3 minutes, stir. Add chicken, covering with mixture. Cover and refrigerate overnight or for at least 3 hours.

When ready to cook: Cover baking dish with waxed paper and microwave on HIGH for 8 to 10 minutes. Turn chicken and microwave on HIGH 8 to 10 minutes more. Let stand 5 minutes before serving.

Servings:
4

Serving Size:
1/4 of recipe

Nutritional analysis per serving:
- Calories: 193
- Fat: 7 gm
- Cholesterol: 73 mg
- Protein: 28 gm
- Carbohydrate: 5 gm
- Sodium: 218 mg

CHICKEN & TURKEY MAIN DISHES

Kung Pao Chicken

Cindy Francois, R.D.; Ann Schenk, R.D.

Kung Pao Chicken is our favorite Chinese dish. This version has a new twist--it's low-fat. Serve over hot steamed rice for a wonderful treat!

COOKING SAUCE:
1 T. soy sauce
1 T. white wine vinegar
1 T. dry sherry
1 1/2 c. water
2 T. sugar
2 T. cornstarch

1 1/2 T. dry sherry
1 T. cornstarch
1/2 tsp. Lite Salt
1/8 tsp. white pepper
2 chicken breasts, boned, skinned & cut into 1/2" cubes

2 tsp. sesame oil, divided
4 sm. dried hot red chiles
1/4 c. unsalted peanuts, dry-roasted
1 clove garlic, minced
1 tsp. minced fresh ginger
6 green onions (including tops), cut into 1 1/2" pieces

Combine ingredients for *Cooking Sauce* and set aside. In another bowl, stir together sherry, cornstarch, Lite Salt and white pepper. Add chicken strips and stir to coat.

Heat 1 teaspoon sesame oil to medium heat in a wok or electric fry pan. Add chiles and peanuts, stir until chiles just begin to char. (Be very careful not to let chiles turn black.) Remove peanuts and chiles from wok and set aside. Heat remaining 1 teaspoon sesame oil in wok and add garlic and ginger, stir, then add marinated chicken strips and stir-fry about 5 to 7 minutes. Add peanuts, chiles, and onions to wok. Stir in *Cooking Sauce* and continue stirring until sauce boils and thickens. Serve warm over large servings of hot steamed rice.

Continued on following page.

TASTEFULLY OREGON

Continued from preceding page.

Servings:
4

Serving Size:
1/4 of recipe

Nutritional analysis per serving (not including rice):

Calories:	219
Fat:	8 gm
Cholesterol:	34 mg
Protein:	17 gm
Carbohydrate:	19 gm
Sodium:	460 mg

This is a picture of a general merchandise store in Dundee, Oregon in 1910, which belonged to Cindy's husband's great uncle, Archie Parrett. Notice the washboards, horse sweatpads and other interesting merchandise hanging from the ceiling. (Courtesy of Marion Brumback's Stories of Old Dundee)

CHICKEN & TURKEY MAIN DISHES

Larch Mountain Lasagna

Mary Baron, R.D.

Serve with French bread and a green salad for a great and filling meal. Tomato lovers may wish to add 1 can of unsalted tomato paste.

1 lb. ground turkey or chicken
1 lg. onion, chopped (1 1/3 c.)
1/2 lb. fresh mushrooms, sliced (4 c. sliced)
2 (15 oz.) cans stewed tomatoes, mashed or well chopped
2 (8 oz.) cans *no-salt-added* tomato sauce
2 tsp. oregano leaves
2 tsp. basil leaves
1/2 tsp. garlic powder
8 oz. part-skim ricotta cheese
2 c. or 8 oz. part-skim Mozzarella cheese, grated
1 T. chopped fresh parsley or dried flakes
11 to 12 lasagna noodles (8 oz. pkg.)

Heat a large nonstick skillet and brown ground turkey or chicken, stirring often, and adding a little water, if necessary. Drain well. Add chopped onion and mushrooms; sauté until lightly browned. Add tomatoes, tomato sauce, oregano, basil and garlic. Simmer 15 to 20 minutes while preparing other ingredients. In separate dish, blend ricotta, grated Mozzarella and parsley. Set aside. Bring 2 quarts water to boil in large skillet. Add lasagna noodles; boil gently, uncovered, 10 to 15 minutes. Drain and rinse.

Preheat oven to 350°. Spray 9x13-inch pan with nonstick cooking spray; layer sauce, 4 noodles, 1/3 cheese mixture, sauce, 4 noodles, etc., ending with sauce. Bake, uncovered, 35 minutes, cover if needed. Let sit 10 minutes before serving.

Servings:
12

Serving Size:
3x3/4-inch piece

Nutritional analysis per serving:
Calories: 285
Fat: 11 gm
Cholesterol: 58 mg
Protein: 20 gm
Carbohydrate: 27 gm
Sodium: 357 mg

TASTEFULLY OREGON

Lemon Chicken

Joyce Gustafson, R.D.

I called my friend for this recipe after a delicious meal at their home. She served it over steamed rice with a green salad and the crowd loved it!

1/4 c. margarine
8 chicken breasts, boned & skinned
2 T. sherry or wine
2 T. grated lemon peel
2 T. fresh-squeezed lemon juice
1 c. fat-free Mocha Mix
2 tsp. cornstarch
2 T. fresh grated Parmesan cheese

Early in the day: Melt margarine in nonstick skillet. Sauté chicken breasts 5 to 8 minutes, turning so all sides are browned lightly. Put chicken, in one layer only, in 9x13-inch baking dish which has been sprayed with nonstick cooking spray. To remaining margarine in skillet, add sherry, lemon peel and lemon juice. Add cornstarch to Mocha Mix; stir to combine. Slowly add to skillet mixture, stirring constantly. Pour lemon sauce over chicken. Sprinkle with Parmesan cheese, cover well; refrigerate until time to cook.

Forty-five minutes before serving time: Preheat oven to 350°. Uncover chicken; bake 30 minutes. Place under broiler 3 to 4 minutes to brown top. *Watch carefully!* Serve chicken warm over hot steamed rice.

Servings:
  8

Serving Size:
  1 chicken breast with sauce

Nutritional analysis per serving:
  Calories: 216
  Fat: 8 gm
  Cholesterol: 70 mg
  Protein: 28 gm
  Carbohydrate: 4 gm
  Sodium: 228 mg

CHICKEN & TURKEY MAIN DISHES

Mediterranean Chicken and Spaghetti

Dawn Kinzel, R.D.

The fat can be lowered by reducing or eliminating the olives and chicken broth. I sometimes add carrots for extra color and flavor.

1 lb. chicken breast, boned & skinned
1/4 c. fresh-squeezed lemon juice
1 T. olive oil
1 clove garlic, minced
1/2 tsp. oregano leaves
1/2 tsp. grated lemon peel
6 to 8 oz. uncooked spaghetti
1/2 c. chopped red bell pepper
1 sm. green zucchini, grated
1 sm. yellow zucchini, grated
1 c. black olives, drained & quartered
2 tsp. cornstarch
1/2 c. chicken broth or water

Cut chicken into thin strips and marinate in lemon juice, olive oil, garlic, oregano and lemon peel for at least 30 minutes. Cook spaghetti in unsalted water according to package directions; drain, rinse and set aside. In a large cooking pot or wok, cook chicken and marinade until no longer pink. Add red pepper and stir-fry until tender. Add grated zucchini and olives. Dissolve cornstarch in chicken broth, add to chicken and vegetables and cook until thickened. Add spaghetti and toss to combine.

Servings:
 4 to 6

Serving Size:
 1/4 to 1/6 of recipe

Nutritional analysis per serving:
 Calories: 330
 Fat: 10 gm
 Cholesterol: 50 mg
 Protein: 25 gm
 Carbohydrate: 38 gm
 Sodium: 360 mg

TASTEFULLY OREGON

Mexicali Medley Burritos
Judy Forest, R.D.

A family favorite; ready in 20 minutes!

- 1/2 lb. ground turkey or finely-ground, cubed chicken breast
- 8 whole wheat flour tortillas
- 1 (16 oz.) can unsalted dark red or black beans, drained, or 2 c. unsalted home-cooked beans
- 1 (16 oz.) pkg. frozen loose-pack vegetables or 3 c. chopped fresh vegetables
- 1/2 pkg. taco seasoning or 1/2 tsp. garlic powder, 1/2 tsp. Lite Salt (opt.), 1 to 2 tsp. chili powder (to taste), 2 tsp. cumin, 1/2 tsp. oregano leaves
- 1/2 c. picante sauce
- 4 oz. grated low-fat cheese
- Optional: chopped tomatoes or fresh salsa, & nonfat sour cream

In a large nonstick skillet, cook the chicken over medium-low heat for about 3 minutes, stirring constantly, until just cooked. Drain off any excess fat. Wrap the tortillas in foil and warm in 300° oven, or heat in microwave. To the chicken, add the beans, vegetables and seasonings. Stir. Cook until most of the liquid is evaporated. Add picante sauce and stir. Heat 1 or 2 minutes more. Place 1/8 of the mixture at one end of a warm tortilla. Place grated cheese on top, then roll. If desired, top with chopped tomatoes, salsa and nonfat sour cream, and serve.

Servings:
8

Serving Size:
1 burrito

Nutritional analysis per serving:
Calories:	251
Fat:	6 gm
Cholesterol:	31 mg
Protein:	17 gm
Carbohydrate:	38 gm
Sodium:	454 mg

CHICKEN & TURKEY MAIN DISHES

Orange Chicken
Nancie Fisher, R.D.

A favorite recipe from my great aunt. Serve this delicious marinated chicken with steamed rice and a salad for a great meal.

1 (6 oz.) can frozen orange juice concentrate, thawed
1/4 c. water
2 T. *lite* soy sauce
1/2 tsp. pepper
1 clove garlic, minced
2 T. chopped, candied ginger
4 chicken breasts, skinned

Early in the morning or the day before serving: Combine first six ingredients in a bowl and pour into plastic bag. Add chicken and marinate 12 hours or overnight.

Preheat oven to 375°. Arrange chicken in a shallow baking dish and cover with marinade. Bake, uncovered, for 45 minutes. Baste occasionally.

Servings:
  4

Serving Size:
  1 chicken breast with sauce

Nutritional analysis per serving:
  Calories: 234
  Fat: 2 gm
  Cholesterol: 68 mg
  Protein: 28 gm
  Carbohydrate: 24 gm
  Sodium: 382 mg

TASTEFULLY OREGON

Parmesan Herbed Chicken
Kathy Schwab, R.D.

This is easily prepared with just a few ingredients.

- 1/3 c. plain bread crumbs
- 1/3 c. fresh grated Parmesan cheese
- 1/4 tsp. pepper
- 1 tsp. fines herbs (it's in the spice section near fennel)
- 1 egg white, lightly beaten
- 4 chicken breasts, boned & skinned

Preheat oven to 350°. Combine bread crumbs, cheese, pepper and herbs in a shallow bowl. Place egg white in a separate bowl. Dip chicken in egg white and roll in bread crumb mixture. Place on a baking sheet which has been coated with nonstick cooking spray, and bake for 20 to 25 minutes or until juices run clear. Serve hot.

Servings: 4

Serving Size: 1 chicken breast

Nutritional analysis per serving:
- Calories: 218
- Fat: 6 gm
- Cholesterol: 80 mg
- Protein: 32 gm
- Carbohydrate: 7 gm
- Sodium: 304 mg

CHICKEN & TURKEY MAIN DISHES

Pasta with Chicken and Asparagus

Donna Oleksa, R.D.

- 2 chicken breasts (about 1 lb.), boned & skinned
- 1 lb. asparagus (broccoli, snow peas or other vegetables work well)
- 1/4 lb. mushrooms
- 3/4 lb. linguine or fettuccine
- 1 tsp. Lite Salt
- 1/4 tsp. freshly-ground pepper
- 3 T. finely-chopped shallots
- 1 c. nonfat milk
- 1 T. flour
- 1 dried hot red pepper or 1/2 tsp. dried pepper flakes
- 1/8 tsp. nutmeg (opt.)
- 1/4 tsp. tarragon
- 1 c. grated low-fat cheese (*Jarlsberg Lite* works well)

Cut chicken breasts into small strips about 1 1/2-inches long by 1/2-inch wide. Cut asparagus on the bias into 1 1/2-inch lengths. Thinly slice mushrooms. Spray a large skillet with nonstick cooking spray. Sauté asparagus and mushrooms, stirring frequently, and adding just enough water to prevent scorching. Cook until asparagus is tender-crisp. Remove from skillet.

Cook pasta in unsalted boiling water until done. While pasta is cooking, spray a large skillet with nonstick cooking spray and add chicken strips. Cook quickly, stirring to separate pieces.

Continued on following page.

TASTEFULLY OREGON

Continued from preceding page.

Cook about 2 minutes or just until the chicken changes color. Add asparagus (or other vegetable) and mushrooms, and stir. Add Lite Salt, pepper and shallots, and cook briefly, about 30 seconds. Add milk (reserving 2 tablespoons), red pepper flakes, nutmeg and tarragon; stir. Add 1 tablespoon flour to reserved 2 tablespoons milk and mix thoroughly. Stir into above mixture; cook until thickened. Add cheese. Heat while stirring, just until cheese melts. Drain the pasta and add to the sauce. Toss lightly to combine; serve immediately.

Servings:
6

Serving Size:
1/6 of recipe

Nutritional analysis per serving:
Calories: 404
Fat: 6 gm
Cholesterol: 53 mg
Protein: 32 gm
Carbohydrate: 54 gm
Sodium: 345 mg

CHICKEN & TURKEY MAIN DISHES

Spinach Chicken Stir-Fry
Peggy Paul, R.D.

Serve this stir-fry with an easy salad to make the meal complete. I suggest alternating slices of tomato and cucumber, and drizzling with flavored vinegar. This is a favorite of ours at the Oregon Dairy Council.

2 chicken breasts, boned & skinned
2 tsp. olive oil
1/2 c. chopped onion
1 T. minced fresh ginger or 1 tsp. ground ginger
3/4 c. chicken broth
1/2 c. plain nonfat yogurt
1 T. flour
2 tsp. country-style Dijon mustard
3 c. fresh spinach, torn into lg. pieces, or 5 oz. frozen spinach, thawed & well drained

Cut chicken into 3/4-inch pieces. Heat olive oil in wok or skillet. Stir-fry chicken, onion and fresh ginger until chicken is browned. (If using ground ginger, add with mustard to the sauce.) Combine chicken broth, yogurt, flour and mustard in a jar with a tight lid. Shake until the flour is thoroughly mixed. Add sauce to chicken mixture. Stir while cooking, for 2 minutes. Add spinach and continue cooking until sauce thickens. Continue to stir. Add water if sauce is too thick. Serve over cooked rice or pasta.

Servings:
2

Serving Size:
1 chicken breast with sauce

Nutritional analysis per serving:
Calories:	287
Fat:	9 gm
Cholesterol:	74 mg
Protein:	36 gm
Carbohydrate:	15 gm
Sodium:	589 mg

TASTEFULLY OREGON

Szechuan Turkey Stir-Fry

Luanna Diller, R.D.

We used lite soy sauce in this recipe to reduce the sodium content.

MARINADE:
- 1 T. *lite* soy sauce
- 1 T. cornstarch
- 1/2 tsp. sugar
- 1 clove garlic, minced
- 1 lb. turkey breast, skinned & cut into thin strips

SOY SAUCE MIXTURE:
- 1 c. water
- 3 T. *lite* soy sauce
- 4 tsp. cornstarch
- 1/2 tsp. crushed red pepper flakes

- 1 T. olive oil, divided
- 3 med. carrots, sliced diagonally 1/8" thick
- 1 c. coarsely-chopped onion
- 3 sm. zucchini, halved lengthwise, sliced diagonally, 3/4" thick
- 2 T. unsalted peanuts

Combine *Marinade* ingredients in medium bowl. Add turkey and stir to coat. Set aside. In another bowl, combine *Soy Sauce Mixture*. Set aside.

Heat 2 teaspoons oil in wok or heavy skillet over medium-high heat. Add turkey mixture and stir-fry until opaque, about 2 minutes. Remove turkey and set aside. Heat remaining oil in wok. Add carrots and onion and stir-fry 3 minutes. Add zucchini and stir-fry 2 minutes. Return turkey to wok with *Soy Sauce Mixture*. Cook until sauce boils and thickens, 1 to 2 minutes. Stir in peanuts. Serve immediately over steamed rice.

Servings:
6

Serving Size:
1/6 of recipe

Nutritional analysis per serving:

Calories:	200
Fat:	8 gm
Cholesterol:	40 mg
Protein:	18 gm
Carbohydrate:	12 gm
Sodium:	449 mg

CHICKEN & TURKEY MAIN DISHES

Thai Chicken Fettuccine

Kathy Cunningham, D.T.R.

A colorful warm summer day entrée. Serve with fruit and roll for a complete meal.

1 c. picante sauce
1/4 c. peanut butter
2 T. honey
1/4 c. orange juice
1 tsp. soy sauce
1/2 tsp. ground ginger
12 oz. dry fettuccine, cooked & well drained
2 c. cooked chicken breast, cut in chunks (3 breasts)
1/4 c. chopped cilantro
1/4 c. chopped unsalted peanuts
1/4 c. thinly-sliced red bell pepper
Iceberg lettuce or savory cabbage leaves for garnish

Combine picante sauce, peanut butter, orange juice, soy sauce and ginger in small saucepan. Cook and stir over low heat until blended and smooth. Reserve 1/4 cup picante sauce mixture; toss remaining mixture with hot cooked fettuccine. Mix reserved picante sauce mixture with cooked chicken pieces. Line large platter with lettuce leaves, if desired. Arrange fettuccine mixture over lettuce; top with chicken mixture. Sprinkle with cilantro, peanuts and red bell pepper. Cool to room temperature before serving, or serve chilled.

Servings:
6

Serving Size:
1 cup

Nutritional analysis per serving:
Calories: 437
Fat: 11 gm
Cholesterol: 37 mg
Protein: 26 gm
Carbohydrate: 59 gm
Sodium: 356 mg

TASTEFULLY OREGON

Turkey Tangine with Vegetables
Chedwah Stein, R.D.

Don't let the list of ingredients scare you, this delicious dish is worth all the effort!

- 1 lb. turkey breast, boned & skinned
- 2 T. olive oil, divided
- 1 med. onion, diced
- 3 cloves garlic, minced
- 1 med. eggplant, cubed
- 3 c. chicken broth
- 1 1/2 sticks cinnamon
- 2 tsp. curry powder
- 1 tsp. cumin
- 1/4 tsp. turmeric
- 1/4 tsp. black pepper
- 1 lg. carrot, cut into 1" pieces
- 1/2 med. acorn squash, peeled & cut into 1" pieces*
- 2 med. parsnips, peeled & cut into 1" pieces
- 1/2 med. green bell pepper, cut into 1" pieces
- 1 (16 oz.) can diced tomatoes & juice
- 1 med. zucchini, cut into 1" pieces
- 1/2 c. golden raisins
- 2 T. chopped cilantro, divided
- Hot steamed rice or couscous

Cut turkey breast into 1 1/2-inch pieces. Heat a large, heavy-bottom pot over medium heat. Add 1 tablespoon olive oil and sauté turkey until opaque. Remove turkey from pot; set aside. Add remaining tablespoon olive oil to pot. Add onion, garlic and eggplant; sauté over low heat until onion is tender, about 10 minutes. Add chicken broth, cinnamon, curry powder, cumin, turmeric and pepper. Stir, bring to boil, reduce heat and simmer, covered, about 10 minutes. Add carrots, squash, parsnips and green pepper. Simmer, uncovered, 10 minutes. Add turkey, tomatoes, zucchini, raisins and 1 tablespoon cilantro. Stir to make sure all ingredients are covered. Simmer, covered, 10 minutes more. Serve in deep bowls on top of hot steamed rice or cooked couscous, garnishing with remaining cilantro.

*To soften rind, place whole squash in microwave oven and cook it on HIGH for 1 1/2 to 2 1/2 minutes. Allow squash to stand for 2 minutes before peeling.

Continued on following page.

CHICKEN & TURKEY MAIN DISHES

Continued from preceding page.

Servings:
6

Serving Size:
1/6 of recipe

Nutritional analysis per serving:
Calories: 313
Fat: 8 gm
Cholesterol: 40 mg
Protein: 24 gm
Carbohydrate: 40 gm
Sodium: 564 mg

TASTEFULLY OREGON

Notes

Beef, Veal & Pork Main Dishes

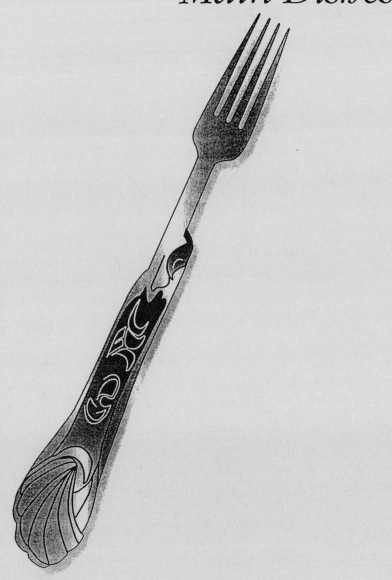

Tastefully Oregon

The Salted Facts

- Sodium is the element in salt most likely to contribute to high blood pressure (hypertension) in people who are predisposed to it.

- People with high blood pressure are more likely to develop heart disease and strokes.

- Salt is 40% sodium. One teaspoon of salt contains about 2000 milligrams of sodium.

- Up to 2000 milligrams of sodium per day (1 teaspoon of salt) is considered safe and adequate.

- People in the U.S. typically consume 4000 to 5000 milligrams of sodium (2 to 2 1/2 teaspoons of salt) a day.

- Most of the excess sodium consumed comes from salt added to food during commercial processing and home cooking.

Shake The Salt Habit

- Use the salt shaker sparingly in cooking and at the table.

- Use *Lite Salt* (Morton is one company that makes such a product) to reduce the sodium in your recipes by one-half, while retaining the same salty flavor. We really like this product because it allows us to include some foods that are high in salt (canned soups, beans and vegetables) and still meet the salt guidelines.

- Use *"no salt added"* products (tomatoes, tomato sauce, etc.) and *"reduced-salt"* products (chicken broth, soy sauce, etc.).

- Rely on fresh or dried herbs and spices as well as lemon juice to add flavor to your foods in place of salt.

BEEF, VEAL & PORK MAIN DISHES

Baked Bowties and Spinach
Sandra Strohmeyer, R.D.

My mom was an excellent cook—this is one of hers that I have changed a bit. It makes a very nice evening meal and great leftovers.

1 (10 to 12 oz.) pkg. bowtie noodles
1 lb. very lean ground beef (9% fat) or ground turkey
1 lg. onion, chopped
1 clove garlic, minced
1 (15 oz.) can tomato sauce*
1 (6 oz.) can unsalted tomato paste*
1/2 c. dry red wine & 1/2 c. water, or 1 c. water
1/4 tsp. each: rosemary, basil, marjoram, oregano, savory & pepper
2 (10 oz.) pkg. frozen chopped spinach, thawed & well drained, or use fresh spinach, chopped
2 c. plain nonfat yogurt
1/2 c. fresh grated Parmesan cheese

Cook noodles in unsalted boiling water until just tender. Drain well. Meanwhile, sauté ground beef or turkey in nonstick skillet. Add onion and garlic and cook until soft. Blend in tomato sauce, tomato paste, wine, water and spices. Simmer slowly, uncovered, until reduced to about 6 cups (about 30 minutes).

Combine drained noodles with meat sauce; let cool slightly. Preheat oven to 375°. Spread half of mixture over bottom of shallow 9x13-inch baking dish that has been sprayed with nonstick cooking spray. Scatter half the spinach over noodles; dot evenly with yogurt, then spread gently to make even layer. Sprinkle with half the cheese. Repeat layers of meat and noodles, spinach and yogurt, top evenly with remaining cheese. Bake, uncovered, for 40 to 50 minutes, until lightly browned on top.

*Lower salt products are suggested to lower the sodium content.

Continued on following page.

Continued from preceding page.

Servings:
8

Serving Size:
1/8th of recipe

Nutritional analysis per serving:
Calories:	350
Fat:	8 gm
Cholesterol:	27 mg
Protein:	26 gm
Carbohydrate:	42 gm
Sodium:	581 mg

BEEF, VEAL & PORK MAIN DISHES

Bean and Burger Casserole

Doris Pavlukovich, R.D.

In years past we used a generous amount of bacon, but with changes it is still a family favorite. Cornbread is great with it!

1 lb. very lean ground beef (9% fat)
1 lg. onion, chopped
1 (8 oz.) can *no-salt-added* tomato sauce
1/4 c. brown sugar (opt.)
2 T. vinegar
1 T. mustard
1 (15 oz.) can kidney beans, drained (use *S & W 50% less salt*)
1 (15 oz.) can butter beans, drained
2 (16 oz.) cans B & M 99% fat-free Brick Oven Baked Beans

Preheat oven to 350°. Heat nonstick skillet; stir and sauté ground beef and onions until onions are soft. Drain well. Spray a casserole dish with nonstick spray. Combine all remaining ingredients with beef and onions and put into prepared casserole dish. Bake, uncovered, for 45 minutes. Serve warm.

Servings:
6

Serving Size:
1 1/3 cups

Nutritional analysis per serving:
Calories: 456
Fat: 7 gm
Cholesterol: 43 mg
Protein: 35 gm
Carbohydrate: 66 gm
Sodium: 649 mg

TASTEFULLY OREGON

Beef or Chicken Fajitas
Kathy Schwab, R.D.

This is one of those great meals that can be on the table in 30 minutes. Lovely to look at too.

- 1/2 c. chopped onion
- 1/2 med. green bell pepper, slivered
- 1/2 c. sliced fresh mushrooms
- 6 oz. flank steak or chicken breast, cut into strips
- 3 T. bottled fajita seasoning (some are labeled *Southwest Seasoning*)
- 4 whole wheat flour tortillas
- 1 med. tomato, chopped
- 1/4 c. *S & W Salsa with Cilantro*

Coat a large nonstick skillet with non-stick cooking spray. Stir-fry onion, pepper and mushrooms until tender-crisp. Remove vegetables and stir-fry flank steak or chicken until browned. Add vegetables back to pan and stir in fajita seasoning. Wrap tortillas in a paper towel and heat in microwave for 10 seconds or until heated through. Fill each tortilla with 1/4 of beef/vegetable mixture. Fold tortilla over and top with chopped tomatoes and salsa. Serve immediately.

Servings:
2

Serving Size:
2 fajitas

Nutritional analysis per serving:
- Calories: 341
- Fat: 8 gm
- Cholesterol: 29 mg
- Protein: 26 gm
- Carbohydrate: 53 gm
- Sodium: 609 mg

BEEF, VEAL & PORK MAIN DISHES

Beef Noodle Bake

Joyce Gustafson, R.D.

My family loves this old standby. I will admit I have skipped refrigerating it for the suggested hour and put it directly in the oven and it seems to turn out just fine. I serve it with salad and fresh crunchy bread.

8 oz. non-egg noodles
1 lb. very lean ground beef (9% fat)
1 (16 oz.) can *no-salt-added* tomato sauce
1 c. low-fat cottage cheese
1/4 c. fat-free sour cream
8 oz. fat-free cream cheese
1/2 c. chopped green onions

Chopped parsley, for garnish

Spray 2-quart casserole dish with non-stick cooking spray. Cook noodles in unsalted water until done. Drain and set aside. Brown ground beef in non-stick skillet, stirring frequently. Drain cooked beef on paper towels to remove any grease. Combine beef with tomato sauce; mix well and set aside.

Preheat oven to 375°. Place one-half of cooked noodles in bottom of prepared casserole dish. In separate bowl, combine cottage cheese, cream cheese, sour cream and green onions. Spread as second layer over noodles. Cover with remaining noodles. Add last layer which is the meat/tomato sauce. Cover; chill 1 hour before baking. Bake, uncovered, 1 hour. Remove from oven and sprinkle top with chopped parsley. Serve hot.

Servings:
6

Serving Size:
1/6th recipe

Nutritional analysis per serving:
Calories: 373
Fat: 8 gm
Cholesterol: 36 mg
Protein: 33 gm
Carbohydrate: 40 gm
Sodium: 461 mg

TASTEFULLY OREGON

Marinated Beef and Vegetable Kabobs
Kathy Schwab, R.D.

Marinate beef cubes overnight and have a special barbecued treat.

MARINADE:
- 3 T. *lite* soy sauce
- 2 T. apple juice concentrate
- 2 T. fresh-squeezed lemon juice
- 2 tsp. sesame oil
- 1 T. Dijon mustard
- 2 tsp. minced garlic
- 1 tsp. grated lemon zest
- 1/2 tsp. dried red pepper flakes

KABOBS:
- 1 lb. boneless beef sirloin tip (about 1" thick), well trimmed
- 1 lg. onion
- 1 med. red or green bell pepper
- 24 mushrooms
- 16 cherry tomatoes

To prepare marinade: Whisk marinade ingredients together in a small bowl. Trim fat from beef and cut into 1 1/2-inch cubes. Add beef cubes to marinade. Stir to coat. Cover and refrigerate for 6 to 24 hours.

To prepare kabobs: If using wooden skewers, soak skewers in water 30 minutes before using. Peel onion and cut into eighths. Cut pepper into 1 1/2-inch pieces. (If not using sweet onions, blanch onions in boiling water for 1 minute to cut hotness.) Place onions, peppers, whole mushrooms and tomatoes in a large bowl and add meat and marinade, stirring to coat the vegetables. If time allows, let vegetables marinate 15 minutes before cooking. Thread 8 skewers, alternating vegetables and meat. When ready to barbecue, preheat grill and cook kabobs over medium-hot coals until meat is no longer pink in center and juices run clear.

Continued on following page.

BEEF, VEAL & PORK MAIN DISHES

Continued from preceding page.

Servings:
4

Serving Size:
2 kabobs

Nutritional analysis per serving:
Calories: 221
Fat: 6 gm
Cholesterol: 54 mg
Protein: 25 gm
Carbohydrate: 18 gm
Sodium: 553 mg

TASTEFULLY OREGON

Flank Steak in Marinade

Joyce Gustafson, R.D.

A great marinade to use on barbecued steak. I like to serve this with twice-baked potatoes, mixed vegetables and a large salad.

MARINADE:
- 1 T. olive oil
- 2 T. water
- 6 cloves garlic, finely chopped
- 1/4 c. fresh-squeezed lemon juice
- 2 T. finely-chopped fresh ginger
- 1 1/2 T. *Lite* soy sauce
- 1 T. coriander seeds, crushed
- 2 tsp. Dijon mustard
- 1 tsp. red pepper flakes

1 1/2 to 2 lb. flank steak

Combine marinade ingredients in a jar with a tight-fitting lid. Put steak in a resealable plastic bag or a shallow pan with a tight lid. Pour marinade over steak and turn meat several times. Refrigerate for several hours, turning meat as often as you think of it.

When ready to broil: Remove meat from marinade and cook under broiler or over hot coals. We like to baste the meat with the marinade as it cooks. When steak is done to your taste, remove to cutting board and slice in thin slices.

Servings:
  6

Serving Size:
  3 to 4 ounces

Nutritional analysis per serving:
  Calories: 228
  Fat: 11 gm
  Cholesterol: 71 mg
  Protein: 27 gm
  Carbohydrate: 3 gm
  Sodium: 238 mg

BEEF, VEAL & PORK MAIN DISHES

Mediterranean Stroganoff

Anne Goetze, R.D.

A beautiful stir-fry to serve over hot steamed rice or pasta. This is adapted from a favorite high-calcium recipe from the Oregon Dairy Council.

3 c. broccoli flowerets
4 med. carrots, peeled & bias-sliced (2 1/2 c.)
1 tsp. olive oil
3/4 lb. well-trimmed beef round steak, thinly sliced
1 lb. fresh mushrooms, thickly sliced
1 med. leek or 1 c. green onions, 1/4" bias-sliced
2 cloves garlic, minced
1/4 c. flour, divided
2 c. nonfat milk
1 T. *lite* soy sauce
1/2 beef bouillon cube
1/2 c. dry wine or water
1 c. nonfat yogurt or sour cream
1 c. fat-free ricotta cheese
1/4 c. fresh grated Parmesan cheese

Combine broccoli and carrots and steam or microwave until crisp-tender. Drain and set aside. Heat oil in a large nonstick skillet. Add sliced meat and brown. Add mushrooms, leeks or green onions, and garlic. Stir-fry over medium heat 3 to 5 minutes. Blend in 3 tablespoons flour. Stir in milk, soy sauce and bouillon cube; cook and stir until mixture is thickened and bubbly. Add wine (or water), reserved broccoli and carrots. In small bowl, combine yogurt, ricotta cheese, Parmesan cheese and the remaining 1 tablespoon flour. Gradually add yogurt/cheese to hot mixture. Cook over medium heat until just heated through. Do not boil. Serve with rice or pasta.

Servings:
6

Serving Size:
2 cups

Nutritional analysis per serving:
Calories: 307
Fat: 9 gm
Cholesterol: 48 mg
Protein: 27 gm
Carbohydrate: 28 gm
Sodium: 436 mg

TASTEFULLY OREGON

Orange Nugget Stir-Fry

Marge Norman, R.D.

This is my husband's recipe. He is the stir-fry cook at our house and he likes to serve this favorite over hot rice. It takes a little effort to slice things, but the actual cooking time is short and the dish is definitely worth it.

SAUCE:
2 T. cornstarch
1 tsp. grated ginger root
1 tsp. minced garlic
1/2 tsp. pepper
1/2 c. water

2 lg. oranges
1 tsp. sugar
2 T. soy sauce

1 lb. flank steak
2 tsp. oil
2 T. water
1 tsp. minced garlic
1 lg. onion, thinly sliced
   & separated into rings
   or cut into wedges
3 stalks celery, sliced
   1/2" thick
1 med. red bell pepper,
   cut into thin strips
1 med. green bell pepper,
   cut into thin strips
8 mushrooms, sliced
   1/2" thick

Combine sauce ingredients, blending until smooth. Set aside. Peel and cut each orange into 6 sections; cut sections in half. Mix sugar and soy sauce and pour over oranges. Let stand for 15 minutes. Thinly slice flank steak diagonally against the grain. Heat oil in wok or nonstick skillet and add water and garlic. Stir-fry flank steak strips, stirring constantly. Remove meat from wok or skillet and set aside, leaving juices in pan. Add sliced vegetables (onions and celery first, then bell peppers and last mushrooms) and stir-fry. Add water, if needed, to prevent sticking. Return meat to wok and stir until mixed. Add sauce to pan and cook until mixture thickens and sauce turns translucent. Add water if you prefer a thinner sauce. Add oranges and heat briefly.

Continued on following page.

BEEF, VEAL & PORK MAIN DISHES

Continued from preceding page.

Servings:
6

Serving Size:
1/6th recipe

Nutritional analysis per serving:
Calories: 201
Fat: 7 gm
Cholesterol: 43 mg
Protein: 18 gm
Carbohydrate: 16 gm
Sodium: 402 mg

This class at Oregon State College in 1925 appears very formal--Preserving Food--Canning and Drying. The copper kettle pictured is a popular collector's item now. (Courtesy of Oregon State University Archives, Harriet's Collection #978)

TASTEFULLY OREGON

Pork Chops Casserole (Costatelle Pasticcio)
Madelyn Koontz, R.D.

This recipe is excellent served with French bread and a green salad. A good make-ahead dish that travels well to a weekend get-away.

2 1/2 lb. (about 8) pork chops, well trimmed
1/4 c. flour
1/2 tsp. Lite Salt
1/8 tsp. pepper
1 T. olive oil
1/2 c. dry white wine
1 low-sodium beef bouillon cube, dissolved in 1 c. hot water
4 med. potatoes, peeled & sliced 1/2" thick
1/2 tsp. Lite Salt
1/8 tsp. pepper

1 lb. fresh mushrooms, sliced
2 med. onions, sliced in thin rings
1 clove garlic, minced
2 T. chopped parsley
1/4 tsp. crushed rosemary

Preheat oven to 350°. Combine flour, 1/2 teaspoon Lite Salt and 1/8 teaspoon pepper in a bowl. Dust chops with flour. Heat oil in nonstick skillet over medium heat. Brown chops about 5 minutes on each side. Remove when browned. In same pan, add wine and bouillon. Bring to boil, stirring to loosen browned bits. Set aside. Place potatoes on bottom of 9x13-inch casserole dish that has been sprayed with nonstick cooking spray. Sprinkle with 1/2 teaspoon Lite Salt and 1/8 teaspoon pepper. Arrange mushrooms and onions over potatoes. Top with chops. Pour wine mixture over all. Sprinkle with garlic, parsley and rosemary. Cover; bake 1 hour and 15 minutes or until chops and vegetables are tender.

This casserole can be assembled one day ahead and refrigerated until ready to cook. If refrigerated, allow 15 to 20 minutes extra baking time.

Continued on following page.

BEEF, VEAL & PORK MAIN DISHES

Continued from preceding page.

Serving:
  8

Serving Size:
  1 pork chop with vegetables

Nutritional analysis per serving:
  Calories: 312
  Fat: 9 gm
  Cholesterol: 89 mg
  Protein: 35 gm
  Carbohydrate: 19 gm
  Sodium: 248 mg

TASTEFULLY OREGON

Pork Chops Diane
Anne Goetze, R.D.

- 4 boneless pork loin chops, about 4 oz. each
- 2 tsp. *Lawry's Lemon Pepper* seasoning
- 1 T. margarine
- 1 T. fresh-squeezed lemon juice
- 1 T. Worcestershire sauce
- 1 tsp. Dijon mustard
- 1/2 lb. fresh mushrooms, sliced
- 1/4 c. dry red wine

Melt margarine in nonstick skillet, or omit margarine and use nonstick spray. Sprinkle surface of each pork chop with lemon pepper; add to skillet. Cook pork chops over medium heat until brown on both sides (about 10 to 15 minutes total). Remove pork chops to warm platter. Stir remaining ingredients into pan juices. Bring to a boil and cook until mushrooms are softened and sauce just begins to thicken. Pour sauce over pork chops.

Servings:
4

Servings Size:
1 pork chop with sauce

Nutritional analysis per serving:
Calories: 232
Fat: 10 gm
Cholesterol: 73 mg
Protein: 27 gm
Carbohydrate: 5 gm
Sodium: 324 mg

BEEF, VEAL & PORK MAIN DISHES

Quick and Easy Veal Scallopini
Nuha Rice, R.D.

*Veal is such a treat and this really shows it off.
I like to serve it with twice-baked potatoes for a special meal.*

1 1/2 T. oil
2 c. thinly-sliced fresh mushrooms (1/2 lb.)
1/4 c. flour
1/2 tsp. Lite Salt
1/4 tsp. black pepper
1 lb. veal cutlets, thinly sliced (1/8" thick)
1/2 c. dry sherry
2 T. water
2 T. chopped parsley

Heat 1 1/2 teaspoons oil in a large skillet over medium heat. Add mushrooms and sauté until tender; remove from pan. Combine flour, Lite Salt and pepper; coat veal with flour mixture. Heat the remaining 1 tablespoon oil in a nonstick skillet and brown veal a few pieces at a time; remove from pan when still slightly pink. Reduce heat and add sherry and water to skillet; stir until liquid is slightly thickened, adding additional water as needed to make a sauce. Return veal and mushrooms to pan and heat through (don't overcook). Arrange on a serving platter and garnish with parsley.

Servings:
4

Serving Size:
1/4th of recipe

Nutritional analysis per serving:
Calories: 241
Fat: 9 gm
Cholesterol: 74 mg
Protein: 19 gm
Carbohydrate: 11 gm
Sodium: 189 mg

TASTEFULLY OREGON

Sweet and Sour Cabbage with Meatballs
Alyce Puppe Waverly, R.D.

A favorite for beach or camping trips. Easy to prepare, allowing time to relax!

- 1 lb. very lean ground beef (9% fat)
- 1/4 c. egg substitute or 2 egg whites
- 2/3 c. uncooked brown rice
- 1/2 tsp Lite Salt
- 2 lb. cabbage, cut in half & sliced
- 1 (14 1/2 oz.) can stewed tomatoes, or 2 c. diced fresh tomatoes
- 1 (8 oz.) can tomato sauce
- 1/2 c. vinegar
- 1/4 to 1/3 c. brown sugar
- 2 T. fresh-squeezed lemon juice
- 1 1/2 c. water
- 1 apple, peeled, cored & cut into chunks
- 1/4 c. raisins

Mix ground beef, egg substitute or whites, rice and Lite Salt. Roll into 16 or more small meatballs. Set aside. Cut cabbage into 1/4-inch strips and place in 4-quart kettle. Add tomatoes, tomato sauce, vinegar, brown sugar, lemon juice, water and apple to cabbage. Put meatballs on top. Heat to boiling. Reduce heat, then simmer for 2 to 2 1/2 hours, stirring gently now and then (try not to break up meatballs). Add raisins the last 10 minutes.

Servings:
8

Serving Size:
1 1/2 cups

Nutritional analysis per serving:
- Calories: 255
- Fat: 6 gm
- Cholesterol: 21 mg
- Protein: 17 gm
- Carbohydrate: 36 gm
- Sodium: 432 mg

BEEF, VEAL & PORK MAIN DISHES

Tollernini

Virginia Harger, R.D.

A quick and easy family favorite.

1 med. onion, chopped
1 lb. very lean ground beef (9% fat)
6 oz. (3 c.) uncooked noodles
1 (15 oz.) can *no-salt-added* tomato sauce
2 c. water
1/4 to 1/2 tsp. pepper
1 (17 oz.) can cream-style corn
1 (4 oz.) can chopped green chilies
1 c. grated low-fat sharp Cheddar cheese

Sauté onion in nonstick skillet. Add a small amount of water, if necessary, to prevent sticking. Add ground beef, brown, and drain off fat. Stir in uncooked noodles, tomato sauce, water and pepper. Cover and cook until noodles are tender, 15 to 20 minutes. Preheat oven to 350°. Spray an 8x12-inch or 9x13-inch baking dish with nonstick cooking spray. Layer ingredients, beginning with 1/2 of the following: meat/noodle mixture, corn, chilies and grated cheese. Repeat layers again with remaining half of ingredients. Bake, uncovered, for 25 minutes, then cover and continue baking another 10 minutes. Remove from oven and let sit for 5 to 10 minutes before serving.

Servings:
6

Serving Size:
1/6th of casserole

Nutritional analysis per serving:
Calories: 378
Fat: 11 gm
Cholesterol: 38 mg
Protein: 27 gm
Carbohydrate: 44 gm
Sodium: 630 mg

TASTEFULLY OREGON

A view of a 1925 Food Science class on meat cutting. Household Sciences classes changed quite a bit after Virginia Harger, who was Head of the Department of Food Systems Management, arrived at Oregon State College. (Courtesy of Oregon State University Archives, Harriett's Collection #978)

BEEF, VEAL & PORK MAIN DISHES

Wild Game Imperial

Joyce Gustafson, R.D.

If you have a hunter in your family, you will be interested in this stroganoff type dish which works well with venison, elk or pheasant breasts.

2 lb. veal tenderloin, pork, venison or elk; veal bottom round steak works well, also
2 c. chopped celery
1/4 c. chopped green bell pepper
1/2 c. chopped onion
1/4 c. chopped pimento
1/2 c. sliced fresh mushrooms
1 (10 1/2 oz.) can Campbell's *Healthy Request* cream of mushroom soup
2 T. *lite* soy sauce
1/2 c. water

8 oz. eggless noodles
1 c. fat-free sour cream (I like to use *Land O' Lakes*)
1 T. sliced almonds

Cut meat in 3/4-inch chunks. Combine meat, celery, green pepper, onion, pimento and mushrooms in cooking pot. In separate bowl, mix soup, soy sauce and water until smooth and stir into other ingredients. Cover with a tight lid; simmer on stove top 30 to 45 minutes or until meat is tender. Veal and pork do not need as long as game. In separate pot, cook noodles in unsalted boiling water while meat is cooking.

Preheat oven to 350°. Combine cooked noodles and sour cream; layer with meat mixture in 2 1/2-quart casserole dish which has been sprayed with nonstick cooking spray. Top with sliced almonds; bake until heated through (takes about 20 to 30 minutes) or cover with plastic wrap and heat in microwave until warm.

Servings:
  6

Serving Size:
  1/6th of recipe

Nutritional analysis per serving:
  Calories: 406
  Fat: 10 gm
  Cholesterol: 118 mg
  Protein: 38 gm
  Carbohydrate: 40 gm
  Sodium: 568 mg

TASTEFULLY OREGON

Notes

Desserts

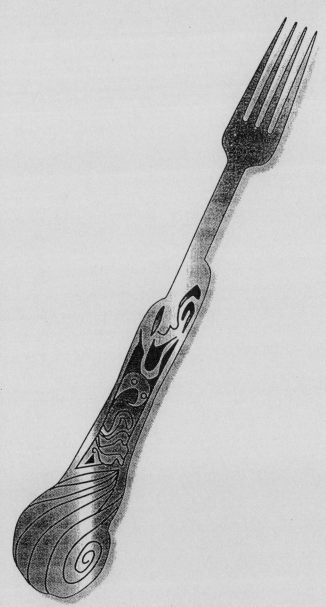

Tastefully Oregon

Baking The Low Fat Way

By now it's no secret that our recipes have a reduced fat content (sugar and salt too). You can alter your favorite recipes as well:

- Use no more than 1/4 to 1/2 cup of fat per recipe.

- Replace up to half the fat with the same amount of applesauce, pureed prunes, banana or nonfat yogurt.

- Use nonfat milk in baking and cooking.

- Use nonfat evaporated skimmed milk or nonfat yogurt in place of cream.

- Use low fat cheeses or experiment with fat free cheeses.

Providing The Low Fat Touch

Reducing the amount of fat in a recipe will affect flavor and texture. Over-baking, which is easy to do, greatly diminishes the quality of low fat baked goods. Be sure to check for doneness at the early side of the indicated baking time. To test for doneness insert a wooden pick in the center of the baked product. It should come out clean. If the item is not completely baked continue baking and retest every 2 to 3 minutes until done.

Because low fat baked goods have a shorter shelf life than high fat ones, they should be eaten as soon as possible or frozen immediately after cooking for future use.

DESSERTS

Cheesecake with Fruit Topping

Madelyn Koontz, R.D.

Delicious! Enjoyed by friends who are fond of French cooking. I estimate it takes me 20 minutes to prepare for baking.

CRUST:
- 1/2 c. graham cracker crumbs
- 2 tsp. melted margarine

FILLING:
- 1 c. nonfat cottage cheese or ricotta cheese
- 2 (8 oz.) pkg. nonfat cream cheese, softened
- 3/4 c. sugar
- 2 T. flour
- 1 tsp. vanilla
- 4 egg whites
- 1/4 c. nonfat milk

To prepare crust: In a small bowl, stir together graham cracker crumbs and melted margarine. Press onto the bottom only of an 8-inch springform pan. Set aside.

To prepare filling: Preheat oven to 375°. Combine cottage cheese or ricotta cheese, softened cream cheese, sugar, flour and 1 teaspoon of the vanilla; beat until smooth. Add egg whites; beat just until combined. (Do not overbeat.) Stir in 1/4 cup milk. Pour mixture in pan over crust. Place on baking sheet or in shallow baking pan. Bake 40 to 50 minutes or until set. (It may need to cook longer. To test cheesecake for doneness, gently shake sides of pan. The center should appear nearly set.) Cool 10 minutes. Using metal spatula, loosen sides of cheesecake from pan. (This helps keep cheesecake edges from cracking.) Cool 35 minutes more, then remove sides of pan. Cover and chill thoroughly.

Continued on following page.

TASTEFULLY OREGON

Continued from preceding page.

TOPPING:
1/4 c. nonfat plain yogurt
1/4 tsp. vanilla
2 tsp. nonfat milk
1 c. fresh sliced strawberries, raspberries or blueberries
1 to 2 T. powdered sugar, if needed

To prepare topping: In a small bowl, combine yogurt, milk and vanilla. If needed, sweeten the berries with powdered sugar.

To serve: Arrange sliced strawberries or other berries on top of cheesecake and drizzle with yogurt mixture.

Servings:
  12

Serving Size:
  1/12th of 8-inch diameter

Nutritional analysis per serving:
  Calories: 143
  Fat: 1 gm
  Cholesterol: 8 mg
  Protein: 10 gm
  Carbohydrate: 22 gm
  Sodium: 360 mg

DESSERTS

Fast Spice Cake
Nancy Oberschmidt, R.D.

I got this recipe from my sister, April. It's fast, easy and great!

1 1/2 c. flour
1 c. sugar
1 tsp. baking soda
1 tsp. cinnamon
1/2 tsp. Lite Salt
1/2 tsp. ground cloves
1/2 tsp. nutmeg
1 T. vinegar
1/4 c. oil
1 c. water
2 T. chopped nuts
1/2 c. raisins

Preheat oven to 350°. Spray an 8-inch square pan with nonstick cooking spray. Mix all the dry ingredients together. Add vinegar, oil and water. Mix just until the dry ingredients are moistened. Fold in nuts and raisins. Pour batter into prepared pan. Bake for 35 to 40 minutes, or until wooden pick inserted in the center comes out clean.

Servings:
  9

Serving Size:
  2 1/2-inch square

Nutritional analysis
per serving:
  Calories: 256
  Fat: 7 gm
  Cholesterol: 0 mg
  Protein: 3 gm
  Carbohydrate: 46 gm
  Sodium: 204 mg

Hazelnut Liqueur Cheesecake

Mary Stansell, R.D.

CRUST:
- 1 c. white flour
- 2 T. chopped toasted hazelnuts or sliced almonds
- 2 T. sugar
- 1/2 tsp. baking powder
- 1/4 tsp. Lite Salt
- 1/3 c. margarine, softened
- 2 T. nonfat milk

FILLING:
- 2 (8 oz.) pkg. nonfat cream cheese, softened
- 1/2 c. nonfat sour cream
- 3/4 c. egg substitute
- 1/2 c. sugar
- 1/4 c. chopped toasted hazelnuts or almonds
- 2 T. hazelnut or amaretto liqueur
- 1 tsp. fresh-squeezed lemon juice

To prepare hazelnuts: (1/2 cup hazelnuts will be needed for entire recipe). Preheat oven to 350°. Spread nuts on shallow baking pan. Bake for 8 to 10 minutes or until skins start to brown. Turn out onto clean kitchen towel. Wrap in towel, and let stand 1 minute. Rub off most of the skins with the towel. Cool before chopping.

To prepare crust: Mix flour, 2 tablespoons toasted hazelnuts, sugar, baking powder and Lite Salt in a large bowl. Cut in margarine with pastry blender or 2 knives until mixture resembles coarse crumbs. Sprinkle with milk; stir until mixture holds together to form a dough. Shape dough into a ball; flatten with hands. Press dough evenly over bottom and 2 inches up the sides of a 9-inch springform pan. Refrigerate for at least 30 minutes.

Continued on following page.

DESSERTS

Continued from preceding page.

TOPPING:
1 c. nonfat sour cream
1/3 c. powdered sugar
1 T. hazelnut or amaretto liqueur
1 tsp. fresh-squeezed lemon juice

2 T. chopped toasted hazelnuts, for garnish

To prepare filling and topping: When crust has chilled, preheat oven to 325°. Thoroughly mix all filling ingredients. Pour over crust. Bake for 50 minutes or until firm. Cool 5 minutes. Mix all topping ingredients until smooth (save 2 tablespoons chopped nuts for garnish) and spread evenly over cheesecake. Return to oven and bake 5 minutes longer. Cool on wire rack for 20 minutes. Refrigerate until chilled (6 hours or overnight).

To serve: Remove from refrigerator and remove sides of pan. Sprinkle top with remaining chopped nuts. Cut into wedges.

Servings:
12

Serving Size:
1/12th of cake

Nutritional analysis per serving:
Calories:	248
Fat:	9 gm
Cholesterol:	7 mg
Protein:	11 gm
Carbohydrate:	28 gm
Sodium:	379 mg

TASTEFULLY OREGON

Hot Chocolate Pudding Cake

Jill Calamar, R.D.

CAKE:
- 1 c. flour
- 1/2 tsp. Lite Salt
- 3/4 c. sugar
- 2 tsp. baking powder
- 4 1/2 tsp. cocoa powder
- 2 T. oil
- 1 tsp. vanilla
- 1/2 c. nonfat milk
- 1/4 c. coarsely-chopped walnuts

TOPPING:
- 1/2 c. sugar
- 1/2 c. brown sugar
- 6 T. cocoa powder
- 1 c. boiling water

To prepare cake: Preheat oven to 350° (325° if using glass pan). Spray a 9-inch square baking pan with nonstick cooking spray. Mix cake ingredients together. Pour into prepared pan.

To prepare topping: Mix sugars and cocoa. Sprinkle over batter. Pour boiling water on top. Bake for 50 minutes. Serve warm.

Servings:
9

Serving Size:
3-inch square

Nutritional analysis per serving:
Calories:	253
Fat:	6 gm
Cholesterol:	trace mg
Protein:	3 gm
Carbohydrate:	50 gm
Sodium:	182 mg

DESSERTS

Lite Cheesecake
Mary Baron, R.D.

A winner! Baking takes a little time, but preparation is easy.

CRUST:
1 1/4 c. graham cracker crumbs (15 squares)
2 T. sugar
3 T. margarine, melted

FILLING:
2 (8 oz.) pkg. nonfat cream cheese
1 c. sugar
2 tsp. grated lemon or orange peel
1/4 tsp. vanilla
3/4 c. egg substitute

TOPPING:
1 c. plain lowfat yogurt
1 c. fresh blueberries or strawberries

To prepare crust: Preheat oven to 350°. Mix graham cracker crumbs, 2 tablespoons sugar and melted margarine. Press into a 9-inch pie plate. Bake 10 minutes and cool.

To prepare filling: Preheat oven to 300°. Beat cream cheese in a large mixing bowl. Gradually add 1 cup sugar, beating until fluffy. Add lemon or orange peel and vanilla. Beat in egg substitute gradually. Pour into crust. Bake approximately 1 hour, or until center is firm. Cool 15 minutes.

To prepare topping: Preheat oven to 425°. Top cheesecake with yogurt. Bake 5 minutes. Cool and refrigerate 3 hours or overnight. Garnish with fresh berries and serve cold.

Servings:
12

Serving Size:
3-inch wedge

Nutritional analysis per serving:
Calories:	217
Fat:	5 gm
Cholesterol:	8 mg
Protein:	9 gm
Carbohydrate:	33 gm
Sodium:	379 mg

TASTEFULLY OREGON

Mom's White "Tough" Cake
Alyce Puppe Waverly, R.D.

This recipe which contains no fat (that's where the name came from) has survived generations of "moms" and has been a family favorite at church potlucks or picnics. I'm not sure if it was around when Great Grandmother had her coffee party, but I have always thought it was served to her friends at the party pictured. For special occasions, Mom would spread a layer of lemon filling over the cake before frosting it with her fluffy "White Mountain Frosting".

2 c. sugar
2 c. cake flour (such as Softasilk*)
1 tsp. cream of tartar
1/8 tsp. Lite Salt
1 c. boiling water
1 tsp. almond extract
6 egg whites
2 tsp. baking powder

Preheat oven to 350°. Spray 9x13-inch baking pan with nonstick cooking spray. Dust sides and bottom of pan with small amount of flour; pour off any excess. Thoroughly combine sugar, flour, cream of tartar and Lite Salt in a large bowl. Add boiling water; mix until cool. Add almond extract and stir. In separate bowl, beat egg whites. When partially stiff, add baking powder; continue beating until whites stand up into firm peaks. Carefully fold beaten whites into flour mixture by taking spoon over and under the mixture repeatedly to get a uniform mixture. Do not stir around and around or egg whites will lose their air. Pour in prepared pan; bake 25 to 30 minutes, or until wooden pick inserted in center comes out clean. Do not overbake. Frost when cake is cool.

Continued on following page.

DESSERTS

Continued from preceding page.

*If cake flour is unavailable, use 2 cups all-purpose flour plus 2 tablespoons cornstarch.

Servings:
12

Serving Size:
3 x 3 1/4-inch piece

Nutritional analysis per serving:
Calories: 205
Fat: trace gm
Cholesterol: 0 mg
Protein: 3 gm
Carbohydrate: 48 gm
Sodium: 120 mg

Alyce's Great-Grandmother (far right) enjoying a coffee party (yes, coffee—they are all Norwegians!) around 1900. They're probably anticipating a piece of Mom's White Tough Cake.

TASTEFULLY OREGON

White Mountain Frosting

Alyce Puppe Waverly, R.D.

A fluffy white cake icing that is wonderful on Mom's White "Tough" Cake. My mom usually used the almond flavoring.

1/2 c. sugar
2 T. water
1/4 c. **light corn syrup**
2 **egg whites**
1 tsp. almond or vanilla extract

Mix sugar, water and corn syrup in a small thin-sided saucepan. Cover and bring to a rolling boil. Remove cover and cook to just 242° using a candy thermometer, or until syrup forms a soft ball in a cup of cold water*.

While syrup is cooking, beat egg whites until stiff enough to hold a point. Pour hot syrup very slowly in thin stream into beaten egg whites. Continue beating until frosting holds peaks. Blend in almond or vanilla extract; frost cake.

*A soft ball stage is when a few drops of hot sugar mixture dropped into a 1/2 cup of cold water sticks together and forms a soft ball when "tickled" with your finger.

Servings:
12 (makes 1 2/3 cups)

Serving Size:
1/12 of 9x13-inch cake

Nutritional analysis per serving:
Calories: 54
Fat: 0 gm
Cholesterol: 0 mg
Protein: <1 gm
Carbohydrate: 13 gm
Sodium: 9 mg

DESSERTS

Maple Syrup Devil's Food Cake
Lorna Vincent Klier, R.D.

This is a 1990's version of a favorite family recipe. Since maple syrup was plentiful in the state of my birth, Michigan, it was used in many ways. Are any of you old enough to remember a so called "burley box"? It was an 8-inch round tin box with a tight-fitting lid, with the original contents being chewing tobacco (I believe). Such a box was used for the baking of this cake and it traveled back and forth during my college days and later to Texas, Mississippi, Illinois, Massachusetts, Kansas and upper New York State, as well as across the Atlantic Ocean. I can vouch for the keeping qualities of this can, as the cake usually came through without even a crack in the icing. I wonder what has happened to the "burley box"?

1/3 c. margarine
1/2 c. sugar
1/2 c. maple syrup
1/2 c. egg substitute
1 1/2 c. flour
1/2 tsp. Lite Salt
1 tsp. baking soda
1 tsp. baking powder
1/4 c. unsweetened cocoa powder
2/3 c. buttermilk

Preheat oven to 350°. Cream margarine and sugar. Add syrup and egg substitute. Beat well. Combine flour, Lite Salt, baking soda, baking powder and cocoa, and add to margarine and sugar mixture alternately with buttermilk. Mix well and pour into an 8-inch square baking pan that has been sprayed with nonstick cooking spray. Bake 30 minutes or until wooden pick inserted in the center comes out clean.

Servings:
9

Serving Size:
2 1/2-inch square

Nutritional analysis per serving:
Calories:	251
Fat:	8 gm
Cholesterol:	<1 mg
Protein:	5 gm
Carbohydrate:	41 gm
Sodium:	381 mg

TASTEFULLY OREGON

Norman's Chocolate Cake
Chedwah J. Stein, R.D.

This was given to my friend when we lived in Micronesia by a gentleman who was sailing around the world. It became very popular because milk and eggs were sometimes difficult to come by and it doesn't require either. This cake is also known as Wacky Cake because of the vinegar. It is easy to make and the finished product is always great. It would be a "no fail" recipe for a beginning cook.

3 c. flour
2 c. sugar
6 T. cocoa powder
1 tsp. Lite Salt
2 tsp. baking soda
1/4 c. oil
1/4 c. applesauce
2 c. water, divided
2 tsp. vanilla
2 T. white vinegar

Preheat oven to 350°. Spray a 9x13-inch baking pan with nonstick cooking spray. In a large bowl, stir together flour, sugar, cocoa, Lite Salt and baking soda. Add oil, applesauce and 1 cup water. Beat until well combined. Add the remaining 1 cup water and the vanilla. Beat well again. Stir in the vinegar (the batter will become foamy). Pour into the prepared pan and bake for 25 to 35 minutes, or until wooden pick inserted into center comes out clean. Cool and cut into squares. Serve as is, or with fresh berries or frozen yogurt.

Servings:
 15

Serving Size:
 3 x 2 1/2-inch piece

Nutritional analysis per serving:
Calories:	235
Fat:	4 gm
Cholesterol:	0 mg
Protein:	3 gm
Carbohydrate:	48 gm
Sodium:	243 mg

DESSERTS

Poppy Seed Cake with Fresh Fruit
Marcia Whitman, R.D.

*No icing is necessary for this great cake;
it is wonderful covered with fresh fruit.*

1 (18.25 oz.) pkg. *light* white cake mix
1 (3.4 oz.) pkg. instant vanilla pudding mix
1/2 c. pineapple juice (it's available in 6 oz. cans)
1/2 c. water
1/3 c. oil
1/2 c. poppy seeds (2 oz.)
1 1/4 c. egg substitute
1 tsp. almond extract

1/2 tsp. cinnamon
2 tsp. sugar

3 c. sliced fresh fruit (strawberries, raspberries, peaches or blueberries, etc.)

Preheat oven to 350°. Mix together dry cake and pudding mixes, juice, water, oil and poppy seeds in a mixing bowl. While beating on low speed, slowly add egg substitute and almond extract. Continue beating until batter is thoroughly mixed. In separate bowl, combine cinnamon and sugar. Spray a bundt pan or tube pan with nonstick cooking spray and sprinkle with cinnamon/sugar. Pour cake batter into pan and bake for 45 to 50 minutes, or until a wooden pick inserted in center comes out clean. Let stand in pan 15 minutes. Loosen sides with knife; wait 15 more minutes before removing from pan.

To serve, cut into wedges and cover with fresh fruit.

Servings:
16

Serving Size:
1/16th cake

Nutritional analysis per serving:
Calories: 246
Fat: 8 gm
Cholesterol: 0 mg
Protein: 4 gm
Carbohydrate: 40 gm
Sodium: 314 mg

TASTEFULLY OREGON

Scandinavian Yogurt Carrot Cake
Peggy Paul, R.D.

3 c. grated carrots
8 oz. plain nonfat yogurt
1 c. sugar
1/2 c. raisins
1/3 c. melted margarine
2 egg whites
2 tsp. vanilla
2 c. flour
2 tsp. baking soda
2 1/2 tsp. cinnamon
1 tsp. ground ginger
1 tsp. ground cardamom
1/2 tsp. Lite Salt

3 T. powdered sugar

Preheat oven to 350°. Spray 2 (8x8-inch) pans or a 9x13-inch pan with nonstick cooking spray. Combine carrots, yogurt, sugar, raisins and margarine in a large bowl. Stir in egg whites and vanilla. Sift together dry ingredients, except powdered sugar, and add to carrot mixture, stirring only until blended. Pour batter into prepared pans. Bake for 30 to 35 minutes. When cool, lightly sprinkle with powdered sugar. Wrap well and refrigerate. Serve at room temperature.

Servings:
  18

Serving Size:
  About 2 1/2-inch square

Nutritional analysis per serving:
  Calories: 159
  Fat: 4 gm
  Cholesterol: trace mg
  Protein: 3 gm
  Carbohydrate: 29 gm
  Sodium: 233 mg

DESSERTS

Special Oatmeal Cake

Ruth Hayden, R.D.

My aunt always made this when we visited.
We seldom have it now and I miss it.

CAKE:
1 1/4 c. boiling water
1 c. dry oatmeal
1/2 c. margarine
1 c. granulated sugar
1 c. brown sugar
1/2 c. egg substitute or
    3 egg whites
1 tsp. vanilla
1 1/2 c. flour
1/2 tsp. Lite Salt
1/2 tsp. baking soda
1 tsp. cinnamon

TOPPING:
3 T. margarine, melted
1/2 c. brown sugar
1/4 c. evaporated skim
    milk
1 tsp. vanilla
1/2 c. dry oatmeal

Servings:
   15

Serving Size:
   2 1/2 x 3-inch piece

To prepare cake: Pour boiling water over oatmeal. Let stand 10 minutes. Preheat oven to 350°. Spray a 9x13-inch baking pan with nonstick cooking spray. Cream margarine and sugars. Add egg substitute or whites and vanilla; blend well. Add oatmeal. Blend in flour, Lite Salt, baking soda and cinnamon. Pour in prepared pan. Bake 30 to 40 minutes, or until wooden pick inserted in the center comes out clean.

To prepare topping: Near the end of baking time, combine melted margarine and brown sugar. Add evaporated milk, vanilla and oatmeal. Spread evenly on top of warm cake. Brown under broiler 3 to 5 minutes, watching carefully.

Nutritional analysis per serving:

Calories:	267
Fat:	9 gm
Cholesterol:	trace mg
Protein:	4 gm
Carbohydrate:	43 gm
Sodium:	204 mg

TASTEFULLY OREGON

Whiskey Cake
Joyce Gustafson, R.D

I often bake this for our annual camping trip on the 4th of July. It goes together quickly, travels well, stays very moist and is delicious. At year-end holiday time it looks lovely decorated with holly and red or green cherries and a dusting of powdered sugar.

- 1 (18.25 oz.) pkg. *light* yellow cake mix
- 1 (4.6 oz.) pkg. vanilla pudding mix, not instant
- 8 egg whites or 1 1/4 c. egg substitute
- 3/4 c. bourbon or apple juice
- 1/2 c. oil
- 1/2 c. maraschino cherries (drained & cut in half) or 1 1/2 oz. dried cranberries
- 1/4 c. coarsely-chopped walnuts or almonds
- 1/2 c. mini chocolate chips

Preheat oven to 350°. Lightly oil a bundt pan and spray with nonstick cooking spray. Combine cake and pudding dry mixes, egg whites or substitute, bourbon or juice, and oil. Mix well. Add cherries, nuts and chocolate chips and blend again. Pour batter into prepared pan. Bake 40 minutes, or until a wooden pick inserted in center comes out clean. Cool 10 minutes and remove from pan.

Servings:
18

Serving Size:
1/18 of cake

Nutritional analysis per serving:
Calories:	270
Fat:	11 gm
Cholesterol:	0 mg
Protein:	3 gm
Carbohydrate:	37 gm
Sodium:	273 mg

DESSERTS

Blueberry Buckle
Margy Woodburn, Ph.D.

This is an old Illinois recipe. Although blueberries are good just as fresh fruit, midwesterners use them in many ways from fruit soup to desserts. We usually serve it as dessert, although it may also be served as a coffee cake.

1/4 c. margarine, softened
1/2 c. sugar
2 c. flour, divided
2 1/2 tsp. baking powder
1/4 tsp. Lite Salt
3/4 c. nonfat milk
2 egg whites, beaten
2 c. fresh or frozen blueberries

TOPPING:
1/2 c. brown sugar
1/2 c. flour
1/2 c. coarsely-crushed corn flakes
1/2 tsp. cinnamon
1/4 c. margarine

Preheat oven to 375°. Cream margarine and sugar together. Stir in one-half of the flour and all of the baking powder and Lite Salt. Add milk and stir well. Add remaining flour and egg whites. Mix thoroughly. Fold in blueberries. Pour batter into a 9x13-inch baking pan that has been sprayed with nonstick cooking spray.

Prepare topping by mixing ingredients until crumbly (mashing with a fork does this well). Sprinkle topping over batter and bake 25 to 35 minutes. The topping should be slightly brown and a wooden pick comes out clean when inserted in center of cake.

Servings:
 12

Serving Size:
 3 x 3 1/4-inch piece

Nutritional analysis per serving:
Calories:	248
Fat:	8 gm
Cholesterol:	trace mg
Protein:	4 gm
Carbohydrate:	41 gm
Sodium:	257 mg

TASTEFULLY OREGON

Dr. Woodburn (past head of the Department of Nutrition and Food Management in the OSU School of Home Economics and Education) helped us reminisce about this picture of a 1907 Cooking Class. The formal caps had been replaced with hairnets by the time many of us arrived for our training. (Courtesy of Oregon State University Archives, Harriet's Collection #978)

DESSERTS

Cranberry Apple Crisp

Kathy Schwab, R.D.

A great recipe. Serve warm, plain, topped with Yogurt Dessert Sauce or frozen nonfat vanilla yogurt.

3 to 4 lg. unpeeled apples, cored, cut in half & thinly sliced
1/3 c. dried cranberries
1/4 c. sugar
1 tsp. cinnamon
2 T. fresh-squeezed lemon juice
1 T. flour

TOPPING:
3 T. flour
1 1/4 c. quick-cooking rolled oats
1/3 c. oat bran
1/3 c. brown sugar
1/4 c. margarine, melted

Preheat oven to 350°. Spray a 9-inch square pan with nonstick cooking spray. In a large bowl, combine apples, cranberries, sugar, cinnamon, lemon juice and 1 tablespoon flour. Transfer mixture to prepared pan. Combine topping ingredients and mix thoroughly. Spread evenly over fruit mixture. Bake 40 minutes or until top is lightly browned.

Servings:
9

Serving Size:
3x3-inch square

Nutritional analysis per serving (without topping):
Calories: 210
Fat: 6 gm
Cholesterol: 0 mg
Protein: 3 gm
Carbohydrate: 39 gm
Sodium: 63 mg

TASTEFULLY OREGON

Fruit Nachos

Alyce Puppe Waverly, R.D.

A 1993 "Berry-Off" finalist which I find to be a great light, easy and fun summer treat.

FRUIT SALSA:
1 c. fresh fruit, crushed
2 c. chopped fresh fruit (strawberries, peaches, raspberries, nectarines, etc.)
1/4 c. honey
1/2 tsp. grated orange rind
1/4 tsp. cinnamon

CINNAMON-NACHO CHIPS:
10 flour tortillas
2/3 c. sugar
2 tsp. cinnamon

Nonfat vanilla yogurt (opt.)

Preheat oven to 500°. Line baking sheet with foil and spray with vegetable oil. Combine salsa ingredients. On a large plate, mix cinnamon and sugar together. Wet both sides of tortilla with water. (I hold it under the faucet and shake off excess water.) Dip each tortilla in cinnamon mixture and cut into 6 wedges. Bake 3 to 4 minutes.

To serve: Spoon salsa on baked chips or dip chips into salsa. May serve garnished with vanilla yogurt, if desired.

Servings:
10

Serving Size:
6 pieces

Nutritional analysis per serving:
Calories:	224
Fat:	3 gm
Cholesterol:	0 mg
Protein:	3 gm
Carbohydrate:	48 gm
Sodium:	170 mg

DESSERTS

Pumpkin Chiffon

Doris Pavlukovich, R.D.

This is one of my family's favorites and a great source of Vitamin A. It is very popular when served at Tuality Hospital in Western Oregon.

1 c. egg substitute
1 (29 oz.) can pumpkin
1/2 c. white sugar
1/2 c. brown sugar
2 tsp. cinnamon
1 tsp. pumpkin pie spice
2 (12 oz.) cans evaporated skim milk
1/2 pkg. l*ight* yellow cake mix
1/3 c. melted margarine

Preheat oven to 350°. Mix together all ingredients except cake mix and margarine. Spray a 9x13-inch cake pan with nonstick cooking spray and pour prepared mixture into pan. Sprinkle dry cake mix over top evenly. Drizzle with melted margarine. Bake for 40 minutes until set. Serve chilled for best flavor.

Servings:
15

Serving Size:
2 1/2 x 3-inch piece

Nutritional analysis per serving:
Calories: 222
Fat: 6 gm
Cholesterol: 2 mg
Protein: 7 gm
Carbohydrate: 36 gm
Sodium: 250 mg

TASTEFULLY OREGON

Pumpkin "Custard" Dessert

Luanna Squires Diller, R.D.

This tastes like pumpkin pie without the crust.

2/3 to 3/4 c. sugar
1/4 c. flour
1 tsp. baking powder
1 (13 oz.) can evaporated skim milk
1/2 c. egg substitute
1 (16 oz.) can pumpkin
1 1/2 tsp. pumpkin pie spice
2 tsp. vanilla
2 T. finely-chopped walnuts

Preheat oven to 350°. Spray a 9x9-inch cake pan with nonstick cooking spray. Beat all ingredients, except walnuts, until smooth (1 minute in blender or 2 minutes on high with electric hand mixer). Pour into pan. Sprinkle nuts over top. Bake 50 to 55 minutes, or until knife inserted in center comes out clean.

Servings:
9

Serving Size:
3-inch square

Nutritional analysis per serving:
    Calories: 145
    Fat: 2 gm
    Cholesterol: 2 mg
    Protein: 6 gm
    Carbohydrate: 27 gm
    Sodium: 129 mg

DESSERTS

Spicy Apple Crisp
Kati DeLaurier, R.D.

This also makes a great breakfast dish. Just warm up the leftovers! If you want to reduce calories a little, use low-calorie syrup.

10 tart baking apples
   (I always use some Granny Smith apples)
1/4 c. maple syrup
2 tsp. fresh-squeezed lemon juice
2 tsp. vanilla
1 tsp. cornstarch
2 tsp. cinnamon
1/4 tsp. ginger
1/8 tsp. nutmeg
1/8 tsp. ground cardamom
1/8 tsp. ground cloves

TOPPING:
1 1/2 c. uncooked quick-cooking rolled oats
3/4 c. whole wheat or oat flour
1 tsp. cinnamon
1/4 tsp. nutmeg
1/4 tsp. ground cardamom
1/4 tsp. ground cloves
1/2 c. chilled margarine, cut into bits
1/3 c. maple syrup
2 tsp. vanilla

Preheat oven to 350°. Spray 9x13-inch baking pan with nonstick cooking spray. Core and slice apples (peel them, if desired). Place apples in large bowl. Combine maple syrup, lemon juice and vanilla; drizzle on top of apples. Combine cornstarch, cinnamon, ginger, nutmeg, cardamom and cloves. Sprinkle over apples and toss well to distribute evenly. Layer apple slices in prepared pan, covering the entire pan.

To Prepare Topping: (Use food processor or two forks to mix.) Mix oats, flour, cinnamon, nutmeg, cardamom and cloves together. Using pastry cutter, blend in margarine until mixture resembles coarse meal. Combine maple syrup and vanilla; add to topping, stirring to combine. Sprinkle mixture evenly over apples. Cover with aluminum foil; bake 40 minutes. Remove foil; continue to bake until top is browned and apples are soft, but not mushy, about 10 minutes longer. Serve warm, or at room temperature.

Continued on following page.

TASTEFULLY OREGON

Continued from preceding page.

Servings:
    12

Serving Size:
    3 1/4-inch by 3-inch piece

Nutritional analysis per serving:
    Calories: 247
    Fat: 9 gm
    Cholesterol: 0 mg
    Protein: 3 gm
    Carbohydrate: 41 gm
    Sodium: 92 mg

DESSERTS

Frozen Vanilla Yogurt
Nancy Oberschmidt, R.D.

This is a favorite among my friends who love yogurt! It's great with fresh berries or cobbler. If you use a Donvier Frozen Dessert Maker, you can have it ready to serve in thirty minutes. (When in season, I add 4 fresh peaches and the juice of 1 lemon to this mix before freezing, to make a winner of a dessert.)

1 qt. plain nonfat yogurt
1/2 of 14 oz. can low-fat sweetened condensed milk
1 1/2 T. vanilla

Mix ingredients well. Chill thoroughly in refrigerator. Freeze in an ice cream freezer according to manufacturer's directions.

Servings:
6

Serving Size:
1 cup

Nutritional analysis per serving:
Calories: 236
Fat: 2 gm
Cholesterol: 11 mg
Protein: 13 gm
Carbohydrate: 37 gm
Sodium: 182 mg

TASTEFULLY OREGON

Pineapple Sherbet
Renée Giroux, R.D.

With a Donvier Frozen Dessert Maker you can achieve instant popularity! Thirty minutes before dinner, put chilled mixture in the Donvier and turn the handle a couple of times every few minutes. A wonderful dessert emerges. I often make this sherbet for social events or potlucks. I turn the freezer-handle every few minutes on the way.

1 (20 oz.) can crushed pineapple, juice-packed, undrained
2 1/2 c. buttermilk
1/2 to 3/4 c. sugar

Combine undrained pineapple, buttermilk and sugar. Chill for several hours. Freeze in an ice cream freezer according to manufacturer's directions.

Servings:
6

Serving Size:
1 cup

Nutritional analysis per serving:
Calories: 162
Fat: 1 gm
Cholesterol: 4 mg
Protein: 4 gm
Carbohydrate: 36 gm
Sodium: 108 mg

DESSERTS

Apricot Date Bars
Kimra Warren Hawk, R.D.

These bars pack and mail well, making them perfect treats for camp, college care packages or holiday gift packs.

3/4 c. flour
1/2 tsp. baking powder
1/8 tsp. Lite Salt
1 tsp. cinnamon
1/2 c. brown sugar
1/4 c. chopped walnuts
1/2 c. chopped, peeled apple
1 c. chopped, pitted dates
1 c. chopped dried apricots
1/4 c. raisins
3 egg whites
2 T. orange juice
1 T. oil

Preheat oven to 350°. Spray 8- or 9-inch baking pan with nonstick cooking spray. In bowl, thoroughly combine flour, baking powder, Lite Salt, cinnamon, brown sugar and nuts. In another bowl, combine all fruits; stir to blend. Add fruits to dry ingredients; mix well with hands, being sure fruit pieces are coated completely with dry mixture. In cup, lightly beat together egg whites, juice and oil. Stir into fruit mixture until thoroughly mixed and moistened. Turn batter in prepared pan; press down on top to spread batter out evenly. Bake about 25 minutes, until golden on top and slightly springy to touch, and wooden pick inserted in center comes out clean. Cool about 10 minutes in pan. Then, using sharp knife, cut into squares. If not serving immediately, cool bars completely; store in airtight container.

Servings:
16

Serving Size:
2-inch square

Nutritional analysis per serving:
Calories: 122
Fat: 2 gm
Cholesterol: 0 mg
Protein: 2 gm
Carbohydrate: 26 gm
Sodium: 38 mg

TASTEFULLY OREGON

Cocoa Brownies
Joyce Gustafson, R.D.

These brownies have no fat AND they are good!

6 T. unsweetened cocoa
1/2 c. whole wheat flour
1 c. white flour
1 c. sugar + 2 T., divided
1 tsp. baking soda
6 egg whites
1 c. plain nonfat yogurt

Preheat oven to 350°. Spray a 9x13-inch baking pan with nonstick cooking spray. In a large bowl, combine cocoa, flours, 1 cup sugar and baking soda. In a separate bowl, beat egg whites until foamy; add yogurt and stir to combine. Add this mixture to dry ingredients. Mix batter thoroughly and pour it into pan. Sprinkle top of batter with remaining 2 tablespoons of sugar. Bake for 30 minutes, or until a wooden pick inserted in the center comes out clean.

Servings:
  24

Serving Size:
  2 1/4 by 2-inch bar

Nutritional analysis per serving:
  Calories: 77
  Fat: trace gm
  Cholesterol: trace mg
  Protein: 3 gm
  Carbohydrate: 17 gm
  Sodium: 75 mg

DESSERTS

Double Chocolate Cookies
Ann Reid, R.D.

"Chocolate Lovers" will be delighted with these tasty treats.

3 T. margarine, softened
3 T. nonfat or light cream cheese
1/2 c. granulated sugar
1/3 c. brown sugar
1 tsp. vanilla
1 c. flour
1/2 c. cocoa powder
1/3 c. mini chocolate chips

Cream margarine, cream cheese, sugars and vanilla. Mix flour and cocoa powder and add to rest of mixture. Blend in chocolate chips. Cover and chill dough in refrigerator for several hours, or overnight.

When ready to bake, remove dough from refrigerator; let soften a few minutes. Preheat oven to 350°. Roll dough into 1-inch balls; place on baking sheets, which have been sprayed with non-stick cooking spray. Flatten cookies with back side of fork, which has been dipped in powdered sugar to keep from sticking. Bake about 8 minutes until slightly puffed and soft to the touch. Let cool on baking sheets a minute before removing to cooling racks.

Servings:
32

Serving Size:
1 cookie

Nutritional analysis per serving:
Calories: 57
Fat: 2 gm
Cholesterol: trace mg
Protein: 1 gm
Carbohydrate: 10 gm
Sodium: 24 mg

TASTEFULLY OREGON

Ginger Cookies

Charlotte Hennessy, R.D.

1/4 c. + 2 T. margarine, softened
2/3 c. + 3 T. sugar, divided
1/4 c. molasses
2 egg whites
2 c. whole wheat flour
2 tsp. baking soda
1 tsp. ground ginger
1 tsp. cinnamon

Preheat oven to 350°. Cream all of the margarine and 2/3 cup sugar at medium speed until light and fluffy. Add molasses and egg whites; beat well. Combine flour, baking soda, ginger and cinnamon; gradually add to creamed mixture, stirring until well blended. Shape dough into 1-inch balls and roll in remaining 3 tablespoons sugar. Place 2-inches apart on cookie sheets which have been sprayed with nonstick cooking spray. Bake for 10 to 13 minutes, or until lightly browned.

Servings:
56 cookies

Serving Size:
1 cookie

Nutritional analysis per serving:
Calories: 42
Fat: 1 gm
Cholesterol: 0 mg
Protein: <1 gm
Carbohydrate: 7 gm
Sodium: 62 mg

DESSERTS

Jelly-Filled "Butter" Cookies

Genevieve Hilley, R.D.*

A delicious party cookie.
They contain no cholesterol and are fun and easy to make.

1/2 c. margarine, softened
1/4 c. sugar
1/2 tsp. vanilla
1 c. flour
2 T. brightly-colored jelly

Preheat oven to 325°. Cream margarine and sugar until creamy. Add vanilla. Mix in flour until thoroughly mixed. Shape dough into 1-inch balls. Make a hollow in center of each cookie with thumb. Bake 12 to 15 minutes, or until lightly browned. Remove from oven, place on cooling rack and fill centers with a favorite jelly. Let cool and serve.

Servings:
25

Serving Size:
1 cookie

Nutritional analysis per serving:

Calories:	63
Fat:	4 gm
Cholesterol:	0 mg
Protein:	1 gm
Carbohydrate:	7 gm
Sodium:	44 mg

*Genevieve was a long-time Oregon Dietetic Association member. She sent us this recipe shortly before she died.

TASTEFULLY OREGON

Oatmeal Hurrahs

James Fox, R.D.

3/4 c. margarine
3/4 c. granulated sugar
1/2 c. brown sugar
1/4 c. molasses
2 tsp. vanilla
2 egg whites
1 1/2 c. flour
1 tsp. cinnamon
1 tsp. baking soda
1/2 tsp. Lite Salt
3 c. uncooked oatmeal
1 c. raisins

Preheat oven to 350°. Cream margarine, sugars, molasses and vanilla. Add egg whites and mix. Combine flour, cinnamon, baking soda and Lite Salt, and add to creamed mixture. Stir to combine; mix in oatmeal and raisins. Drop by tablespoons onto a baking sheet that has been sprayed with nonstick cooking spray. Bake 12 minutes, or until lightly browned. Cool for a minute or two on baking sheet, and remove to cooling racks.

Servings:
64

Serving Size:
1 cookie

Nutritional analysis per serving:
Calories:	71
Fat:	2 gm
Cholesterol:	0 mg
Protein:	1 gm
Carbohydrate:	12 gm
Sodium:	59 mg

DESSERTS

Mom's Gingersnaps
Martha Hirsch, R.D.

Combine the dough ahead of time, then bake when needed.

2 1/4 c. flour
1 T. ground ginger
2 tsp. baking soda
2 tsp. cinnamon
1/2 tsp. Lite Salt
1/4 c. margarine
1/2 c. prune purée*
1 c. brown sugar
2 egg whites
1/4 c. molasses

1/4 c. granulated sugar

Combine flour, ginger, baking soda, cinnamon and Lite Salt; set aside. Cream margarine and prune purée together. Add sugar gradually. Beat in egg whites and molasses. Add flour mixture slowly; beat. Cover and chill dough at least 3 hours in refrigerator, or overnight.

Preheat oven to 350°. Form teaspoons of dough in small balls; roll in granulated sugar. (Flour hands when forming balls.) Place 2-inches apart on nonstick baking sheet, which has been sprayed with nonstick cooking spray. Bake 12 minutes, or until tops are slightly rounded and crinkly.

*To prepare prune purée: Combine 1 1/3 cups (8 ounces) pitted prunes and 6 tablespoons hot water in blender or food processor; purée until smooth. Makes 1 cup; keeps up to 2 months in a tightly-sealed container in refrigerator.

Servings:
36

Serving Size:
1 cookie

Nutritional analysis per serving:
Calories:	71
Fat:	1 gm
Cholesterol:	0 mg
Protein:	1 gm
Carbohydrate:	14 gm
Sodium:	106 mg

TASTEFULLY OREGON

Pumpkin Cookies
Christie Digman, R.D.

- 1/3 c. margarine
- 1 c. brown sugar
- 1 c. granulated sugar
- 2 egg whites, slightly beaten
- 1 tsp. vanilla
- 1 1/2 c. canned pumpkin
- 2 c. flour
- 1 tsp. baking soda
- 1 1/2 tsp. cinnamon
- 1 c. uncooked oatmeal
- 1/2 c. semi-sweet mini chocolate chips

Preheat oven to 350°. Lightly spray cookie sheets with nonstick cooking spray; set aside. Cream margarine, sugars, egg whites and vanilla. Mix in pumpkin. Add flour, baking soda and cinnamon. Fold in oatmeal and chocolate chips. Drop onto prepared cookie sheets (about 1 tablespoon per cookie). Bake for 15 to 20 minutes.

Servings:
60

Serving Size:
1 cookie

Nutritional analysis per serving:
Calories:	61
Fat:	2 gm
Cholesterol:	0 mg
Protein:	1 gm
Carbohydrate:	11 gm
Sodium:	36 mg

DESSERTS

Jennie's Yogurt Pie

Jeanne Bristol, R.D.

Some people like to use fructose, which is sweeter than our usual sugar.

3 egg whites
1 1/2 c. plain nonfat yogurt
1/3 to 1/2 c. sugar or fructose
1 (8") prepared graham cracker pie shell
1 c. fresh berries, or other fruit
2 T. cornstarch
1/4 c. honey (opt.)

Preheat oven to 350°. Beat egg whites in mixing bowl until thoroughly blended. Stir in yogurt and sugar or fructose. Pour mixture into pie shell. Bake 30 minutes, or until pie looks set. The middle should be quite soft when you jiggle it. Remove from oven; let cool.

Put berries in saucepan with small amount of water; simmer a few minutes to soften berries. Strain berries. Return berry liquid to pan and heat until boiling. Add honey, if desired. Mix cornstarch with a small amount of water and stir into boiling juice mixture. Reduce heat and cook until sauce is thick and clear. Remove from heat and add berries. Top pie with berry mixture. Chill thoroughly before serving.

Servings:
  8

Serving Size:
  1/8th of pie

Nutritional analysis per serving (including honey):
  Calories: 219
  Fat: 5 gm
  Cholesterol: <1 mg
  Protein: 5 gm
  Carbohydrate: 39 gm
  Sodium: 151 mg

TASTEFULLY OREGON

Layered Banana-Pineapple Dessert

Doris Pavlukovich, R.D.

1 1/2 c. graham cracker crumbs (about 16 sq.)
1/4 c. sugar
1/4 c. margarine, melted
3 bananas, sliced
1 (8 oz.) pkg. fat-free cream cheese, softened
3 1/2 c. nonfat milk
2 (3.4 oz.) pkg. vanilla instant pudding
1 (20 oz.) can crushed pineapple, drained
1/2 of 12 oz. tub *Lite Cool Whip*, thawed

Mix graham cracker crumbs, sugar and margarine. Press onto bottom of a 9x13-inch pan, which has been sprayed with nonstick cooking spray. Arrange banana slices on crust. Beat cream cheese in large bowl, until smooth. Gradually add milk and mix well. Add dry pudding mix and beat until well blended. Spread evenly over banana slices. Spoon well-drained pineapple evenly over pudding mixture. Spread whipped topping over pineapple. Refrigerate at least 3 hours, and cut into squares to serve.

Servings:
 15

Serving Size:
 3-inch by 2 1/2-inch square

Nutritional analysis per serving:
 Calories: 245
 Fat: 6 gm
 Cholesterol: 4 mg
 Protein: 5 gm
 Carbohydrate: 42 gm
 Sodium: 419 mg

DESSERTS

Lemonade Yogurt Pie

Anne Goetze, R.D.

CRUST:
1 1/2 c. graham cracker crumbs (about 16 sq.)
2 T. sugar
1/2 tsp. ground ginger
1/4 c. margarine, melted

FILLING:
1/3 c. frozen lemonade concentrate, thawed
2 env. (1 T. each) unflavored gelatin
1/3 c. sugar
1/4 tsp. vanilla
2 c. nonfat lemon-flavored yogurt

1 c. fresh fruit (kiwis, raspberries, strawberries and blueberries)

To prepare crust: Preheat oven to 350°. Stir graham cracker crumbs, sugar and ginger together in a small bowl. Add melted margarine and mix well. Press into bottom and up sides of a 9-inch pie plate or springform pan. Bake for 10 to 12 minutes. Cool.

To prepare filling: Pour lemonade into small saucepan, sprinkle in gelatin. Stir, then let stand to soften gelatin. Add sugar; heat mixture gently to dissolve gelatin and sugar. Stir in vanilla. Refrigerate until cold. When beginning to set, whip lemonade mixture until fluffy, stir in yogurt and whip again. Pour into crust and chill until firm.

To serve: Decorate top of pie with kiwi slices, raspberries or strawberries and blueberries.

Servings:
8

Serving Size:
1/8 of pie

Nutritional analysis per serving:
Calories: 281
Fat: 8 gm
Cholesterol: <1 mg
Protein: 6 gm
Carbohydrate: 47 gm
Sodium: 250 mg

Yogurt Dessert Sauce

Kathy Schwab, R.D.

I like this sauce on <u>Cranberry Apple Crisp</u>; it also tastes great on any cut-up fresh fruit.

1/2 c. nonfat ricotta cheese
1/2 c. plain nonfat yogurt
3 T. sugar
1 tsp. vanilla

Combine all ingredients in a food processor and blend until smooth. Chill several hours to thicken sauce, before serving.

Servings:
16

Serving Size:
1 tablespoon

Nutritional analysis per serving:
Calories: 25
Fat: <1 gm
Cholesterol: 3 mg
Protein: 1 gm
Carbohydrate: 3 gm
Sodium: 16 mg

Especially for Children

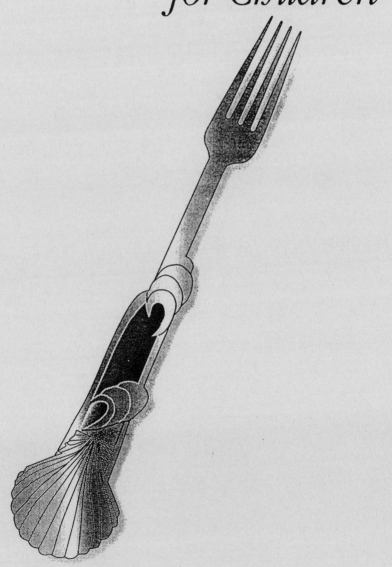

Tastefully Oregon

Getting Children Off To A Healthy Start

Can proper nutrition during childhood pave the way for admission to Harvard? While there's no guarantee, giving young people a great start on eating will help them to learn and perform at their best.

Young people do best when they follow the recommendations of the Food Guide Pyramid. Just as a real pyramid is built on a strong foundation, the basis of good health is a nutritious diet. Including a wide variety of foods from all five food groups, limiting fat and sugar intake, and drinking plenty of water will optimize the growth and activity of young people.

Recipes on the following pages are ones that young people enjoy making as well as eating. Involving young people in cooking builds skills in food handling, nutrition, math, reading, and clean-up. Successfully making a recipe builds confidence. Most of all, cooking is fun and the end product tastes delicious!

Speedy Ideas For Young People

- *Make-your-own-mini-pizza* is a big hit with young people. Set up an assembly line of split English muffins, pizza or pasta sauce, grated low fat cheese, and their favorite toppings (sliced olives, mushrooms, green or red pepper rings, lean ham or turkey slices, etc.). Place finished pizzas on a baking sheet and broil for 3 to 5 minutes.

- A trick for parents: sneak vegetables into a pocket bread sandwich. Cut a pocket bread in half and fill with 2 ounces of lean turkey, tomato slices, leafy lettuce, and sprouts. Add mustard or family's favorite reduced fat dressing.

ESPECIALLY FOR CHILDREN

Apple Pie Popsicles
Robin Stanton, R.D.

1 c. nonfat vanilla yogurt
1 c. applesauce
1/2 tsp. cinnamon
6 paper cups
6 popsicle sticks

Blend yogurt, applesauce and cinnamon. Pour into paper cups. Cover with foil. Make slits in center of foil and insert popsicle sticks into each cup. Freeze 4 to 8 hours.

Servings:
6

Serving Size:
1 popsicle

Nutritional analysis per serving:
Calories: 55
Fat: trace gm
Cholesterol: 4 mg
Protein: 2 gm
Carbohydrate: 12 gm
Sodium: 29 mg

Apple Smiles
Anne Goetze, R.D.

A fun snack idea from the Oregon Dairy Council which does, indeed, bring smiles.

1 red apple
2 (1 oz.) wedges, *Light Laughing Cow* cheese
1 sm. jicama cut in about 32 (1/2") cubes*

Cut apple in quarters; remove core. Cut each quarter into four slices. If not using soon, prevent browning by dipping apple slices into a mixture of 1/4 cup lemon juice and 1/4 cup water.

Peel jicama. Then cut jicama into 1/2-inch cubes.

To assemble: Using 2 slices of apple, spread cheese on one side of each apple slice. Place 4 jicama cubes on cheese side. Put other apple slice, cheese side down, on top of jicama cubes. Peelings should both face same way, making lips. The jicama cubes are teeth.

*Jicama is pronounced heé cah mah. It is a root vegetable and available in produce department of most supermarkets.

Servings:
8

Serving Size:
1 "smile"

Nutritional analysis per serving:
Calories: 50
Fat: 1 gm
Cholesterol: 4 mg
Protein: 2 gm
Carbohydrate: 9 gm
Sodium: 64 mg

ESPECIALLY FOR CHILDREN

Chocolate Pudding
Patricia Rose, R.D.

Easy for children to make with supervision.

3 T. cornstarch
1/4 c. cocoa powder
2 1/4 c. nonfat milk
1/3 c. sugar
2 tsp. vanilla

Combine cornstarch and cocoa in medium saucepan. Add milk slowly, and stir until blended. Cook over medium heat, stirring constantly, until smooth and thick.

Remove from heat and stir in sugar and vanilla. Be sure the sugar is completely dissolved in the hot pudding. Pour into dessert dishes and chill.

Servings:
  6

Serving Size:
  1/2 cup

Nutritional analysis per serving:
  Calories: 102
  Fat: <1 gm
  Cholesterol: 2 mg
  Protein: 4 gm
  Carbohydrate: 21 gm
  Sodium: 49 mg

TASTEFULLY OREGON

Focaccia Bread Pizza
Connie Evers, R.D.

On especially busy days, I use commercial pizza sauce in place of the sauce I have listed here, which works well, also.

- 1 loaf whole wheat or white focaccia bread
- 1 (6 oz.) can *no-salt-added* tomato paste
- 1 (8 oz.) can *no-salt-added* tomato sauce
- 1/2 tsp. garlic powder
- 1 tsp. oregano leaves
- 1 tsp. basil leaves
- 1 tsp. dried parsley flakes
- 2 c. chopped vegetables or your choice: green pepper, onions, mushrooms, tomatoes, etc.
- 1 3/4 c. (or 7 oz.) grated part-skim Mozzarella cheese

Preheat oven to 375°. With a bread knife, carefully slice the focaccia bread in half horizontally. In a separate bowl, mix together tomato paste and tomato sauce (you will have extra sauce which can be refrigerated and used for another pizza). Spread tomato mixture evenly over the two bread halves. Sprinkle spices on top. Place vegetable toppings on pizza and cover with Mozzarella cheese. Bake until cheese is slightly browned (15 to 20 minutes). Cool for a minute and cut into 16 wedges to serve.

Servings:
  8

Serving Size:
  2 pieces

Nutritional analysis per serving:
  Calories: 318
  Fat: 11 gm
  Cholesterol: 13 mg
  Protein: 13 gm
  Carbohydrate: 42 gm
  Sodium: 737 mg

ESPECIALLY FOR CHILDREN

After this great salmon trip, Kenny and Tommy Gustafson were very hungry for a pizza treat! Their fishing buddy is Chick Hawk.

TASTEFULLY OREGON

Fruit Parfaits
Lynn Guiducci, R.D.

A good, tasty way to get fruit and yogurt in kids' diets and they love to help make them! Help them choose one of the suggested combinations and then have them follow the directions below.

COMBINATION #1:
- 2 c. fresh strawberries, sliced
- 2 bananas, sliced
- 2 c. nonfat strawberry banana yogurt

COMBINATION #2:
- 2 kiwis, sliced
- 2 c. mandarin oranges
- 2 c. nonfat vanilla yogurt

COMBINATION #3:
- 2 c. mandarin oranges
- 2 bananas, sliced
- 2 c. nonfat orange yogurt

COMBINATION #4:
- 2 c. fresh strawberries, sliced
- 2 c. fresh blueberries
- 2 c. nonfat vanilla yogurt

Choose small dishes for the dessert. Slice fruit if necessary. Layer fruit, then yogurt, then fruit; alternating fruits. Place dollop of yogurt on top with a whole berry or mandarin orange.

Servings:
4

Serving Size:
1 parfait

Nutritional analysis per serving:
Calories:	156
Fat:	<1 gm
Cholesterol:	2 mg
Protein:	6 gm
Carbohydrate:	34 gm
Sodium:	53 mg

ESPECIALLY FOR CHILDREN

Frozen Yogurt Saucers
Kimra Warren Hawk, R.D.

This is a fun version of frozen ice cream sandwiches. All you have to do is assemble these and freeze; they are ready at a moment's notice.

2 c. nonfat frozen yogurt, any flavor
1 c. *Grape-Nuts* cereal
32 Nabisco *Famous Chocolate Wafers*

Remove the frozen yogurt from the freezer and soften slightly for about 10 minutes. Meanwhile, line a shallow pan with aluminum foil. Pour *Grape-Nuts* into a shallow saucer or bowl. Place 2 tablespoons yogurt on a chocolate wafer, cover with another wafer, and compress the "sandwich" slightly. Set it on its edge and roll it in the *Grape-Nuts*. Place the *yogurt saucer* on the foil-covered pan and repeat. Freeze the sandwiches until hard, then wrap individually in foil or plastic for storing in the freezer. They soften quickly, so serve soon after removing from the freezer.

Servings:
16

Serving Size:
1 saucer

Nutritional analysis per serving:
Calories: 100
Fat: 2 gm
Cholesterol: 1 mg
Protein: 3 gm
Carbohydrate: 19 gm
Sodium: 144 mg

TASTEFULLY OREGON

No-Fry Chicken Fingers
Connie Evers, R.D.

1/2 c. plain nonfat yogurt
2 T. prepared mustard
2 c. crushed corn flakes
4 chicken breasts, boned & skinned

Preheat oven to 400°. Mix together yogurt and mustard. (For a strong flavor and if your child likes it, try Dijon or other gourmet mustards). Cut chicken into strips. Dip chicken strips in mustard mixture. Coat both sides with cornflake crumbs. Place on a baking sheet coated with nonstick cooking spray. Bake for approximately 15 minutes, turning once during baking.

Servings:
4

Serving Size:
3 ounces chicken

Nutritional analysis per serving:
Calories: 218
Fat: 4 gm
Cholesterol: 66 mg
Protein: 29 gm
Carbohydrate: 15 gm
Sodium: 327 mg

ESPECIALLY FOR CHILDREN

Peanut Butter Cereal

Patricia Rose, R.D.

This disappears from my kitchen very quickly. It is a good kids' recipe that is very easy to make.

3 T. reduced-fat peanut butter
2 T. honey
3 c. ready-to-eat cereal (Kix, Chex or Corn Bran)

In a glass bowl mix peanut butter and honey together. Microwave on MEDIUM for 1 to 2 minutes until soft. Stir in cereal until well coated. Preheat oven to 300°. Place mixture on nonstick baking sheet. Bake 5 minutes. Stir and continue baking another 5 minutes, until crunchy. (Total baking time in oven is 10 minutes.)

Servings:
6

Serving Size:
1/2 cup

Nutritional analysis per serving:
Calories: 105
Fat: 3 gm
Cholesterol: 0 mg
Protein: 3 gm
Carbohydrate: 15 gm
Sodium: 135 mg

Popcorn Cake

Charlotte Hennessy, R.D.

A great dessert for kids' parties and a welcome change from cupcakes.

2 qt. popcorn, air-popped
8 oz. marshmallows
1/4 c. margarine
1/8 tsp. Lite Salt
1 c. (6 oz.) gumdrops
1/2 c. unsalted peanuts

On the day before: Pop the popcorn, using no additional fat or salt, and set aside in a large bowl. In 2-quart microwave dish, heat marshmallows, margarine and Lite Salt for 2 to 3 minutes, until melted. Watch closely because it melts rapidly. Add gumdrops and peanuts to the popcorn. Stir marshmallow mixture into popcorn mixture. Press into springform or bundt pan which has been coated with nonstick spray. Allow to stand overnight before turning out of pan. Slice like regular cake, serve and have fun with all the reactions!

Servings:
24

Serving Size:
1 slice

Nutritional analysis per serving:
Calories: 102
Fat: 4 gm
Cholesterol: 0 mg
Protein: 1 gm
Carbohydrate: 17 gm
Sodium: 36 mg

ESPECIALLY FOR CHILDREN

Luscious Slush

Merri Lynn Coleman, R.D.

A group of young people tested this recipe and they gave it a score of "10".

1 c. nonfat milk
1/2 c. frozen pineapple juice concentrate (use frozen)
1/2 tsp. vanilla
1 c. berry-flavored nonfat yogurt (raspberry yogurt is great)

Place milk, frozen juice concentrate and vanilla in blender. Blend quickly to mix only. Add yogurt and blend for 10 seconds. Served immediately. If not slushy enough for you, serve over crushed ice.

Servings:
4

Serving Size:
1/2 cup

Nutritional analysis per serving:
Calories: 143
Fat: trace gm
Cholesterol: 2 mg
Protein: 6 gm
Carbohydrate: 30 gm
Sodium: 75 mg

TASTEFULLY OREGON

Notes

Index

Appetizers & Beverages

Baked Garlic 1
Marinated Mushrooms 2
No-Guilt Nachos 3
Special Shrimp 4
Hummus Dip 5
Moroccan Eggplant 6
Party Vegetable Dip 7
Russian Bean Dip 8
Spicy Garbanzo Bean Dip 9
Tangy Dip 10
Tofu Paté 11
Tzatziki 12
Hot Crabmeat Appetizer 13
Salmon Paté 14-15
Shrimp Dill Dip 16
"Smoked" Salmon Ball 17
Breakfast Smoothie 18
Favorite Gin Fizz 19-20
Hot Apple Cider 21
Hot Spice Tea 22
Lemon Velvet 23
Peachy Soy Cooler 24
Special Citrus Iced Tea 25
Summertime Strawberry
    Smoothie 26-27
Tofrutti Smoothie 28
Wedding Punch 29

Breads & Muffins

Apple Cranberry Muffins 31
Blueberry Bran Muffins 32
Cereal Bran Muffins 33
Dorothy's Muffins 34
Fresh Apple Muffins 35
Pumpkin Apple Muffins 36
Raisin Bran Muffins 37
Banana Bran Bread 38
Blueberry Coffee Cake 39
Cherry Banana Bread 40-41
Cherry Bran Bread 42

Date Nut Bread 43
French Breakfast Puffs 44
Old World Bread 45
Overnight Raisin Bread 46
Pumpkin Cornbread 47
Rieska 48
Whole Wheat Walnut
    Bread with Raisins 49
Zucchini-Pineapple
    Raisin Bread 50-51
Iced Cinnamon Rolls 52-53
Oatmeal Raisin Rolls 54
Quick Wheat Bread 55

Breakfasts, Brunches & Lunches

Bulgur and Apples 57
Familia 58
Vispipuuko "Whipped
    Pudding" 59
Dutch Babies 60
Fruity French Toast 61
Gingerbread Pancakes
    Topped with Lemon
    Sauce 62
Wheat Hearts Pancakes 63
Baked Chicken
    Sandwich 64-65
Puffy Chile Relleno
    Casserole 66
Garbanzo Spread 67
Hummous 68
Gyros 69
Hearty Meatball Submarine
    Sandwiches 70-71
Thai Salad Rolls 72
Middle Eastern Salad
    Rolls 73

Soups, Stews & Chili

Asopao (Puerto Rican
    Rice and Chicken) 75
Butternut Ginger Soup 76
First Prize Western
    Lentil Soup 77

Garden Split Pea Soup 78
Grandpa's Beef and
    Barley Soup 79
Hearty Spinach Meatball
    Soup 80-81
Hearty Vegetable and
    Lentil Soup 82
Lentil Soup 83
Mexicali Stew 84
Moroccan Vegetable Stew ... 85
Navy Bean Soup 86
On-The-Mark Black
    Bean Soup 87-88
Quick Minestrone Soup 89
Rice and Bean Soup 90-91
Soupe au Pistou (Bean and
    Basil Soup) 92-93
Split Pea and Herb Soup 94
Summertime Gazpacho 95
Tomato Florentine Soup ... 96-97
Vegetable Barley Soup 98
Zesty Black Bean Soup 99
Zucchini Tomato Soup 100
Champion Chili 101-102
Chicken Chili 103
Chili Molé 104
Quick and Easy Black
    Bean Chili 105
White Bean Chili with
    Hot Peppers 106

Salads & Salad Dressings

Blue Ribbon Potato Salad .. 107
Chilled Potato and
    Green Bean Salad ... 108-109
Hot Potato Salad 110
Bean Salad Supreme ... 111-112
Black and White Bean
    Salad 113
Fiesta Salad with
    Black-Eyed Peas 114
Heart of Texas Black-Eyed
    Pea Salad 115
Navy Bean and Tomato
    Salad with Balsamic
    Vinaigrette 116

White Bean and Garlic
    Salad 117
Apple and Greens with Garlic
    Dijon Dressing 118-119
Chicken Salad with Grapes
    and Almonds 120
Fresh Mushroom Salad 121
Marinated Vegetable Salad .. 122
Rice and Vegetable Salad ... 123
Summer's Best Salad 124
Bing Cherry Salad 125
Lemon Supreme Salad 126
Oregon Raspberry Salad ... 127
Chicken Ravioli Salad
    with Fruit 128-129
Colorful Vegetable and
    Pasta Salad 130
Macaroni Salad 131
Somen Oriental Salad .. 132-133
Oriental Chicken
    Salad 134-135
Berry Vinegar 136
Cucumber Yogurt Dressing
    (Tzatziki) 137
Homemade Ranch-Style
    Dressing 138
Rice Vinegar Dressing 139
Yogurt Vinaigrette
    Salad Dressing 140
Quick Ranch-Style
    Dressing 141

Side Dishes, Sauces
& Condiments

Picnic Three-Bean
    Casserole 143
Southwestern Red Beans
    and Rice 144
Basmati Rice Pilaf 145
Cheesy Rice with
    Green Chiles 146
Italian Risotto 147
Pimiento Rice 148
Broccoli-Corn Casserole 149
Mediterranean
    Vegetables 150

Baked French Fries 151
Kate Aaloo 152
Roasted Potatoes 153
Fruit Sauce 154
"Lite" Hollandaise
    Sauce 155
Marinara Sauce 156
Fresh Strawberry Chutney ... 157
Berry Freezer Jam 158

Vegetarian Main Dishes

Brown Rice Skillet
    Medley 159-160
Cajun Red Beans
    and Rice 161
Lentil Casserole 162
Mexi Tamale Pie 163-164
Pasta with Garden
    Vegetables 165-166
Pasta with Black Beans
    and Tomatoes 167
Pasta Primavera 168
Spinach Lasagna 169
Spinach Manicotti 170
Szechuan Broccoli 171
The Six-Minute Meal 172
Three-Bean and Rice
    Casserole 173
Tofu Baked Beans 174
Tofu Patties 175
White Beans Provencale 176

Seafood Main Dishes

Bouillabaisse 177-178
Fish Fillets in Red Wine 179
Fish Gumbo 180-181
Lemon-Lime Salmon 182
Mexican-Style Marinated
    Flounder 183
Orange Roughy with
    Sun-Dried Tomatoes 184
Shrimp Creole 185
Sesame Halibut 186-187
Steamed Halibut with
    Black Bean Sauce 188

Chicken & Turkey
Main Dishes

Asian Chicken and
    Vegetable Kabobs 189
Broiled East Indian
    Chicken 190
Chicken with Mustard
    Sauce 191
Chicken with Caramelized
    Onion Marmalade 192
Chicken Cordon Bleu 193
Chicken Diane 194
Chicken Fajitas 195
Chicken Meatballs 196
Chicken Paprika 197
Chicken and Wild Rice 198
Company Chicken 199
Cranberry Curry Chicken ... 200
Diane's Mexi-Chicken
    Casserole 201
Herbed Chicken 202
Kung Pao Chicken 203-204
Larch Mountain Lasagna 205
Lemon Chicken 206
Mediterranean Chicken
    and Spaghetti 207
Mexicali Medley Burritos 208
Orange Chicken 209
Parmesan Herbed
    Chicken 210
Pasta with Chicken
    and Asparagus 211-212
Spinach Chicken Stir-Fry ... 213
Szechuan Turkey Stir-Fry .. 214
Thai Chicken Fettuccine 215
Turkey Tangine with
    Vegetables 216-217

Beef, Veal & Pork
Main Dishes

Baked Bowties and
    Spinach 219-220
Bean and Burger
    Casserole 221
Beef or Chicken Fajitas 222

Beef Noodle Bake 223
Marinated Beef and
　　Vegetable Kabobs ... 224-225
Flank Steak in Marinade 226
Mediterranean Stroganoff ... 227
Orange Nugget
　　Stir-Fry 228-229
Pork Chops Casserole
　　(Costatelle
　　Pasticcio) 230-231
Pork Chops Diane 232
Quick and Easy Veal
　　Scallopini 233
Sweet and Sour Cabbage
　　with Meatballs 234
Tollernini 235-236
Wild Game Imperial 237

Desserts

Cheesecake with
　　Fruit Topping 239-240
Fast Spice Cake 241
Hazelnut Liqueur
　　Cheesecake 242-243
Hot Chocolate Pudding
　　Cake 244
Lite Cheesecake 245
Mom's White "Tough"
　　Cake 246-247
White Mountain Frosting 248
Maple Syrup Devil's
　　Food Cake 249
Norman's Chocolate Cake ... 250
Poppy Seed Cake
　　with Fresh Fruit.............. 251
Scandinavian Yogurt
　　Carrot Cake 252
Special Oatmeal Cake 253

Whiskey Cake 254
Blueberry Buckle 255-256
Cranberry Apple Crisp 257
Fruit Nachos 258
Pumpkin Chiffon 259
Pumpkin "Custard"
　　Dessert 260
Spicy Apple Crisp 261-262
Frozen Vanilla Yogurt 263
Pineapple Sherbet.............. 264
Apricot Date Bars 265
Cocoa Brownies 266
Double Chocolate
　　Cookies 267
Ginger Cookies 268
Jelly-Filled "Butter"
　　Cookies 269
Oatmeal Hurrahs 270
Mom's Gingersnaps 271
Pumpkin Cookies 272
Jennie's Yogurt Pie 273
Layered Banana-Pineapple
　　Dessert 274
Lemonade Yogurt Pie 275
Yogurt Dessert Sauce 276

Especially for Children

Apple Pie Popsicles 277
Apple Smiles 278
Chocolate Pudding 279
Focaccia Bread
　　Pizza 280-281
Fruit Parfaits 282
Frozen Yogurt Saucers 283
No-Fry Chicken Fingers 284
Peanut Butter Cereal 285
Popcorn Cake 286
Luscious Slush 287

ORDER FORM for *Tastefully Oregon*

Name _____

Address _____

City & State _____

How many copies? _____ Amount enclosed $_____

Price per book (postage & handling included) $15.95

Please make checks payable to:

OREGON DIETETIC ASSOCIATION
Mail Orders to: Oregon Dietetic Association
P.O. Box 6497
Portland, Oregon 97228

- -

ORDER FORM for *Tastefully Oregon*

Name _____

Address _____

City & State _____

How many copies? _____ Amount enclosed $_____

Price per book (postage & handling included) $15.95

Please make checks payable to:

OREGON DIETETIC ASSOCIATION
Mail Orders to: Oregon Dietetic Association
P.O. Box 6497
Portland, Oregon 97228

EXCELLENT FUNDRAISING IDEAS

In addition to printing cookbooks for fund raising organizations, JUMBO JACK'S COOKBOOKS also offers the proven successful fund raising products shown below. The products shown below are just a few of the many items you might select for your next fund raising project, or perhaps in conjunction with your cookbook project. Any of these will be beautifully imprinted with your organization's logo and name.

If you are interested in helping your organization make money with these successful fund raising products, just mark the products you'd like more information about, give us your name and address.

Name _____

Address _____

Tear out this page and mail it to: JUMBO JACK'S COOKBOOKS
301 Broadway • P.O. Box 247 • Audubon, Iowa 50025

☐ OVEN MITT
☐ HOT PAD
☐ TOTE BAG
☐ COOKBOOK
☐ APRON
☐ T-SHIRT
☐ MUG
☐ PLACE MAT

Or if you prefer, give Mike, Mitzi or Jeanne a toll free call at 1-800-798-2635
FAX 1-712-563-3118   COLLECT: 1-712-563-2635

We hope you are enjoying using this cookbook and find it useful in your kitchen. This book was printed by JUMBO JACK'S COOKBOOKS. If you are interested in having cookbooks printed for your organization, please write us for prices and details.

A cookbook is a good way for YOUR organization to make money.

If you are interested in more information, just tear out this page and mail it to us with your name and address, or just call us toll-free 1-800-798-2635.

Featuring the 3-ring easel binder

We also do hardback covers, square back wire covers, and other types of binding

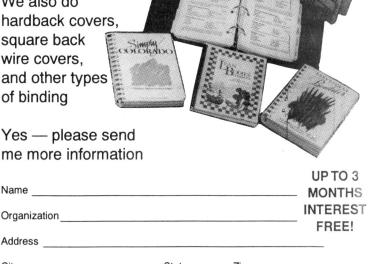

Yes — please send me more information

Name _____

Organization _____

Address _____

City _____ State _____ Zip _____

Phone _____

UP TO 3 MONTHS INTEREST FREE!

Or, if you prefer give Mike, Mitzi or Jeanne a call:
Toll free: 1-800-798-2635; Collect: 1-712-563-2635
FAX: 1-712-563-3118

JUMBO JACK'S COOKBOOKS
AUDUBON MEDIA CORPORATION
AUDUBON IA 50025 • 1-800-798-2635